Advance Praise For
A Brief History *of a* Perfect Future

"This book reminds us that the future is our choice. It inspires the bold thinking and creativity required to change our world for the better. This is a must read for public and private sector leaders with the awesome opportunity to shape the trajectory of progress."

—*Kristine Martin Anderson, EVP and leader,*
Civil Services, Booz Allen Hamilton

"This book provides clear and constructive action and direction for individuals, companies, and governments. If you fall into any of these categories (and who doesn't?), it is well worth reading."

—*Vince Barabba, Commissioner, California Citizens Redistricting*
Commission, former Director of the U.S. Census Bureau (twice), former
senior strategy and marketing executive at General Motors, Kodak,
and Xerox, past president of the American Statistical Association, and
member of the Market Research Council's Hall of Fame.

"If you are an unapologetic optimist who believes mankind's tough challenges are made to be solved, this book is for you. For the pessimist in search of a cure, read this first!"

—*Kathleen Blake, MD, MPH, Vice President,*
Healthcare Quality, American Medical Association

"As one who has seen first-hand how even one tool can change the world, it's exciting to read the future histories of the seven drivers laid out in this insightful book. We can combine them for a wonderful future—if we take the right steps!"

—*Dan Bricklin, inventor of the spreadsheet*

D0972225

"A thoroughly readable, enjoyable and stimulating book. Future histories are a clever way to stimulate thought-provoking discourse and focus innovation on areas that will be of importance to the quality of life to come."

—Larry Cohen, CEO, Health2047

"What a timely book. Even techno utopians have become techno cynics, wondering whether technology has caused more harm than good. By imagining how we can do better, the authors propose histories of what our future can be through the creative technique of drafting news articles set far in the future, after we have fixed today's problems. One is headlined, 'Even Zuckerberg Can Be Redeemed,' reporting that Facebook eventually provided its users with information about the credibility of news and other sources appearing in their feeds, finally giving people the tools to overcome the infodemic of misinformation and hoaxes that back in 2021 made social media such a cesspool. Bring some optimism to the reading of this book: In the perfect-history news story about Mark Zuckerberg's retirement in 2050, his children were even able to say they were proud of him."

—L. Gordon Crovitz, co-CEO of NewsGuard and
former publisher of The Wall Street Journal

"*A Brief History of a Perfect Future* presents us with a rare gift in this era of pervasive negativity, anonymous grousing, and divisiveness. It offers a positive and optimistic view of our future, grounded in facts and the lessons of history. It is both inspirational and aspirational on how we can make this vision a reality. Highly recommended! Reading it should put a spring in your step and a smile on your face!"

—Bran Ferren, Chief Creative Officer, Applied Minds, and former
President of Research and Development, The Walt Disney Company

"We are the designers of our future. The authors help us be idealistic, yet pragmatic, in reimagining our future. Most importantly, they show us a smart path forward; the time has come to "think big, start small, and learn fast." Thanks to the unprecedented speed of innovation, "near-miracles" are possible. We can get to our Future Perfect, *if* we start now to make the right choices."

—Linda A. Hill, Wallace Brett Donham Professor of Business Administration, Harvard Business School, and author of Collective Genius: The Art and Practice of Leading Innovation

"My dad wrote a great book! Please read it. Better yet, ask your kids to read it."

—Zoe Jenkins-Mui

"This book is a must read for private and public sector leaders and individuals looking to expand their insight, frame the future, and accelerate their thinking. Here's a better reason to read it: My 14-year-old son asked to read the whole book after I had him read a section or two. What fascinated me was his strong engagement in the concepts discussed and prior knowledge of some of the key Laws of Zero. It made for a great father/son moment! I hope you'll not only read this important book but also talk about it with your kids."

—Gordon Jones, Dean, College of Innovation + Design at Boise State University, and inaugural Director, Harvard University Innovation Lab (i-lab), 2011–2015

"This book is a great read for anyone interested in participating in the design of the future. The Laws of Zero offer hope in a volatile and divided world. Science has saved us before and, armed with the blueprint offered by these very smart yet pragmatic authors, can help us all create the only legacy that truly matters…a better world for our children and grandchildren."

—Arlene Kern, Innovation Leader, Munich Re

"A few years ago, Chunka Mui and Paul Carroll introduced me to the value of writing about my endeavor as a Future Perfect headline and story (motivational) and a Future Pathetic headline (scary...). Both were invaluable. In this book, they, together with Tim Andrews, equip us with the science and the formulas to create not just the headlines and stories of the Future Perfect but to actually create that world....to step up and step into it (exciting!)."

—*Karen Kmetik, Group Vice President,*
Improving Health Outcomes, American Medical Association

"What happens when once-scarce resources become free and freely available? This book looks past the immediate trends of today and presents a provocative look at the implications of our technological future, peppered with eye-popping examples. A readable must-read for all ages."

—*Andy Lippman, cofounder and Associate Director, MIT Media Lab*

"This book takes a future-back approach in which commonly perceived constraints on the future state are released, permitting the starting point of that perfect future. I really liked the illuminating stories, how this feels like a logical extension of the authors' previous books, and the great writing paired with the imaginative Law of Zero concept. A compelling, interesting read that is also quite a bit of fun!"

—*James Madara, MD, CEO, American Medical Association*

"Life feels polarized by geopolitical, global, and local social events, and it often seems like we don't have much say in the future ahead of us. *A Brief History of a Perfect Future* starts by removing the fog of over-information and noise that clouds our minds by reminding us of incredible advances our societies conquered across topics as diverse as technology, healthcare, and societal matters. The authors level the playing field and allow us to regain the ability to envision the future we want as individuals and community and business leaders and act to achieve the future we desire. They leave us with tools and refreshing thought-provoking considerations on how we achieve the future we desire."

—*Florian Quarré, Chief Strategy Officer, Exponential AI*

"This book is a must read. It connects the rapid changes of the next few years to the next 30 and shines a light on the emerging possibilities, risks, and responsibilities that will determine success or failure, vibrancy or chaos."

—Toby Eduardo Redshaw, CEO, Verus Advisory, and former SVP, Enterprise Innovation and 5G Solutions, Verizon

"Inventing a better future requires deep learning from the past and optimistic viewpoints that embrace an ever-increasing speed of change. This book gives shape to awe-inspiring possibilities from advanced science that can be easily consumed by the reader."

—Paul Roma, Global General Manager, IBM Watson Health

"I appreciate the optimism being applied throughout this book to the grand challenges we face as human beings in shaping our world and sustaining our planet for our children and future generations. Optimism is a requirement for engaging with an innovator's mindset to ask the questions: What if, why not, and how might we—and the authors consistently present a fact base for optimism to thrive in exploring these questions. Through exploring the 'Laws of Zero,' I found my mind racing with the possibilities of these questions and allowing my thinking to diverge from the present day's challenges to the art of the possible of the future possibilities enabled by exponential change. The 'future histories' then enabled my thinking to converge on ways to concentrate deeper exploration of the actions and innovations required to reach an optimistic future."

—Stuart W. Rosenberg, Chief Innovation and Strategy Officer, Westfield

"The authors have outlined a positive view of the future and ask us to envisage an optimal pathway to it. A refreshing and novel approach to guide our actions and plans as a society and as individuals."

—Ken Sharigian, Chief Strategy Officer, American Medical Association

"Yogi Berra famously said, 'The future ain't what it used to be.' This wonderful book is a practical companion for the curious soul about what may come. It combines a keen analysis of fundamental trends in technology and practical imagination to help us all navigate a world disrupted."

—John Sviokla, partner, Manifold Group, and former US Chief Marketing Officer, PwC Advisory

"… a tremendously fun journey through a future that's both plausible and necessary if we want to create a thriving world. This book provides a much-needed jolt of optimism about humanity's ability to overcome our greatest challenges."

—Andrew Winston, sustainability strategist, author of Green to Gold *and* Net Positive

A Brief History
of a Perfect Future

Inventing the world we can
proudly leave our kids by 2050

A Brief History
of a Perfect Future

Inventing the world we can
proudly leave our kids by 2050

Chunka Mui
Paul B. Carroll
Tim Andrews

**FUTURE
HISTORIES
PRESS**

Copyright © 2021 by Paul B. Carroll and Chunka Mui

All rights reserved. No part of this book may be reproduced or used in any manner without written permission of the copyright owners except for the use of quotations in a book review. For more information, address: chunka.mui@gmail.com

This work contains elements of creative nonfiction. Names, characters, places, and incidents in the book's "future histories" either are the product of the authors' imaginations or are used fictitiously in varying degrees, for various purposes.

Cover and interior design by Alan Barnett
Cover design guidance from Mark Maltais
Cover illustration by Brian Stauffer

Published by Future Histories Press
www.perfectfuturebook.com

From Chunka, Paul, and Tim

*To our kids, Zoe, Kai, Clare, Shannon, Tyler, and Brett
(and, of course, to their moms, Beth, Kim, and Valerie).*

To our kids' kids—and to theirs, on down the line.

To your kids.

CONTENTS

PART 3: JUMPSTARTING THE FUTURE

INTRODUCTION

Inventing the Future

When Xerox CEO C. Peter McColough established the Palo Alto Research Center (PARC) in 1970, Xerox executives were, naturally, curious to know what their corporate crystal ball would tell them about the future of computing. When Alan Kay, a team leader at PARC, was asked for the umpteenth time to say what the future would hold, he snapped there was no easy way to know. "The best way to predict the future is to invent it," he said.*

That line became a mantra for Alan and for PARC, which did unbelievable amounts to invent the future by laying the foundation of today's computing experience. It also became a mantra for the three of us, as we worked with Alan for decades, and it drives the narrative of this book. In the following pages, we'll lay out ways that we, as a society, can harness the technological marvels at our disposal and invent a sparkling future.

At PARC, starting in 1971, the mantra played out over five glorious years as researchers invented many of the core elements of information technology. Alan's team contributed to the development of the first personal computer and gave it the overlapping windows and graphical user interface that Steve Jobs copied for the first Apple Macintosh. Alan invented (with Dan Ingalls) what today would be called dynamic

---

* Alan tells us that while his well-known line was a spontaneous utterance in 1971, "the idea is a simple one, sure to be invented many times." Alan nods to many who came up with variations of it previously, including Abraham Lincoln, Peter Drucker, and Dennis Gabor.

1

object-oriented programming (which is a big reason you have so many apps on your smartphone; developers can easily incorporate software "objects" others have already written, rather than having to write all the code from scratch). Other teams at PARC developed desktop publishing, the laser printer, peer-to-peer and client-server computing, and Ethernet, which enabled corporate networks of personal computers.* And, while PARC didn't invent the internet, its researchers made such significant advancements that PARC deserves considerable credit for it.

A half-century later, most of the information-technology industry and much of global culture and commerce still depends on PARC's inventions. Technology companies and many others in downstream industries have collectively realized trillions of dollars in revenue and tens of trillions in market value because of PARC's work.

When PARC began its work in 1971, what most people thought of as a computer weighed more than a ton, needed to be cooled with water in a heavily air-conditioned room, took about 15 minutes to boot up, and was surrounded by a sort of priesthood of lab technicians in long, white coats to cater to the needs of the machine. Data was entered with punch cards, and results were produced on clackety printers as words and numbers—there was maybe the occasional graph, but certainly no images, and the idea of video on a computer was positively silly. The internet existed, but barely—while tens of billions of devices are connected these days, only four computers were tied together in the early days. Not four billion. Not four million. Not four thousand or even four hundred. Four.

Computers in 1970, with far less power than today's phones, looked like the ones shown in Figure 1.

But Alan had developed a series of very different ideas as a graduate student in the 1960s, and they would lead to what he eventually called Dynabook—a battery-powered laptop with wireless access to a network

---

* While Xerox is often derided for not capturing anything close to the full value of PARC's inventions, we think McColough is one of the unsung heroes of innovation. He invested in PARC for years, taking money out of the bonus pool for himself and other executives, even though Xerox didn't see the big payoff until after he retired in 1982. That payoff was enormous: more than $100 billion in sales of laser printers. For what it's worth, McColough also established one of the first affirmative action programs at a major corporation.

FIGURE 1. A typical data center circa 1970

that let you communicate with anyone and have access to all the world's information.

In a world full of mainframes, Alan imagined computers more like the ones pictured in Figures 2 and 3.

Then he and the team at Xerox PARC invented that future.

Alan didn't wait 30 years to say, "Wow, I sure have access to a lot of computing power now; what should I do with it?" He and his colleagues at PARC envisioned a radically different educational tool that they could build around that power and use to provide a new kind of literacy and new meanings for "reading" and "writing" so children could discuss, play with, and learn powerful ideas. Then Alan and PARC imagined all the pieces that would be needed. Some related to the computer itself— the kind of operating system that would tap into the new power, the windows that would let users flip easily between tasks, etc. Some related to supporting devices, in particular to capabilities for networking

FIGURE 2. The Flex Machine, drawing by Alan Kay, 1968

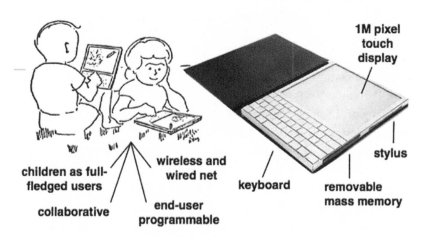

FIGURE 3. The Dynabook, drawing by Alan Kay, 1972

computers and for printing. PARC then moved in a host of directions at once. The whole computing environment, not just the processor, gained momentum quickly. We're all better off as a result.

Alan invented a future a second time, too.

As an Apple fellow, he helped pull together a vision for a so-called Knowledge Navigator, unveiled in a video in 1987. The device bears an eerie resemblance to the iPad, introduced 23 years later. While Steve Jobs obviously shaped the iPad in his own brilliant way, the vision in the Knowledge Navigator videos clearly guided research in Apple's labs for years before Jobs got involved.

For good measure, Apple's work on the iPad gave the company the biggest gift in the history of business: the iPhone. According to Jobs, when he decided the iPad wasn't ready for production, he realized the technology could be packaged into something much smaller—a revolutionary phone.[1]* *Et voilà!* Neither Apple nor the world has yet recovered.[2] (In the pre-iPhone world, in 1996, Apple almost sold itself to Sun Microsystems for about $4 billion; as of this writing, Apple's market value is $2.34 trillion.)

The idea of inventing the future surfaced anew for the three of us as we tried to make sense of the dysfunction in the U.S. in recent years—on politics, race, the pandemic and other public health issues, social media and disinformation. As we write this in the summer of 2021, the Gulf of Mexico is on fire, a condo building just collapsed in south Florida and killed scores of people, and a town in Canada burst into flames and burned down as a "heat dome" repeatedly settled over much of North America. One of Paul's daughters sent him a panicked text: "There is no Planet B!" One of Tim's sons told him, "You're worried about whether your Social Security benefits are going to be cut; we're worried about whether there's going to be a planet left by the time that's an issue for us!" Chunka's daughter noted that he's often described as a futurist and once quipped to him, "Well, then you'd better not mess mine up."

Can we reassure our kids, honestly, or are we doomed to a dystopian future? There sure is a lot going wrong.

---

* When Jobs introduced the iPhone in 2007, he explained Apple's decision to build its own phone by quoting Alan as saying: "People who are really serious about software should make their own hardware."

As is our nature, we've settled on hope. We think we can envision a grand future, putting a stake in the ground for our kids and their kids, then draw on our decades of experience evaluating technology trends to start inventing what we're calling a Future Perfect.

We're not saying we can predict the future. We very much abide by the oft-used line that "it is difficult to make predictions, especially about the future." Besides, at their best, predictions represent the most likely outcome, and in pivotal times like today's, the most likely scenarios might well be ones that we want to avoid. No, rather than predict the future, we want to draw on what we've learned from Alan Kay. We want to invent it. More precisely, we want to help you invent it.

Following the pattern Alan has laid out for us, we'll use this book to take you 30 years into the future and describe technological marvels that will be available to us all. These marvels are hard to envision today. While we can all get our heads around a two-fold improvement in something, it's extraordinarily hard to imagine three decades of the sorts of two-fold improvements in computing power *every 18 months* that Moore's law was providing to Alan and his colleagues at Xerox PARC. How do you even process the idea of the MILLION-fold increase in computing power over 30 years that they were designing into their work? So, we're going to try to do that imagining work for you and describe seven so-important-as-to-be-almost-magical technological building blocks that will be available to all of us in 2050.

We'll then paint some pictures of how those building blocks could be supplemented by other technological improvements and novel ideas that, together, will let us construct that Future Perfect. As amazing as these technological marvels will be, the building blocks are not the building. In fact, they could lead to an infinite number of buildings. So, we'll apply "systems thinking" as much as possible to consider how all factors interact and to point us toward a future that is optimized as broadly as possible, not optimized for each of its parts. As we'll explain more in the introduction to Part Two, too much planning has historically been done in silos—so we wind up with city streets optimized for traffic, for instance, but not for people (and we care much more about people than we do about cars). We all need to make this difficult mental effort (ecosystems are really complex), or we may waste the fabulous power these building blocks will provide us. We want you to get excited about the possibilities of these technological marvels while also seeing the sort of work we all should be doing now to prepare for their possibilities.

Technology will give us great gifts by 2050 no matter what we do, so we could let development happen on its own and then figure out how to react. But we think it would be much better to start planning for the implications—like experimenting now with how cities could be rethought based on driverless cars and some other technological wonders. Why wait 30 years to start learning when we can already see at least the outline of what's coming?

To provide the groundwork for that planning, we'll not only describe the technological marvels but will paint visions of 2050 based on what we call "future histories"—short, provocative "news" articles set in 2050 that describe how key aspects of the world might look in areas such as transportation, health care, and the electric grid. We'll then provide you with tools you can use to envision and write your own future history, for whatever part of the world you think is especially important and that you could help invent by 2050.

Then we'll hand the keys over to you, encourage you to start right away on inventing your piece of the future, and wish you luck. So, yes, we're leaving the hard part to you.

But we hope that, along the way, we'll have stretched your thinking a bunch and given you a powerful way to get started. If we all do our part, we can at least get close to that Future Perfect. If not, we may stumble our way into what we call the Future Pathetic—think *Brave New World* or *1984*. As we all see from what's happening around us today, technology can cut both ways. It can produce great gains—but dystopia is out there, too.

Let's harness the future, rather than just taking our chances.

• • •

We've done this sort of Future Perfect planning for major corporations for years, both separately and together, since the three of us were partners at Diamond Management & Technology Consultants, which pioneered the idea of "digital strategy" in the mid-1990s. After we all left the firm, Paul and Chunka collaborated on a massive research project that led to their 2008 book, *Billion Dollar Lessons: What You Can Learn From the Most Inexcusable Business Failures of the Last 25 Years*. They then founded a boutique consulting firm, the Future Histories Group, where they help companies spot potential pitfalls, then project out several years to envision an idealized, but plausible, world. Tim went the big-firm route, taking on senior technology roles that led him to his current position at Booz Allen. When the three of us began working together on a project in 2019, and Booz Allen agreed to collaborate on a book related to it, we decided to write a future history for those who really matter: our children and theirs.

Booz Allen became the final piece of the puzzle. The firm provided access to a broad array of experts who sharpened our thinking in numerous ways and encouraged us to expand our scope to include the future of trust, security, privacy, and government services. Given the firm's long history of consulting with government on major projects, Booz Allen also enriched our understanding of how government entities can play the key role that we need them to play to get to our Future Perfect. (Although we won't call out each one, Booz Allen is involved in most of the government examples we cite in the book.)

When writing this book, we took some encouragement from what some are calling "the optimism beat"—a growing body of literature that shows that, despite the pessimism created by the drumbeat of negative news, the world is becoming a much better place. Poverty is way down. Life expectancy has fully doubled globally in the past 100 years. Educational levels are way up, even in developing countries. Crime is down. So are deaths from wars—from terrorism, too, even though it worries so many of us.* Now, the gains from all this good news are spread far too inequitably. For instance, while infant mortality is down in the U.S., the improvement is much greater for whites than for Blacks and other minorities. While incomes are rising, the disparity between Blacks and whites has not narrowed since the 1960s. Gender disparities in wealth and income also stubbornly persist. But there are still broad gains around the world, and they justify optimism.

---

* A plethora of books provides stats and analysis both for the trends and for why they're occurring. Among our favorites are: *The Better Angels of Our Nature: Why Violence Has Declined*, by Steven Pinker; *Abundance: The Future Is Better Than You Think*, by Peter H. Diamandis and Steven Kotler; and *Factfulness: Ten Reasons We're Wrong About the World—and Why Things Are Better Than You Think*, by Hans Rosling, with Ola Rosling and Anna Rosling Rönnlund.

Our tracking of technology trends underscores the cause for hope. The trends are creating so many, many, many more resources for the world to use to tackle its problems. We've been around long enough that we aren't Panglossian about technology—watching something like virtual reality come and go and then come and go again as an all-purpose solution over the past 30 years provides cause for being careful. But we can still look at the future and say, based on the technological marvels we expect to see: "Okay, 30 years from now, what would it be crazy for society not to have?"

We've created what we call the Laws of Zero to summarize the seven main building blocks that we've promised you and that can be used to invent the future—costs are dropping so fast in these seven areas that you can think of them as heading toward zero(ish), meaning that an infinite(ish) amount of that resource will be available. These areas are: computing, communication, information, genomics, energy, water, and transportation.

The easiest Law of Zero to grasp concerns the cost of computing, because we've all seen the stunning and unrelenting improvements in cost/performance for decades now. The cost of a gigabyte of memory, for instance, fell from $500,000 to just two cents over 30 years. We use so much memory these days that no one would say it's free, but if you're thinking about something costing you $500,000 per unit today and can imagine a price of two cents, well, that feels pretty close to free, right? You'd certainly be inclined to use a lot more of that resource to address a problem or opportunity. The cost of phones and bandwidth follows the same sort of plunging curve as computers, giving us our second Law of Zero. Because of the plummeting costs of computers and phones in all their forms—including satellites and tiny sensors—the world will be so wired that the cost of information will also head toward zero cost, and any information you want will be available.* The rapid reductions in the

---

* Yes, we're waving our hands over some real economic issues here. In some cases, we're talking about zero total cost. In more cases, we're talking about zero marginal cost—or a combination, such as when someone primarily buys a smartphone to use an app like TikTok or Google Maps and basically gets the ability to make phone calls thrown in for free. For now, it's enough just to note the trend toward zero. We'll be more precise as we get into the specifics of the Laws of Zero and the chapters on their implications in key areas of life and business.

cost of genomic sequencing (which have fallen even faster than that of computing) give us our fourth law and provide enormous reason for optimism about our health. There's even reason to project that energy costs are headed toward zero (with some significant caveats). If energy costs plunge, then so does the cost of providing water—which becomes ubiquitous even in many areas that are currently arid. And autonomous vehicles will erase so many considerations of time and distance that the costs of transportation will plunge, meaning it can be envisioned as a nearly unlimited resource. The idea of zero cost may be discomfiting, especially for energy, water, and transportation. We explain our thinking at length in the next section.

Here's another way to think about why we should come to grips with the Laws of Zero and start planning now for 2050: Do we want to be like Norway or like Venezuela?

Both had windfalls from the discovery of enormous oilfields, but Norway used its strategically, while Venezuela used its tactically and meandered into a disastrous future.[3] When Venezuela began discovering massive oilfields during World War I, they led to an economic boom that gave Venezuela the highest GDP per capita in Latin America by 1935, and that boom lasted into the 1980s. But there was no planning for the long term, just reactions to what was happening in the present—and then oil prices crashed in the 1980s. With nothing beyond oil production to rely on, Venezuela descended into social, economic, and political chaos that led to the authoritarian Hugo Chavez and now Nicolas Maduro. Even though Venezuela has the greatest oil reserves in the world, it had a GDP per capita of just $1,700 in 2020. The country ranks 92nd in the world in life expectancy and last in the Americas, at 72 years. By contrast, when Norway discovered rich oilfields in the North Sea in the late 1960s, it strategically invested in ways designed to increase social benefits, including one of the best education systems in the world and a health system so good that life expectancy is nearly 82 years. Norway even poured money into experimenting its way toward a model prison system. It spends roughly three times as much per prisoner as the U.S. does, largely to focus on preparing prisoners to live a crime-free life once they are released—as a result, Norway has one-tenth as many prisoners per capita as the U.S. does.[4] The Social Progress Index ranks Norway as No. 1 in the world, while Venezuela ranked No. 81 out of the 168 countries in 2016 and wasn't ranked in 2018 because its situation was deteriorating so rapidly that a ranking couldn't be assigned. (The U.S. ranks 28th.)[5]

We'd rather plan like Norway, and we can.

We realize we seem to be swimming against the political tides at the moment. Political factions can barely agree on what day of the week it is, and the 2020 elections have left us with a polarized government (often, a really, really polarized government) at every level. So, this may seem like an inauspicious time to try to rally people around big ideas that will shape our future. But we take encouragement from history. In 1961, when President Kennedy first told Congress of his audacious plan to land a man on the moon by the end of the 1960s, the response was tepid, and 58 percent of Americans opposed the plan.[6] Yet Kennedy managed to pull support together, and the 1969 moon landing is remembered as one of his and the country's great achievements. Even though the political climate in the 1960s was at least as fractious as today's, Congress managed to pass landmark civil rights legislation. And it doesn't matter in the long run whether margins of victory in Congress were small, as with civil rights, or huge, as with the Interstate Highway Act passed under President Eisenhower in 1956.

In fact, we think that right now is a perfect time for discussions on a vision like the Future Perfect. Sure, our political divisions can make it hard to sort through all the near-term issues on, say, health care—"pre-existing conditions," "Medicare-for-all," "the public option" … the list of terms, alone, is onerous. But it's pretty easy for everyone to agree that, in 2050, it'd be crazy for us as a society to not have affordable care available to everyone that keeps them healthier and lets them live longer. If, for the moment, we set aside the question of who should pay—the big issue that divides us—it's straightforward enough to see how the Laws of Zero and breakthroughs in medical technology can get us to both far better care and much lower costs. Long-term discussions simply aren't freighted the way the short-term fights are, and thinking more about the future can actually get people nodding their heads in ways that build rapport. The resulting discussions can then provide context for the actions that need to be taken and for the milestones that need to be reached in the next 10 or 15 years, which can then be turned into factors that need to be considered in our current planning.

The federal government will obviously play a fundamental role by establishing the rules of engagement, conducting basic research, and sparking markets. In recent decades, federal research has given us the internet, the Global Positioning System (GPS), and the core of what's now Google Maps, and it will give us much more by 2050. President Biden believes so much in basic science that he elevated his science adviser to a cabinet-level position for the first time in the nation's history. That new national science adviser, geneticist Dr. Eric Lander, said, "Our country stands at the most consequential moment for science and technology since World War II. How we respond will shape our future for the rest of this century." State and local governments will have a big role to play, too, and they're huge drivers of both the supply and demand for technology through their policy, regulatory, and procurement choices. Business will play its crucial role bringing innovations to market, as companies chase those tens of trillions of dollars of market valuation that exist out there. We individuals will have to do our part, too, as citizens, consumers, employers, employees, and so on.

So, let's set aside the short-term differences for the next 200-plus pages and find a vision that we can all agree on. And let's get excited. The future can be a great place.

On to a Future Perfect!

PART ONE

THE LAWS
OF ZERO

While people often cite the drastic improvement James Watt made to the steam engine in 1765 as the beginning of the industrial revolution and the march to modernity, we don't often think about a key intellectual force behind all this progress: the concept of zero.

These days, we use the number zero all the time, but history shows that the notion of counting nothing was far from obvious. Almost all counting systems started with the number one; why are you counting if there's nothing there? Look at how rarely zero was discovered (some say "invented") and at how long it took to flesh out the concept. The idea has arisen only three times among all the world's civilizations.

First were the Sumerians, in roughly 2000 BC. They eventually spread a nascent form of the idea, but they didn't spread it that far— Greek and Roman engineers used the concept,* but even the ancient Greeks' great mathematicians never codified it. The Mayans followed in about 350 AD, but their idea never went beyond Mesoamerica. Finally came India, where the idea percolated for some time. Aryabhata did pioneering work in the early 500s, and Brahmagupta codified the use of zero, including a symbol for it, in 628 AD. This time, the idea took. It spread to the Arab world, whose mathematical system has become the basis for what we do today. (Hence, "Arabic numerals.") In the ninth century, zero allowed for the invention of *al-jibr*, which the English-speaking world knows as "algebra" and which spread during the Islamic conquests in subsequent centuries, including into Europe. The inventor of algebra also gave us the algorithm, a shortcut for solving a problem that's so important in today's computing world.

Imagine if we were still stuck with the Roman system, without a zero. Divide MDCXLIV by XLVIII. Go ahead. We'll wait. Or, imagine the language of today's digital world, the binary code represented by ones and zeros—but without the zeros.

---

* While the Greeks and Romans didn't have a name for zero, the idea was implicit in the abacus they'd use for calculations—the counting on an abacus starts from nothing. The idea of zero was also implicit in Greek geometry, just not expressed.

As recently as 400 years ago, the notion of zero was still in its infancy. It turns out that the concept of nothing, while intuitive at one level, is hard to come to grips with in all its mathematical implications. René Descartes came along in the early 1600s and helped us visualize zero through the graphs we all use today, with x- and y-axes that meet at (0,0) and extend in both positive and negative directions—the graphs are known as Cartesian coordinates, in his honor. Then, in the second half of the 1600s, Isaac Newton and Gottfried Leibniz began independently imagining a form of mathematics that, among other things, explored the idea of dividing by zero. Not really dividing by zero, because that makes no sense—but what if you divided by numbers that got smaller and smaller and smaller, heading toward zero; what sorts of results would you get? There was certainly one key result: calculus. While dreaded by many high school and college students everywhere, calculus provided a new system for understanding the physical world.

So, when James Watt made his crucial improvement to the steam engine in 1765, about a century after calculus was invented, the intellectual horsepower was already developing in ways that would unleash the physical horsepower that Watt's engines provided. Zero provided the anchor for basic calculations, and calculus was available for engineering, architecture, and complex calculations in so many other arenas, including those that have driven our biggest businesses and our economies. From Roman times through the start of the industrial revolution, economic growth had been so slow that an average European was only about twice as wealthy as an average subject of Julius Caesar had been, some two millennia earlier. In the 250 years since the start of the industrial revolution, that average European's wealth jumped 13-fold[7]—and that calculation doesn't adequately account for some things that can't really be quantified, like indoor plumbing, the benefits of electricity, or the joy of the latest gadget from Apple. The intellectual structure based on the concept of zero played a major role in those leaps forward.

Zero will also play a key role in the Future Perfect.

Certain key drivers of mankind's progress are heading toward zero cost. (Remember, your mileage may vary, and we'll explain the caveats shortly.) If something is free, you can throw as many of those resources as you want at a problem. We may struggle with the idea of a cost heading to zero (ZERO!!!), but if we can understand what zero cost really does, we can design a remarkably different and better future.

We think of these cost trends as the Laws of Zero. The first few—for computing, communication, and information—will seem familiar, because we've all felt the trends for years or even decades. The fourth basically combines the first three laws with biological advances that will put genomics on a curve headed toward zero cost, with profound implications for our health. The final three laws are more speculative—we're not likely to get nearly as close to zero as with energy, water, and transportation—but the trends toward rapid declines in cost are real and powerful and will make a lot of the considerations for even things like time and distance go away.

We'll explain.

CHAPTER 1

The First Law of Zero: Computing

In 1965, a journal commissioned a forecast on progress in electronics, and, as unlikely as it might seem, that scientific paper largely laid the base for today's digital world. In the paper, Intel co-founder Gordon Moore merely observed that the number of transistors in an integrated circuit was doubling every year. (The number of transistors is a rough proxy for the processing power of a chip.) Moore speculated that the pace could continue for at least a decade. That was enough.

What has come to be known as Moore's law became the metronome for the semiconductor industry. That scientific paper went from being an observation to being almost a mandate, a self-fulfilling prophecy. The semiconductor industry would produce doubling after doubling after doubling, and anyone whose product or, eventually, business tapped into the growing power of electronics was on notice to be ready. The pace of the doubling has varied—Moore amended the time span to every two years, and Intel later put it at 18 months—but the power had been unleashed. Intel's chips went from a few dozen transistors when Moore made his observation to billions today; Intel no longer even provides a count. That one observation became a road map for the entire computing world. Whatever the exact pace, the exponential improvement in power meant that capability was headed toward infinity, and the cost of a unit of computing power was headed toward *zero*.

The ability to throw computing power at any problem has driven the Information Age, putting that smartphone in your pocket that powers all your apps and provides your instant connections to friends and associates, as well as your access to all the information you can imagine. You aren't really asking Siri or Alexa for help. You're asking Gordon Moore.

While computing obviously isn't free, it looks almost free from any historical distance. The latest smartphones contain more processing power than the top-end, multimillion-dollar supercomputers circa 1990—which required a special export license from the U.S. government, because giving a foreign organization access to even one was thought to endanger national security. On Intel's first microprocessor, in 1971, the 2,300 transistors cost $1 apiece; today, transistors cost less than a millionth of a penny each. That's an improvement of a factor of more than 100 million in price/performance in less than five decades. The same kind of improvement has occurred in anything with a chip in it.

How powerful are exponentials? A classic video, made in 1977 by IBM, demonstrated the concept by showing a picnic filmed from overhead at a distance of one meter (10^0 meters) and then panning out. By the time the "camera" gets to 10^{12} meters, it's outside our solar system. By 10^{16}, the "camera" is a light year away. Then, the "camera" zooms back in—way in. By the time it gets to the 10^{-10} level (0.0000000001 meter), the "camera" is showing something an angstrom wide—about the width of two hydrogen atoms.[8] With just 27 steps in an exponent, you can go from a distance of two atoms to a light year.

The exponential improvement in computing power will continue, too. Yes, the pace of Moore's law has slowed. Some say it's even stopped because the need to keep increasing the density of the electronics on chips is running up against some fundamental principles of physics.[9] But there are still miles of runway for improvement. Among other things, while most devices have run off general-purpose chips, because they've had so much speed to burn, special-purpose processors for phones, laptops, tablets, etc. will be developed that can offload work from the central processor and run applications far faster than is possible today.[10] In addition, while chips have been designed as essentially flat surfaces, a third dimension can be added that would allow for layers of transistors and multiply the number on a single processor.[11] Meanwhile, moving so much of the work of computing to the "cloud" allows for removing all sorts of software bottlenecks that slow computing at the moment.[12]

Whole new forms of computing, such as quantum computers, promise improvements far beyond Moore's Law for some uses.[13, 14] Google already claims it's achieved "quantum supremacy," referring to using the bizarro-world characteristics of quantum physics to build a machine that can solve a problem no conventional computer could have solved in any reasonable time. Google says its machine performed a calculation in 200 seconds that would have taken the world's most powerful conventional supercomputer 10,000 years.[15]

Other "laws" kick in, too, that pour gasoline on the increase in computing power. You may have heard of "network effects," based on Metcalfe's law.[16] It says the value of a network increases in proportion to the square of the number of users. In practical terms, that means that the internet wasn't terribly useful when the first four computer systems were connected in late 1969[17] but that the billions of devices connected to the network today make the internet incredibly powerful. And network effects will continue to amplify the raw power of computers in innumerable ways as billions more devices connect with each other. By 2050, trillions of devices will be connected in a network, making the so-called Internet of Things (IoT) millions of times more important than it already is. (And it's already incredibly important.)

Something called Bell's law will also contribute. Formulated by our longtime friend and colleague Gordon Bell, the developer of the first minicomputer, the law roughly says a new form of computing will appear every decade. There were mainframes in the 1960s, minicomputers in the 1970s, personal computers in the 1980s, cellphones in the 1990s, early smartphones and tablets in the 2000s, and wildly impressive smartphones in the 2010s. In the 2020s, we're likely moving into the Internet of Things, building on ever-smaller connected devices and on AI-driven voice input assistants such as Alexa, Google Home, and Siri, which not only take commands but can act as sensors in a myriad of ways, including detecting illnesses and providing home security. Progress won't stop there, either. Robots could extend our presence: Just slap on some virtual reality goggles and "inhabit" a robot in your kid's, parent's, or friend's room (only with permission, of course). Computing could be implanted in our bodies: A chip right below the jaw and near the ear could capture our voices while vibrating in ways that our ears would easily pick up as sound. There's even talk of chip implants that would plug directly into our brains and give us instant access to essentially all the world's information. People may turn into a form of centaur, except that, instead of being half-human and half-horse, we'll be half-person and half-computer.[18] *Jeopardy!* will never be the same.

While artificial intelligence isn't a device, you could say AI is the next form of computing. The improvement in just one part of AI—machine learning (ML)—is exponential and accelerating, because, within boundaries set by programmers, the machine trains itself at its own, wildly fast speed. For example, an AI developed by Google's DeepMind went from knowing nothing about the game of Go to quickly beating the world champion. While AI is still a long way from many kinds of human thinking, including the Holy Grail known as "general intelligence," AI is already approaching human reasoning in areas like speech recognition, image recognition, and understanding/generating written language. ML gets better with more/faster processors and storage produced by Moore's law, and there's no upper limit on the number/speed of processors or storage that can be applied.

Just as we can imagine exoskeletons making superhumans, ML can make super-intelligent reasoning possible. If you remember the movie *Short Circuit*, where an AI robot read a gazillion books and watched a gazillion shows to become super smart very quickly, you're not that far off track.

To get a feel for how good AI is already, look at OpenAI's GPT-3, which can mimic human writing. For instance, a human provided this to the AI as a prompt:

> "In a shocking finding, scientists discovered a herd of unicorns living in a remote, previously unexplored valley in the Andes Mountains. Even more surprising to the researchers was the fact that the unicorns spoke perfect English."

The AI was asked to continue the story, and it added:

> "They also were found to have perfectly coiffed hair and wore what appeared to be Dior makeup.
>
> 'We were shocked to discover the unicorns,' said anthropologist Daniel St. Maurice. 'They were like nothing we had ever seen before. We had heard legends of the unicorns, but never thought they actually existed.'

When the scientists first arrived in the valley, the unicorns were surprised and startled by the presence of humans but were also excited. The unicorns welcomed the researchers and explained that they had been waiting for them for a very long time."[19]

Whoa, right?

Here's where the combination of AI and computing power gets really interesting: The gains can be recursive. Computationally intensive techniques are allowing for much faster and better design for the processors and everything else about electronics. And we're already at a "lather, rinse, repeat" stage. The underlying electronics get so much faster that they allow for huge improvements in artificial intelligence, which improve the design of the underlying electronics, which....

The notion is that we shape our tools, then our tools shape us*—and the effects will reach well beyond computers themselves. Bell Textron recently used virtual reality to iterate through countless possibilities and design a helicopter in less than six months, a process that previously took five to seven years.[20] Simulations for materials design that used to take a year have been shortened to 15 minutes; this creates opportunities to greatly accelerate breakthroughs in areas such as optics, aerospace, and energy storage, where the ability to design new components has greatly outpaced the ability to design the materials that are required to make them.[21]

The AI won't stop at physical design, either—the AI will be able to design the AI. Sam Altman, CEO of OpenAI, describes this sort of super-recursion as "Moore's Law for Everything." AI gains the potential to keep adding and adding and adding computer-based intelligence to any task, driving the cost of performing that task toward that magic number: zero.

Yes, there will always be costs for computing—Apple et al. will all make sure we pay—but the cost will be so low and the capability so high that, if we're planning from today's perspective, we can almost imagine that computing power is free and that we can throw a nearly infinite amount of it at any problem we want to address in that Future Perfect.

"Hey, Siri, please text Gordon Moore and say, 'Thank you.'"

---

* The idea is often attributed to Marshall McLuhan, who never quite said this, and is more accurately attributed to Winston Churchill, who said, "We shape our buildings, and then our buildings shape us," or Henry David Thoreau, who said, "Men have become the tools of their tools."

CHAPTER 2

The Second Law of Zero: Communication

The first message that inventor Samuel Morse sent on his experimental telegraph line between Baltimore and Washington, DC, in 1844 was, "What hath God wrought?" Some form of that astonishment has been expressed time and again as communications have moved from the telegraph to the telephone to the ubiquitous texts, emojis, and other digital communications of today.

Within living memory, operators on roller skates manned huge boards (or, more accurately, "womaned" the boards, because most operators were young women). They needed the skates to speed up and down the boards to plug in long cords that completed analog circuits and physically connected the phones of two people who wanted to talk. Operators completing calls might grandly announce, "Hold for long distance," and the cost could be dollars per minute. Today, while communication is hardly free—just look at your cellphone and internet bills—the marginal cost certainly is. That's why we can spend all day on a smartphone, using apps and sucking up all kinds of data, even including streaming movies, for an all-you-can-eat, monthly fee. Those of us of a certain age remember how exotic Dick Tracy's wristwatch video phone was in the comics. But, these days, what's exotic about FaceTime? Ho-hum.

We saw the drive toward zero communication cost up close and personal when we published a column in the late 1990s in *Context*, a magazine we produced while the three of us were partners at Diamond Management & Technology Consultants. The column, by our friend David Reed, noted that telecommunications firms were depreciating their copper-wire networks slowly, based on standard tables for physical assets like buildings, but that they should actually depreciate exponentially, based on Moore's law, because the fiber networks that were replacing copper were essentially massive computers. Lots of telecom companies squawked about the column (including, awkwardly, some clients). Then, they wrote off almost the entire value of their multibillion-dollar copper networks.

Reach will keep expanding, too. The fifth-generation technology (5G) that's beginning to be rolled out may provide greater wireless bandwidth than what the vast majority of the population gets via fiber today. No more messy wires and poles needed, just massive bandwidth everywhere. Even without 5G, Wi-Fi will continue to expand its reach and capacity, at no increase in cost. Satellites will provide bandwidth to everyone on the planet—Elon Musk's SpaceX launched 895 satellites into low-Earth orbit by October 2020 and plans to launch 60 more every two weeks on its way to as many as 42,000[22], so the Earth will soon be blanketed with communications capabilities. Driven by the need to make sure everyone has access to broadband (so they can buy lots of goods and services), Microsoft and other companies plan land-based efforts, too, to reach rural communities.[23] So-called mesh networks will extend the reach both in rural America and in less-wired parts of the world by letting every device with communications capability act as a relay for any other device.

Communications will reach into every corner of the globe, as tens of billions of devices and trillions of sensors are incorporated into a tapestry of communication. In other words, we aren't just talking about humans connecting with each other. We're also talking about humans talking to devices and devices talking to each other—anywhere, because, with a little solar power, maybe a bit of battery, and a tiny antenna, any device can connect to the internet these days. Basically, you can assume that you, or any device affiliated with you, will be able to reach any person, any home, any device, anywhere in the world, at any time—at zero marginal cost.

Communication will become richer, too, as having bandwidth to burn means video can be part of every connection.* Think of how easily the world moved from voice calls to Zoom calls during the pandemic. Now imagine having thousands of times more bandwidth available by 2050. And think about what even a bit of video can add. Poker has been around for a long, long time, but it only became a major spectator game with tournaments broadcast on ESPN when cameras became so tiny they could show the two down cards as each player inspected them in a game of Texas Hold 'Em. In the past, all you could watch was the betting and the faces of players as you tried to figure out what was going on. But the players had spent years learning to show zero emotion, and there was no rule that players had to show their cards at the end of a hand, so a lot was left to the imagination of the TV viewers. Now, with the increased use of cameras, you can see whether players are bluffing, can see whether they are bluffed out of a hand, and can generally play along with them. Poker became a huge TV event, and interest in the game soared, all because of a little (literally) video.

That richness of bandwidth will allow for such fast response times that it will be possible for many decisions to be made in real time. Cars, for instance, will communicate with each other and with infra-structure that monitors and controls traffic, coordinating their actions in milliseconds. No human involvement needed. To see the potential ramifications, think of the profound changes in your own behavior that occurred when the world of personal computing went from dial-up to "always-on" some 20 years ago. You used to have set times when you'd go to your computer, dial in to a server, and check your email, maybe visit a news site, and perhaps poke around in other ways. Then you'd log out, maybe for hours. Now, you not only have a computer but a phone that keeps you immersed in the online world at all times, and your use of texts, consumption of alerts and TikToks, etc. have transformed the ways in which you communicate. Super-fast response times will have the same sort of profound—and rather unpredictable—effects for the coordination among devices in the IoT.

---

* Results will be unpredictable. The telephone grew out of an effort to let wires carry more telegraph traffic and was initially viewed as a way to broadcast into homes, but the capability for exchanging audio turned out to be more important than anyone initially imagined.

Before too long, response times will be so fast they'll create novel issues, such as new types of warfare. Today's fighter planes are amazing, but some uses are limited by the pilot—he or she has to be able to withstand the G-forces and still control the plane, and a plane won't be sent into a situation that carries too much risk for the human pilot. But if computers, sensors, and communications create a fast-enough cycle for gathering and processing information, planes no longer need a pilot—removing lots of physical limitations for the plane, while raising all sorts of questions about when or whether a machine should be able to act in certain ways, in particular being authorized to kill a bad actor without approval from a human.

History suggests some of our expectations about communication should be tempered. The advent of the telegraph, for instance, was expected to bring world peace.[24] Seriously. In the 1840s, in the age of sailing ships, a message between the English government and Washington could take eight weeks or more to go round-trip, from communication to answer. But with the telegraph, an urgent exchange of messages might take just an hour or two. So, it's easy to see how thoughts of a golden age in communication might have let people get carried away. As things turned out, exchanging confrontational messages quickly didn't make them any less bellicose, and the world marched right on toward World War I and then World War II.

The internet created similar delusions in the 1990s. The line of thought went that we'd all understand each other better and communicate more freely, so everything would be rainbows and unicorns and…. Clearly, no one imagined Twitter in those early days. No one realized how much Facebook and other social media could increase tribalism and exacerbate divides.

Still, whatever winds up flowing through the pipes in our future—whether priceless data or raw sewage—the pipes will be almost infinitely wide, and the cost will be a flat, low rate. Draw the graph of cost vs. performance from today's perspective, and the cost in the Future Perfect will be so low that, well, let's call it zero.

What hath God wrought, indeed?

CHAPTER 3

The Third Law of Zero: Information

In the late 1990s, during the internet's initial heyday, it started to become clear just how much information could be collected on people's online behavior. But Nicholas Negroponte, the founder of the MIT Media Lab, defiantly told us that, while his credit card company or someone else might know that he went to see a certain movie, "They won't know whether I liked it!"

No longer.

These days, just a few buildings away from the Media Lab, researchers can monitor motion, heartrate, breathing, and even emotions simply by how people reflect ambient radio waves, such as Wi-Fi. So, sensors in a movie theater could now get a read on how Negroponte and the rest of an audience feel about a film.

The topic of wiring the world with sensors has drawn attention mostly for its dystopian possibilities. We're learning just how much information Facebook, in particular, but Google and others have on us—and are happy to sell. In the 2016 U.S. presidential election, we saw how effectively people could be manipulated based on that information. China has also stirred up concern with a plan to use facial recognition to identify people no matter where they are and to assign them "social credits" based on their behavior (à la the "Nosedive" episode on the TV series *Black Mirror*). Jaywalk, and you lose credits. Obey all laws, and you gradually accumulate credits. But this scenario isn't limited to China. The prospect of governments or even private companies aggregating information from both the physical and online worlds into profiles that would determine people's access to credit, to jobs, to transportation, to everything isn't hard to imagine. Don't think you could run away, either. Someone sitting in a public place could call up the profiles of those nearby and collect a bounty by turning in someone who has, say, defaulted on a debt. That scenario is about as creepy as it gets, right?

It's not all doom and gloom, however. The ability to monitor everything and everywhere has plenty of potential benefits, especially when combined with the powerful AI capabilities that are coming along. With computing and sensors shrinking in size and increasing in power, AI will be able to perform feats in real time. Think of a situation we're all familiar with: the daily commute. Every car and every street will soon be so wired that traffic will be managed in ways that aren't conceivable today. Even leaving aside for the moment the prospect of driverless vehicles, information will be everywhere. Cars will be able to travel in platoons, just a foot or so apart, because, the instant the first car hits the brakes, all the cars behind it will be notified and will also hit the brakes. Just because you can't see what might be coming at you from the sides at an intersection doesn't mean another car can't do it for you and relay that information to your car—e.g., a camera on a car could spot a vehicle zooming at a red light and automatically alert all cars in the vicinity to halt and wait for the danger to clear the intersection. Cars will, in any case, communicate with each other at intersections and work out who goes when, so stop signs and traffic lights will become anachronisms; you might slow a bit as you approach an intersection, but you'll never have to stop again. The presence of ice or any other danger on the road will be immediately communicated to all other cars in the area.

Car theft, already dropping rapidly, will virtually disappear. Why try to steal a car when the owner can be notified instantly if the car moves, with police being notified moments later? Drunk driving violations will drop dramatically, too. Even if those under the influence of drugs or alcohol haven't summoned an autonomous vehicle for their ride home, the limitless cameras on the road will immediately notice erratic driving and report it to police. They would also learn immediately of many instances of road rage and any contests by those who somehow see driving as a form of the "Grand Theft Auto" video game. Accidents will plummet, and most remaining claims will be resolved instantly. Who needs claims adjusters when the cars' sensors and cameras can report exactly what happened?

Basically, traffic will be managed as a single, highly efficient digital system, rather than by setting a modest number of laws and letting hundreds of millions of individual actors sort things out.

Sensors will supply information from everywhere else, too, including our bodies. Already, sensors built into contact lenses can measure blood sugar levels. A cuff about the size of a smartwatch can report on blood pressure in real time. The Apple Watch can do an electrocardiogram to look for abnormalities in heartbeats (though not yet at a level that is clinically useful, so please don't say we told anyone otherwise). Tiny cameras can now be sealed into a capsule the size of a cod liver oil tablet that someone can swallow; the cameras screen for cancer as they pass through the person's bowel, meaning the person can avoid the dreaded colonoscopy.[25] In addition, chips the size of a grain of salt are being developed that could be swallowed and provide real-time data on our vital signs from our bloodstreams—sort of an Internet of Me, to go along with the Internet of Things that's connecting billions of devices to the Internet.

As sensors zoom in, they'll also zoom out, thanks to shrinking and ever-cheapening satellites, and telecom companies won't be the only ones putting more things in the sky. While a commercial satellite used to be perhaps the size of a school bus and cost $1.5 billion to $3 billion to design, build, and launch, today's CubeSats are about the size of a loaf of bread, and a "constellation" of 20 to 36 of the satellites costs $25–$40 million for the entire project.[26] And that's today. These satellites will keep getting smaller, more powerful, and cheaper. Today's resolution allows for the inspection of images down to about 25 cm, or the length of an average man's shoe, but that's an artificial limit established by the U.S. government—10 cm (roughly four inches) and even sharper resolution is on its way. Images that go beyond the visual, via radar and electromagnetic techniques, are coming soon, too.[27]

As satellites blanket the globe, they'll allow for new levels of navigation, whether that's by tracking North Korean ships as they try to evade embargoes or by helping that Amazon delivery drone make it to your front doorstep without hitting any of the other drones flying around.

The additional, more powerful satellites will greatly improve weather forecasting, too, and farmers will be able to monitor crops like never before. They'll be able to check each morning to see what part of the field might need more fertilizer, more water, or more of some other sort of attention. In other sectors, satellites mean businesses will be able to track operations, employees, and customers as never before. (Yes, there will be plenty of privacy issues to sort out.)

Governments will be able to use the new satellite capabilities to track the effects of climate change, such as rising sea levels or erosion, and spot any number of other sorts of problems. For instance, while environmentalists have pieced together information on thousands of illegal gold mining sites in the Amazon, whose activities often lead to mercury poisoning and increases in malaria,[28] having thousands of cheap satellites would allow those sites to be spotted in days as they develop and then be shut down. Deforestation, overfishing in the ocean, and certain forms of pollution will be tracked in real time and can thus be reduced.[29] Al Gore says that by late 2021 all major sources of greenhouse emissions will not only be measured but will have most sources updated every six hours, providing an unprecedented amount of feedback on how we are—or aren't—doing on climate change.[30] Artificial intelligence can then use this new ocean of data to make ever-better predictions of the course and effects of climate change. Human rights abuses will be observed to a new degree. Even now, while the Chinese government has claimed that Muslims in the western part of the country are being placed in "vocational schools," human rights activists have shown that watchtowers and razor wire surround many of the "schools."[31] A drone captured video of hundreds of the Muslim Uyghurs, blindfolded and handcuffed, being led from trains.[32]

Ubiquitous sensors, enhanced by artificial intelligence and drawing on limitless sources of information, will give you a sort of digital overlay of the world—the entire world, and everything in it. You'll be able to manipulate that overlay and view it however you want, even through a set of goggles that allow for virtual, or at least augmented, reality. Kevin Kelly, a founder of *Wired* magazine, has written of a "mirrorworld," where every physical object will have a digital twin and where all information is updated instantaneously. Want to fix something? Put on your AR goggles, and you can see inside what you're trying to repair, all the while getting instructions on what you need to do. Want to see what happened yesterday, last week, or last year in the exact spot where you're standing? Just put on your goggles and hit rewind. "History will become a verb," Kelly writes.[33]

Yes, this sort of worldwide nakedness can be—and is—a scary prospect. Big Brother is a real possibility—"Asleep or awake, working or eating, indoors or out of doors, in the bath or in bed—no escape. Nothing was your own except the few cubic centimeters inside your skull," *1984* says. Corporate monopolies could develop that would allow, at the least, for wild riches and, at the worst, for harmful distortions of markets. Technology lends itself to monopolies. There was IBM and its near-monopoly on mainframes from the 1960s through the 1980s. Microsoft then became the 800-pound gorilla through its near-monopoly on the personal computer operating system. Google and Facebook now are so dominant that they worry many, and Amazon is sure trying hard to get there in terms of shopping. A monopoly could certainly develop in the gathering, organizing, and disseminating of the world's information.

But, remember, we're designing a Future Perfect, not a Future Pathetic. There are ways to navigate the potential problems, if they're acknowledged up front, and avoid either too much government control or too much business control. We'll get to how to avoid those pitfalls.

For now, just imagine a world where every bit of information is available that would let you design and manage a Future Perfect.

CHAPTER 4

The Fourth Law of Zero: Genomics

Our ability to understand and map genetic structures traces back to the garden of an abbey in Moravia in 1856, where an Augustinian monk raised peas. That monk, Gregor Mendel, spent seven years purifying his strains of peas based on seven characteristics, then cross-pollinating the peas to slowly deduce the properties of inheritance. He published a paper in 1865 on a novel theory of what he called dominant and recessive genes—and that was pretty much the end of it. Mendel soon became the head of the abbey, in what is now the eastern part of the Czech Republic, and set aside his scientific work. The paper was promptly forgotten: It was cited all of three times in the next 35 years.[34]

It's fair to say genomics—the branch of molecular biology concerned with the structure, function, evolution, and mapping of genomes—got off to a slow start. But, remember, that's how exponentials work: slow start, overwhelming finish.

Mendel's paper was rediscovered in 1900 and led to a series of discoveries that built on each other and ignited the interdisciplinary branch of science that we now call genomics.* If DNA is "the language in which

---

* The science of genomics also stands on the shoulders of many other genius researchers, many of whom became well-known but some others who deserve much more recognition beyond scientific circles. Albrecht Kossel discovered the nucleic acids that are the chemical building blocks (called "bases") of DNA and RNA. James Watson and Francis Crick, building on the work of Rosalind Franklin, deciphered the double helix

God created life," as President Clinton once put it, then genomics' acceleration has brought us to the point that we can read and write in the language of life. And in recent decades, the progression, moving even faster than Moore's law, suggests we're very much looking at a Law of Zero: The benefits will keep expanding so fast that we're barely able to discern their outline at this point.

Let's resume the story in 1975, when Frederick Sanger and Walter Gilbert separately unveiled techniques for decoding genes by directly determining the sequence of the bases that make up DNA.[35] The sequencing processes, while miraculous, were arduous. Sequencing required expert laboratory skills and the precise use of dangerous chemicals, including acrylamide (a neurotoxin), chloroform (a carcinogen), and hydrazine (a rocket fuel). Initially, there were no computer programs to analyze the results; researchers had to interpret the results by eye. The entire process of preparing, sequencing, and analyzing even small fragments of the genome was novel and complex enough to earn one a Ph.D.

Tom Maniatis, the head of the New York Genome Center, observed that, when he was a postdoctoral fellow in Sanger's lab, it took him a year to sequence a piece of DNA that was about 35 base pairs. At that rate, it would've taken him 86 million years to sequence the full human genome. Sequencing the COVID-19 virus would have required about 860 years.

But the Laws of Zero feed off each other. And advances in computing, in particular, kept speeding up sequencing. In 1990, the U.S. led the formation of an international cooperative, the Human Genome Project, to sequence the entire genome. Francis Collins was put in charge, and the venture was funded with $3 billion through the Department of Energy and the National Institutes of Health. In 1998, Craig Venter decided that the government effort wasn't moving fast enough and announced a rival, privately funded attempt. A race ensued, and both groups declared success in June 2000, five years ahead of the original timeline for the Human Genome Project.

What had once been a messy problem for scientists handling test tubes and making slides in the lab soon enough became a problem for

---

structure of DNA. Marshall W. Nirenberg and Har Gobind Khorana cracked the code on DNA by showing how the bases determine protein synthesis. And many more.

computers, not just lab technicians—and, as we've seen, computers have become unbelievably fast. Thirty years after Maniatis was a post-doc, the Illumina NovaSeq 6000 machines in Maniatis' center can sequence an entire human genome overnight.

From 86 million years to overnight. Yeah, that works.

Cost comparisons are similar. It cost billions of research dollars to sequence the first human genome in 2003. Today, sequencing a genome costs roughly $600. You can see the plunge in Figure 4. Note that it's logarithmic. The line based on Moore's law doesn't show a steady decline of maybe 50 percent in the cost of computing over the past two decades, as the line would if the chart were using normal, Cartesian coordinates. Each of the horizontal markings represents an order of magnitude, so the chart shows that Moore's law has brought a decline of roughly a factor of 1,000 since 2000—and the cost per human genome has declined far, far faster.

We're not even close to done, either. Multiple makers of sequencing machines predict the path to a $100 genome test doesn't even require further breakthroughs, just incremental technical improvements.

In mid-2021, as we write this, the high-end NovaSeq 6000 in Maniatis' lab costs roughly $1 million, and there are only about 1,000 of them in the world. They're the sequencing supercomputers of the moment. But those prices will come down, and there's no reason sequencers need to stay in labs—think of all the mainframes in computer labs in the 1970s

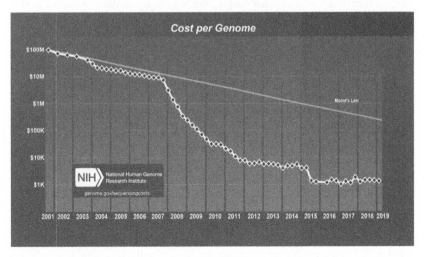

FIGURE 4. Sequencing Cost Per Human Genome 2001–2020

and 1980s, then look at the (more powerful) smartphone in your hand. Even now, lower-power desktop sequencers cost only around $10,000, and there are early versions the size of smartphones, which cost about $1,000. Oh, and there are already attachments that let you sequence a genome from an app on your smartphone.

When will some version of genomic sequencing be embedded in every smartphone (or whatever device the smartphone morphs into)? We don't know exactly, but we're pretty sure that some version of Dr. Bones McCoy's *Star Trek* tricorder is in our future.

In the Future Perfect, you can safely bet the cost of testing will drop so low that you can imagine throwing as much genomic sequencing at a problem as you'd like.* Gordon Sanghera, CEO of Oxford Nanopore Technologies, the company that makes the $1,000, phone-sized sequencing device, describes his company's ethos as "the analysis of anything, by anyone, anywhere."

For a dramatic illustration of the real-world benefits of genomic sequencing today, consider our experience with COVID-19. The genome of the offending SARS-CoV-2 virus was isolated, sequenced, and shared with researchers across the globe within days of when a patient was admitted to the Central Hospital in Wuhan, China, with symptoms of the yet-to-be identified disease. Then, days—we repeat, days—after the sequence was shared, the genetic code of the virus was being used to design the first vaccines, formulate treatments, create testing kits, and monitor for mutations of the virus.

Less than a year later, emergency-use authorizations were approved for multiple vaccines that showed more than 90 percent effectiveness. Soon, millions of shots of those vaccines were being poked into arms to protect those at a high risk from COVID-19, and billions of shots have since followed. Before genomic sequencing, developing and distributing a vaccine could have taken more than a decade—if one ever succeeded.

---

* We'll still have to face the fact that more and better testing isn't always a good thing. Mammograms keep improving, but breast cancer mortality hasn't declined. More and more cases of thyroid cancer are being diagnosed, and more surgeries are being done, but the fatality rate here also isn't decreasing. MRIs to diagnose back pain have made it easier to spot spinal deformities and justify surgeries—that all too often do nothing to alleviate the pain. We'll still have to correlate and make sure that fixing the issues surfaced by genomic testing lead to real benefits and that those benefits outweigh risks and other costs.

The fact that one succeeded, and so quickly, saved hundreds of thousands or even millions of lives worldwide.

And turning back viruses is absolutely just the beginning of what's possible—the very beginning. Even more powerful is the potential ability to write in (or at least edit) the language of life. And we're starting to take baby steps at doing so. Those baby steps are being enabled by a tool named CRISPR/Cas9, called CRISPR, for short.*

CRISPR was invented by Emmanuelle Charpentier and Jennifer Doudna in 2012. The duo and their teams developed it by deciphering and adapting a technique bacteria use to fight viruses. Viruses reproduce by injecting themselves into host cells and taking over the cells' metabolism to reproduce. The host can then fight back by snipping the infecting virus' DNA out of the host's DNA, where the virus has embedded itself—and Charpentier and Doudna figured out how a bacterium's immune system accomplishes that feat. They then designed a process to chemically reprogram that mechanism to cut out any stretch of DNA at a predetermined spot in a bacterium's genome and replace it with a molecule of the scientists' choosing. (They shared the Nobel Prize in Chemistry in 2020.) Other researchers soon developed methods to edit the genomes of any other organism, including ours. (Zhang Feng at MIT deserves special recognition.)

Yes, CRISPR is almost like magic.

Other techniques existed for editing DNA before CRISPR, but they were much less precise and could take months to prepare. CRISPR was a generalized, programmable method that was easily repeatable and cut the time to hours—or even minutes. The Nobel committee called the CRISPR advance "epoch-making" and dubbed it "a tool for rewriting the code of life."[36]

Already, the applications are wide-ranging. CRISPR is being applied to major staple foods in Africa, such as wheat, cassava, and banana, to help them resist disease.[37] Another group showed that CRISPR can snip

---

* CRISPR/Cas9 is short for "Clustered Regularly Interspaced Short Palindromic Repeats and CRISPR-Associated Protein 9." This clunky phrase was chosen more to fit the acronym than the other way around, according to Francisco Mojica, the Spanish molecular biologist who coined it. He thought that "CRISPR" sounded friendly and that the dropped "e" gave it a futuristic sheen. His wife thought CRISPR was a great name for a dog.

out a family of viruses in pig DNA and potentially increase the opportunity to use pig organs for human transplants. A third group has developed a CRISPR-based treatment that appears to fix the genetic mutation responsible for muscular dystrophy in dogs.[38] And CRISPR-enabled technology is poised to revolutionize medicine: Researchers are developing CRISPR/Cas9 therapies for a wide range of diseases, including inherited blood and eye diseases, neurodegenerative conditions such as Alzheimer's and Huntington's disorders, and even non-inherited diseases such as cancer and HIV.[39]

Now, think more broadly: Imagine what's called a gene drive, a genetic engineering approach designed to spread a gene across an entire species. A gene drive could potentially spread an advantageous trait—or could even wipe out an entire dangerous species.[40]

A gene drive tool changes the genes of a single creature in a way where those genes become dominant, are passed on to all offspring and, eventually, are spread to the entire species. A gene drive could alter female mosquitoes to not bite—the males don't bite, so the alteration would end malaria. A gene drive could produce rats that only have male offspring, eliminating a threat to, say, the native bird and turtle populations of Galapagos. Gene drives could fight invasive crop pests like the fruit flies that eat up the raspberry patch of one of your authors every season, no pesticides required.

Actually, you don't have to imagine any of these things. All these possibilities have been demonstrated. CRISPR lets us alter both individuals and entire species.

We're not saying we should make any of these fundamental changes. Ecosystems are remarkably complicated, and there are loads of examples of attempts to handle a pest by introducing a predator for that pest—only to find that the predator created many more problems than it solved. Even if you go after something as clearly vile as rats, well, what animals feed on the rats and will now struggle for food? What animals feed on the animals that feed on the rats? What else did the rats feed on, besides the eggs of the species you want to protect? And so on.

We favor slow changes so that we can see what the full ramifications turn out to be for an ecosystem. We're taking great strides and baby steps at the same time. And many of our steps are in the dark—or, at the very least, the fog.

While we still have much to learn even about the meaning of the genomes we can read, genomics already provides hope for addressing a number of diseases caused by variation in a single gene. These diseases include sickle cell anemia, cystic fibrosis, Huntington's disease, and Duchenne muscular dystrophy—debilitating diseases that afflict some 400,000 people just in the U.S. CRISPR is helping researchers to better understand these diseases, and a number of therapies are currently in the midst of clinical trials for treating and even curing them.

Eric D. Green, who heads the National Human Genome Research Institute (NHGRI), a part of the National Institutes of Health (NIH), wrote in *Wired* in late 2020 that he believes genomics will provide a platform for discovery that broadly accelerates the pace of biology research.[41]

"A lot of times people hear CRISPR and think of therapies for people. But by far the bigger use is at the bench. With CRISPR, we can make edits to little pieces of DNA that never go into a person—they go into cell lines or bacteria, which then get tested to see if those edits have functional consequences. The combo of genome editing and genome synthesis methods getting better, coupled with better and better computational tools, is really going to change the pace of biological discovery. Right now, we rely on one paper being published about one genomic variant to give us one drip of information at a time. That doesn't scale.

So we've got to get to a point where we're making millions of changes, generating massive amounts of data, and then hopefully we can use AI to train computers to look for patterns. At that point, we won't even have to do the experiments, because we can make predictions about what a mutation means based on the last 1,000 times we've done this. Going forward, those are the sorts of tools that might make the difference."

Think of his approach as science in hyperspeed. Progress in genomics rides on the coattails of the Laws of Zero in computing, communications, and information. If Green is right that research can increasingly move from the lab bench to the computer, then progress can happen at the speed of electrons. That means the Laws of Zero can exponentially amplify the capabilities in genomics, enabling a platform for discovery about the workings of life itself.

And who knows where that takes us?

In medicine, almost every new drug and vaccine is already based on genomics,[42] which is also a foundational tool in almost every field of science related to biology, including agriculture, environmental studies, health, and zoology. So, the Law of Zero for genomics will exponentially amplify science and engineering's impact over the next half century to a degree that will likely surpass the impact of the computing platform it's built upon.

Just in the next five to 15 years, Green, Collins (the director of NIH), and their colleagues predict genomic testing will become as routine as complete blood counts and will guide prevention, diagnosis, and therapy. They expect that the biological function(s) of every human gene will be known and that studies involving analyses of genome sequences will be so routinely available they'll appear at school science fairs.[43, 44]

The sorts of techniques and computing power that are opening up genomics will allow for other "-omics" with extraordinary potential, too—proteomics, metabolomics, and other fields that will provide deep understanding of how our cells function.

One limiting factor for genomics lies in the difference between a genotype and a phenotype. A genotype is the genetic characteristics of an organism as detailed by its genome, while a phenotype refers to the actual physical characteristics of that organism. It's analogous to the difference between a blueprint for a house and the actual house itself. The physical characteristics of an organism are determined not just by the genetic blueprint described in the genome but by the complex interaction between an organism's many genes and environmental factors beyond the genome itself.* This complex interaction, known as epigenetics, very much affects health, albeit in complex ways. Even when we have all the data in front of us, as we do with many cancer genomes, the epigenetics are so complex that we can't yet decipher the diseases.

---

* The Department of Veterans Affairs (VA), with help from Booz Allen, has a program doing exactly this kind of genomics/epigenetics work. The goal of the program is to sequence the genomes of 1 million vets and match them to the 30-plus years of phenomic data contained in the VA's electronic health records. The work, which created electronic health records decades ahead of the private sector, provides a treasure trove of phenomic data.

But the Law of Zero on genomics, building on the Laws of Zero on computing, communication, and information will steadily advance our understanding—at an ever-accelerating pace.

We can also envision harnessing the power of genomics to create healthier foods; to eliminate the microbes that cause disease; to eradicate the most dangerous pests; to correct the genetic errors that cause disease; and to do all of the above in an ethical and equitable manner with a deep understanding of the implications of our choices.

We are truly writing in the language of life—and we're getting better at an exponential rate. Mendel would be proud. Stunned, but proud.

CHAPTER 5

The Fifth Law of Zero: Energy

A joke in the world of energy imagines Alexander Graham Bell and Thomas Edison coming back to life today. Bell would be amazed by wireless communications, by the small size of phones, by texting, by emojis, by TikTok, and by all sorts of other apps. What would he even do with an iPhone? With Snapchat? With FaceTime? Where would he start?

By contrast, Edison would look at the electric grid and say, "Yeah, that's about where I left things."

Fortunately, big change is finally afoot.

When Bell Labs developed the first solar photovoltaic panel in 1954, the cost was $1,000 per watt produced. That means it cost $75,000 to power a single reading lamp—a little pricey. The technology might have gone nowhere, at least for decades, except that the Soviet Union launched the Sputnik satellite in 1957, and, suddenly, the U.S. needed to launch satellites, too. National pride was at stake. Satellites needed a power source, but batteries weigh a lot, and every ounce matters when something has to be lifted into orbit. Batteries, of course, run out of power, and they also don't much like super-cold environments such as space. But space has lots of access to sunlight, and NASA had nearly unlimited access to money in those days, so it kept working on solar technology it could use to power satellites. By the early 1970s, the price for a solar panel had fallen to about $100 a watt. Then the oil scare hit, making solar power a more intriguing prospect, and a burst of research drove the price down again. By 2008, solar had fallen to $3.50 a watt. When the Great Recession hit, the Stimulus Act included $36.5 billion for the Department of Energy, which poured money into solar research right about the same time China decided to invest heavily in manufacturing solar panels. By 2017, solar was down to 25 cents a watt.[45] The International Energy Agency's annual report for 2020 said solar power was already "the cheapest electricity in history."[46]

Now we're talking.

A drop in price by a factor of 3,000 over six decades, as shown in Figure 5, isn't Moore's law, but it's certainly headed toward that magic number: zero.

Even as things stand now, buying fuel for a natural gas plant costs about the same as building new solar capacity.[47] A solar project that will supply seven percent of the electricity to Los Angeles promises power at less than two cents per kilowatt hour,[48] while the national average for electricity charges to consumers in the U.S. is nearly seven times that.[49] Plus, there's still loads of room for improvement in solar technology. There have even been breakthroughs in generating "solar" power from heat, removing the basic complaint: that solar panels can't generate power when the sun doesn't shine. In fact, these new panels can even generate power at night. Panels will also increasingly be built into roof tiles, road

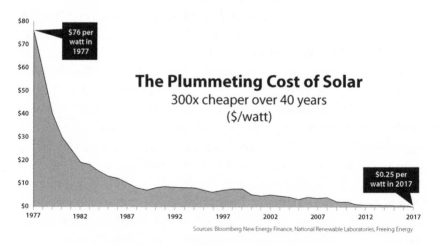

FIGURE 5. The Plummeting Cost of Solar

surfaces, and almost anything else you can imagine, including windows (which will still be transparent).[50] There's even work being done on solar paint. Not only will the new forms of solar power make it ubiquitous, they'll reduce what's rapidly becoming the biggest cost for solar: installation. Essentially, when it comes to any product you can imagine that will have a surface outdoors, the question will be: Want a little solar with that?

As a result, solar power is producing a consistent doubling in production; the amount of solar power generated has doubled every two years or less for the past 40 years. If that rate continues, solar is less than 12 years away from generating all the energy the world needs. Even Asia, which is known for keying growth to fossil fuels, has seen a surge in renewable energy sources, including solar.[51] A recent project that used machine learning to search through satellite data found 1.47 million solar installations in the 48 contiguous U.S. states, almost 50 percent more than was previously thought.[52] Exponentials are powerful things.

Wind power is also on an aggressive move toward zero—prices are down nearly 50 percent in just the past year-plus. Contracts were recently signed for wind power in Mexico and Brazil at two cents per kilowatt hour (kwh), which is less than a third of the average of 6.8 cents per kwh worldwide for coal, the cheapest of the conventional energy sources. The cost of wind power will continue to decline as the technology improves, and it's being pushed in plenty of promising directions. Turbines are being developed that can float and can thus be deployed farther offshore, where winds are stronger—experiments have even been done with wind turbines that would float in the air. Superefficient turbines that stand more than 850-feet tall will soon be deployed. Turbines without blades are being developed; they generate electricity by vibrating in place as the wind hits them. These devices, referred to as "skybrators," don't need to be large, like the wind turbines we see now, so they could be stationed almost anywhere, even in a backyard.[53] ARPA-E, part of the Department of Energy, is researching underwater turbines that are driven by currents and tides. Currents turn out to be highly reliable and are often close to areas with lots of power demand. And, of course, unlike with coal, you don't have to strip mine any more wind and transport it or burn it once a skybrator or wind turbine is put in place.

The key holdup for energy has been batteries. There has to be some way to store solar and wind energy for when you need it, which means lots and lots and lots of battery capacity. Fortunately, costs here are also plunging. The cost of industrial batteries dropped by nearly a factor of 12 between 2009 and 2018.

The room for improvement in batteries is enormous, too, partly because the little buggers are so complicated chemically that there are a ton of ways to improve them. For instance, makers are adding sensors to monitor the chemical reactions happening inside the batteries, then using software to tweak the interactions and optimize output. In an example of how the tools shape us after we shape the tools, AI is sifting through the essentially infinite combination of materials and chemicals to identify promising possibilities and greatly accelerate improvements. Researchers at Stanford, MIT, and the Toyota Research Institute, for instance, optimized the fast-charging capability of a lithium-ion battery in a month using AI, rather than the normal two years trial-and-error would have required.[54]

Merely increasing the number of batteries produced will reliably lead to big reductions in cost per output and per weight, too—which is where Elon Musk and his plans for massive manufacturing at his Gigafactory in Reno come in. India has also signed up for a huge increase in battery making as part of a goal of having all vehicles be electric by 2030.[55]

There are also lots of possible improvements in the basic chemistry of batteries. For instance, several companies recently announced they figured out how to use silicon as the anode to store the ions that provide the electricity in batteries. Silicon can store 25 times as many ions as the materials used today, and that may actually just be the beginning of the benefits from using silicon.[*]

Massive batteries for grid-level storage are being developed based on radically new ideas and will look nothing like what we currently think of as batteries—such as a battery based on molten salt that began as a Google "moon shot" and recently drew a $26 million investment from a fund whose investors include Michael Bloomberg.[56] Overall, as

---

[*] As with most issues related to batteries, changing to silicon won't be simple. Storing ions in it tends to crush the structure of the silicon, making it hard to reuse the battery. As a result, the initial uses of silicon are only promising gains of 15–40 percent in storage, but the switch to silicon looks like a fundamental shift in capability. https://www.wsj.com/articles/the-battery-boost-weve-been-waiting-for-is-only-a-few-years-out-1521374401

some batteries become enormous, others may disappear. Just as solar may migrate from separate panels and become part of the windows or paint on a house, why build a battery and put it in a car when you could have the battery be an integral part of the chassis?[57]

So, with batteries, solar, and wind, we have at least three cost curves in the energy realm that are very much headed in the right direction.

Now, the trend toward zero isn't anywhere close to as clear in energy as it is with computing, communication, information, and genomics. Not even close.

For one thing, these newly low prices for solar and wind include government subsidies. The plunge in their cost is real, but governments are pushing the numbers lower so they can try to narrow (or even eliminate) the price advantage of fossil fuels and can try to drive renewables to critical mass as soon as possible. In addition, while the cost curves have looked positively Moore's law-like in recent decades, it's not clear how much longer solar, wind, and batteries can maintain that progress. There will need to be breakthroughs, especially with batteries, if the trend is to continue.

In addition, the electric grid is wildly complex and delicate, as we all saw during the freeze in early 2021 that pretty well shut down Texas, killing at least 151, leaving 4.5 million homes without power and many without water, and doing $195 billion to $295 billion of damage.[58] Even having a breakthrough in batteries doesn't solve the whole problem for the grid. Batteries could become good enough to provide backup power almost all the time when the sun isn't shining and the wind isn't blowing, but the word "almost" matters a lot. There's no current prospect for batteries that could power an entire grid through a lengthy storm, let alone through a long, dark winter with diminished wind power. So, for now, some power source will still have to be available at least as a backup. That doesn't have to mean coal, oil, natural gas, and pollution—an argument is growing for new, much smaller, and far safer nuclear reactors. The Department of Defense's Project Pele is funding the development of small, portable fission reactors (which split atoms) that can be assembled in days and can generate one to five megawatts of power, enough for as many as 4,500 homes. Use of such reactors could especially help the underserved in the U.S. and around the world by enabling the quick installation of significant power generation. There's even progress in fusion (which combines atoms and generates power as the sun does). Whatever the solution, the cost curves for solar, wind, and batteries—as impressive as they are—aren't enough.

But there's still loads of reason for optimism. While we've explained why the numbers on solar, wind, and batteries aren't yet as good as they may seem, when they're looked at another way—the way economists say is the right way—the cost reductions are actually far more dramatic.

The key here is what economists call "externalities." At the moment, the price of power generated from coal, oil, and natural gas doesn't have to include the costs to society from the harm caused by the greenhouse gases they emit. *Scientific American* said in 2017 that between 7,500 and 52,000 Americans die every year from illnesses caused by power plant emissions.[59] That figure suggests hundreds of thousands more get sick. The greenhouse gases also contribute to climate change, whose effects we're increasingly able to see in concrete economic terms, based on more frequent and more violent storms, raging wildfires, and rising sea levels. Those externalities from illness, death, and environmental damages represent real costs—but not for the power companies that are largely responsible.

A study by the Brookings Institution found that making electricity powered by coal and natural gas carry the cost of those externalities would add 5.6 cents a kilowatt hour to the price of electricity.[60] You also have to account for the expense of the heavy U.S. political and military involvement in the Middle East, largely designed to protect our oil supply. Add up all the externalities and the total cost of carbon-based power is maybe 50 percent higher than what we pay now. So, just getting renewables—with their zero output of greenhouse gases—close to parity with fossil fuels is already a huge improvement in costs.*

Once carbon emissions cease being a consideration, people can use all the electricity they want. You don't have to worry about taking on a state or national government to get approval to double the output of your coal-fired plant. Once you have a solar panel or wind turbine installed,

---

* Yes, there are externalities associated with renewables—in particular, the need for land for solar farms; pollution associated with mining some of the materials, especially for batteries; and issues associated with dismantling and disposing of batteries and equipment at the end of their life—but they pale in comparison with the externalities associated with fossil fuels.

you can generate as much power as the equipment can possibly produce. It's hard to know exactly how people will use the electricity once they have power to burn (or, rather, power not to burn), but we know people tend to be creative. Think of all the memes and YouTube videos people send on their phones now that they have so much more computing power and bandwidth than they need for talking with each other.

The benefit of renewables won't just be all that carbon-free energy, either. The benefit will also be that all sorts of parts of the world will be able to operate unplugged from the grid. Think of the emergency phones you see along some freeways, powered by a solar panel with a bit of battery (though who really needs those phones in today's cellular age?), or the street lights that have a solar panel attached to the pole and operate independently of any outside electrical source. Parts of the world will look a lot like those emergency phones or street lights.

In some cases, there'll be neighborhoods or remote towns that operate based on "micro grids" that produce all their own power and can either tolerate the occasional lapse in power or will have some sort of backup—perhaps an emergency connection to a neighboring grid or perhaps some sort of generator. In parts of the world without electricity today, the arrival of any sort of sustained solar or wind power would be a straight-up gain.

These micro grids, too, will operate far more efficiently than the grid does today. Some six to eight percent of electricity is lost during transmission from the power plant to your home, and that's just the beginning of the inefficiencies. There are problems with planning that lead to much more electricity production than is needed. Power plants come online and go offline during the day, a process that can take many hours and is extremely inefficient.* Traffic jams occur frequently on power lines, preventing available power from being delivered to homes and businesses. Power is lost as voltage is stepped way up (to some 700 times the voltage you need in your home) to make transmission efficient and is then stepped down again so your appliances don't blow up. So on and so on. The power grid also presents a big, fat target for enemies of

---

* Some plants, known as "peakers," are online for only some dozens of hours per year to handle peak demand for air conditioning. They are the least efficient of plants—even charging the highest allowable rates, utilities typically lose money on power from these plants. Peakers are also the biggest polluters.

the U.S.—Russian hackers could take down large portions of the grid in a heartbeat and basically pick any number they want as a ransom demand—and it's vulnerable to severe solar storms.

If the grid goes away, then so do all these inefficiencies and vulnerabilities,* so the tendency will be to shift toward micro grids wherever possible.

That shift will greatly accelerate if nuclear power has, in fact, overcome its previous safety issues. A new style of nuclear reactor, based on thorium, produces far less nuclear waste than a uranium-based reactor, doesn't have to be fed with fuel after startup, and is designed to make a meltdown impossible. If a chain reaction gets out of control, a plug in the bottom of the reactor melts, and the fuel—which is less volatile than uranium—drains into a safety container. For good measure, thorium is nearly as plentiful as lead, and its use doesn't produce the sorts of byproducts that can be used in nuclear weapons. While thorium reactors are still in the research stage, they could be small enough to power a town of a few thousand people, at low cost and without carbon emissions.

Bill Gates argues there are plenty of other "energy miracles" to be found that will drive our Law of Zero on energy. He organized the Breakthrough Energy Coalition, which has brought together 20 billionaires who have pledged to, in total, spend at least $2 billion on research. Gates notes that the pharmaceutical industry spends 20 percent of revenue on research and that the information technology world spends 15 percent, while the energy industry historically has spent just 0.23 percent.[61] For its part, Google has invested in kite-based electricity generators (shades of Ben Franklin).[62] Lots of companies and researchers are working on geothermal, which the Department of Energy says could provide as much power as 60 large nuclear power plants in the U.S. by 2050.[63] As we've said, nuclear fusion might even make it out of the lab after decades of work.[64, 65] Japan is counting heavily on hydrogen fuel cells, which provide clean power for everything from cars to commercial buildings.[66] Other forms of hydrogen are drawing attention as potential carbon-neutral fuels[67]—Saudi Arabia is spending $5 billion on a plant where wind and solar energy will extract hydrogen from water,

---

* Developing countries have a chance to leapfrog developed countries here because they don't have to adapt a creaky, ancient network to fit today's realities.

and the European Union is spending $500 billion on infrastructure to support the use of hydrogen as a fuel.[68] The list of potential innovations for energy sources is long.

The U.S. government established ARPA-E in 2019 to do energy research that tries to emulate DARPA,[69] an adjunct of the Defense Department that launched the internet and GPS and spurred the early work on driverless cars. A Bank of America report argues other governments will also invest heavily in energy innovation as part of a global competition for what analysts see as $6 trillion of market capitalization available to the companies that most effectively tackle climate change.[70]

Meanwhile, Amory Lovins, in his important book *Reinventing Fire*, argues that radical improvements in the efficiency of equipment will greatly reduce the need for electricity. *The Wall Street Journal* recently painted a vision of a near-term future of "net-zero homes" that are so energy-efficient that adding "a little solar with that" would let them require zero electricity or natural gas from the grid. The article notes homes and commercial buildings use 40 percent of all the energy consumed in the U.S.[71]

Some of the approaches to energy efficiency read like science fiction. For instance, an outfit called SkyCool is working on a device you could install on your roof that would turn heat from your house into a type of radiation that would use a narrow slice of the spectrum of light and would be transmitted up through the atmosphere into space; your house would be cooled by as much as 70 percent, and the heat would leave the planet permanently.[72] The Air Force is experimenting with putting a vast solar array into orbit, where it could operate far more efficiently than on the ground, and then beaming the energy back to Earth.[73] The vast majority of these think-big approaches will fail, but enough will work that we'll see breakthroughs in energy efficiency.

Energy powers every living thing, and, together, all these possibilities for innovation will produce a sort of Law of Zero for energy that will create unfathomable benefits for the Future Perfect.

Edison wouldn't know what hit him.

CHAPTER 6

The Sixth Law of Zero: Water

Water is becoming so scarce and precious that many say it's "the new oil." Demand for water will grow with population, urbanization, and wealth, taxing traditional fresh water supplies while also polluting them.

But there's hope.

To see how that hope could play out, let's look back into the mid- to late-1800s and the world's obsessive need for bird guano—yup, we're going to talk about bird poop. Economist Thomas Malthus famously wrote in 1798 that, essentially, we were all doomed to die in a famine because food production couldn't keep up with population growth. Jonathan Swift's epic satirical essay, "A Modest Proposal," said that, because all the poor kids were going to die and rich people would be hungry, why not just feed the poor kids to the rich people? Then bird poop came to the rescue—once the wonders of nitrogen-rich guano were discovered, the world's farmers had all the fertilizer they needed. Poor kids—and everybody else—were safe.

But the competition for guano became fierce—so fierce the U.S. passed a law during the Lincoln administration that promised the protection of the U.S. Navy to any citizen who found an island covered in bird guano that could credibly be claimed as a U.S. possession. Spain went to war with former colonies Chile and Peru in the mid-1860s over the guano-rich Chincha Islands. Chile and an alliance of Bolivia and Peru fought a five-year war over the Atacama Desert, which had become covered with especially nice, dry bird poop.

By the late 1800s, bird guano was running out. Pessimism about the food supply set in again as the 20th century began.

Then Fritz Haber came along and, in 1909, invented a process that literally pulled nitrogen out of thin air*, and Carl Bosch made the process scale. The food crisis was over.

All that was needed for the Haber-Bosch process was a catalyst and lots of energy. The Law of Zero for energy should now allow for some of that same sort of magic with water.

Water won't be pulled right out of thin air in great quantities any time soon, but that technology is under development.[74] One group won a $1.5 million XPRIZE by developing a generator that can be used in any climate and can extract at least 2,000 liters of water a day from the air at a cost of less than two cents a liter, using entirely renewable energy.[75] Cody Friesen, founder of SOURCE Global, says one to two percent of the world's carbon footprint comes from mass-purifying today's water; that carbon dioxide goes away when water is drawn from the air and is purified at your doorstep by the sorts of solar-powered SOURCE Hydropanels he produces.[76] (Friesen's company has its naysayers, who believe the technology will never be inexpensive enough at scale.[77]) Think of all the time and effort people in developing countries could save if they didn't have to trudge miles to and from wells every day. Then think about what they can do with all that newly available time.

By the time the Future Perfect arrives, anyone near a body of salt water will certainly benefit from technology breakthroughs. Desalination has always been possible but prohibitively expensive because of the energy costs, whether done by filtering out the salt through osmosis or by evaporating the water and leaving the salt behind. But cheap energy makes desalination more plausible at a time when many cities are getting desperate. Cape Town, in South Africa, was on watch for Day Zero for a year—Day Zero being when water for the city of 4.3 million people

---

* While Haber's process provided a remarkable service for humanity, history doesn't always proceed as we might hope. Haber, a German, went on to lead the development of the poison gas that Germany used on the battlefields in World War I and personally supervised its early use. Apparently in protest, his wife committed suicide. Their son later died by suicide, too, as did the son's eldest daughter. Scientists working for Haber developed an early version of the poison used in the Nazi gas chambers during the Holocaust.

would run out, even as limitless salt water from the Atlantic Ocean sits cheek by jowl with the city.[78] (Slashing water consumption in the city by 50 percent bought time, and rains eventually began to refill reservoirs.) Chennai, a city of 11 million that is India's sixth-largest, hit Day Zero in mid-2019 even though it's on the coast of the Bay of Bengal.[79] Chennai has been in a state of emergency ever since. Dubai, a city of about 2.5 million, is so desperate that it's explored the possibility of towing a 100 million-ton iceberg to the city's shore from 5,500 miles away in Antarctica.[80] San Diego has already opened a $1 billion desalination plant that provides water for about 300,000 people, and there are some 20,000 desalination plants around the world already that provide water for about 300 million people.[81] The cost of the desalinated water is twice as high as the cost of water from other sources,[82] but remember: Energy costs are following a Law of Zero. If costs fall far enough, suddenly desalination isn't just plausible at scale; it's positively economic.

Many states and countries will transport the desalinated water well beyond the coast. Already, California uses about a third of its energy output to transport water from the wet northern part of the state to the arid south. So the Law of Zero for water has the potential to create the kind of effect air conditioning did in the early 20th century. At the time, the American Southwest, for instance, was considered barely habitable because of the heat; then air conditioning tamed it. Now, cities like Phoenix are among the fastest-growing in the country. Just imagine the possible population shifts if water becomes abundant almost anywhere within striking distance of an ocean.*

Water reuse will also become far more common. Taking effluent from wastewater plants and treating it to drinking-water quality has long been possible but hasn't been done at any scale because of the "yuck" factor. People can't fathom drinking water that came from raw sewage, even though it's perfectly fine in every way. But the increased demand for water as climate change dries up many areas (including the American West) will push water reuse into the mainstream. We'll have no choice. Water reuse will become a major factor in agriculture, industry, and human consumption.

---

* Desalination must still cope with, in particular, the problem of brine waste: The liquid left behind after the fresh water is produced is extremely salty and must be disposed of carefully. Simply dumping it back into the ocean can kill an ecosystem.

Technology advances will let water reuse happen all over the place—not only at centralized facilities but in small, distributed ways, much as the gains we detailed in the Law of Zero for energy allow for micro grids. For instance, the Janicki Omni Processor generates electricity and water simultaneously, while also attacking sanitation problems in developing countries—three wins at once. The device is a sort of self-contained plant whose input is a slurry of raw sewage. The machine boils the sewage, producing fresh water—waste from 100,000 people would provide enough water for 43,000 of them. The residue from the water, now dry, is then burned to boil more sewage and to produce electricity. The fire produces ash that has no odor and no microbes that could cause disease; the ash can be used as a soil amendment or additive for construction material.[83]

If water fades as an issue, political tensions would drop in many areas. China is currently damming up the Mekong River, claiming much of its water and angering those the river feeds throughout Southeast Asia. Israel and its Arab neighbors are arguing over the water from the Jordan River. There are rumblings of war between Egypt and Ethiopia over a dam Ethiopia has nearly completed on the Nile. Southwestern states in the U.S. tussle over the Colorado River, which is tapped so heavily it runs dry before reaching the sea. More access to more plentiful water would drastically ease concerns and tensions.

Where there's abundant water, along with the energy that comes from that Law of Zero, there can be food, so all sorts of possibilities arise. For instance, people are experimenting with "vertical farming," growing food on the sides of tall buildings or using artificial photosynthesis to grow food in warehouses,[84] so city dwellers could have access to fresher produce transported over shorter distances.

That kind of controlled, indoor farming could also produce the sort of radical improvement in efficiency for water usage that Lovins, the author and conservationist, foresees for energy usage—and farming accounts for 80 percent of water consumption in the U.S.

In any case, just as electricity no longer needs to tie into an elaborate grid, water could be produced independent of the massive, municipal pipeline projects we rely on now. In the Future Perfect, the basics of life will be available everywhere, even to the far corners of the Earth.

CHAPTER 7

The Seventh Law of Zero: Transportation

Although the enthusiasm for autonomous vehicles (AVs) took a hit for a couple of years—they're a really hard problem—momentum is building again, and the multitude of startups and brilliant scientists tackling the issues make us confident the Future Perfect will include an unlimited number of fully autonomous vehicles.

The implications are mind-boggling. The cost of driving, in terms of the time you devote to it, will essentially disappear once we reach full autonomy. With time no longer a factor, distance won't be one, either. Even if you have to travel a couple of hundred miles or spend two to three hours in a vehicle, you'll take your world (your phone, computer, and VR goggles) into the vehicle with you and can act just as you would sitting on your couch at home or your desk at the office.

Now, a lot of metal will need to be shaped and maintained even in an autonomous future, so transportation won't be free. The power for the cars won't be free, either, but it should cost much less than it does today because all cars will be electric, and energy prices will benefit from that Law of Zero.

Still, all in all, the costs of transportation will be so much lower than they are today that we can be profligate in throwing transportation resources at anything we want to design for the Future Perfect.*

---

* We acknowledge measuring progress on the Law of Zero for transportation is fuzzier than for the other laws. There isn't a straightforward measure, like cost per transistor

You won't need to go get things—they'll come to you. That ingredient you forgot for a dinner dish, or, for that matter, the dinner itself? Just summon it. You'll pay a monthly fee to be part of the circuit for those who, like you, forget things, but you won't need to spend 20 minutes on a trip (more if you have to wrestle small kids into the car with you).[85] Everything you'll need will come based on a sort of Amazon Prime to the nth degree. You won't need to take your kids to soccer practice. The cars will do it (only opening their doors once a coach or other designated adult has acknowledged the kids are accounted for). The elderly parent whose keys you've had to take away or the physically challenged relative who can't drive? No problem. That person can now get around just like anyone else.

Autonomous drones will kick in, too. They'll not only drop off packages at your doorstep but will provide emergency help. Imagine drones stationed throughout neighborhoods that could do CPR or administer naloxone to someone suffering from an opioid overdose. Or imagine drones that could deliver a flotation device to someone adrift at sea; provide food, water, and medical supplies to someone lost in the mountains; or airlift out individuals trapped by a wildfire or flood.

You may even get that flying car we've all been hearing about for decades.* You still won't be George or Jane Jetson and be able to be-bop anywhere—helicopter-like flying cars are mechanically probably too tricky to be deployed widely, and car/planes require runways for taking off and landing, even if you can figure out what to do about the wings as the car/plane drives down the highway. But the airways should certainly open up to new forms of passenger traffic. The limitations of flying cars

---

on a chip, watt of energy, or liter of water. Transportation involves tradeoffs among speed, cost, and quality, depending on the what, how, and why of the person or thing being transported. But, in spite of all the provisos and difficult-to-exactly-measure ambiguities that economists and historians will rightly point out, it's clear that quantitative improvements in the time and cost of moving people and things have repeatedly driven qualitative changes in the long arc of human history. And, viewed from the vantage point of that long arc, both time and cost are now moving rapidly down that trendline toward zero.

* ARPA-E is working with researchers to fund various renewable energy approaches to aviation, including the REEACH and ASCEND programs. Ammonia-powered engines and more powerful electric engines are among the areas being pursued. https://arpa-e .energy.gov/sites/default/files/documents/files/REEACH_Project%20Descriptions_ FINAL.pdf, https://arpa-e.energy.gov/sites/default/files/documents/files/ASCEND_ Project_Descriptions_FINAL.pdf

up to this point have really been a computing problem—it's so hard to keep track of all those objects in the air that major airlines still fly primarily via the equivalent of freeways that criss-cross in the sky, rather than just going straight from the starting point to the landing spot. But the Law of Zero for computing means we'll have orders of magnitude more computing power and can manage far more objects in the sky, without them running into each other. And you have a lot more room for vehicles when you're working in three dimensions rather than two. There's also no need to pour concrete to create those routes in the sky.

The Law of Zero for transportation means you could very well take an AV to a local airport in the Bay Area, catch a flying car for the half-hour flight to Truckee, California, and have an AV take you to the resort where you're staying in Lake Tahoe—avoiding what today could be two hours sitting in bumper-to-bumper traffic on the San Mateo Bridge over the San Francisco Bay on a Friday afternoon in winter, followed by a potential slog through a snowstorm as you climb into the mountains.*

Sometimes, nothing will even have to move in the Future Perfect. While virtual reality has had its fits and starts over the past 25 years, it will have so much more computing power and bandwidth that it will let you "drop in" to some situations without ever having to leave your home or office—and the pandemic greatly accelerated remote work, both in terms of the technology and in terms of general acceptance.

All these changes will be phased in, of course. The dangers of having a drone drop something on you from 150 feet in the air, for instance, are great enough that restrictions will be severe until the technology really proves itself—never mind the restrictions that will govern autonomous planes filled with people. But the changes will happen soon enough that they can be assumed for a Future Perfect world.

So much will change about transportation, time, and distance that the interactions are hard to project with certainty. But don't be lulled into complacency: Changes that may seem like simple, linear improvements can produce decidedly nonlinear effects.

Consider an example as unsexy as the Erie Canal, known as "Clinton's Big Ditch" or even "Clinton's Folly" after the New York governor who

---

* Not that we're smarting from personal experience or anything, but what is, under decent conditions, a 3½-hour drive from the Bay Area to Tahoe City once took one of the authors 14 hours.

championed it in the early 1800s. All the canal did was provide a faster connection between Buffalo and Albany once it was completed in 1825. Travel time over the 363 miles dropped from 45 days by wagon to nine days by barge (still a long trip, but a lot less long). The cost of cargo declined 99.5 percent because a team of two mules, which could pull a wagon carrying about 500 pounds, could pull a barge laden with 100,000 pounds of cargo. But the changes the canal caused stretched far beyond what those improvements would suggest. Boom towns exploded along the canal—including at Buffalo, Rochester, Syracuse, and Albany—that grew into major cities. Even more important was that having the canal connect the Great Lakes port of Buffalo to the Hudson River port of Albany by water, 150 miles upriver from New York City, opened the interior of the continent up to settlement and transformed New York City into a dominant port and a world commercial center.

All because of a "ditch."

We've seen new forms of transportation cause tectonic shifts repeatedly. James Watt's dramatic improvement to the steam engine enabled the river steamboats, steam-driven trains, and ocean steamships that drove expansion, integration, and global trade throughout the 19th century. The car—initially seen as merely a better version of a horse—reshaped cities and created suburbs. The internal combustion engine that powered those early cars also produced trucks and, enabled by the interstate highway system, reshaped commerce and just about everything else about how we live, work, and play. The jet engine enabled planes that shrank world travel into a day—forget about getting from Buffalo to Albany in nine days; you can get from Buffalo to *Moscow* in nine *hours*.

AVs will provide the next such step-change in transportation and will transform how we live and work. We can already see that vast amounts of space will open up in cities, where nearly a third of space is devoted to parking cars that will no longer need to be parked—cars will just drop people off and then move on to their next user or head to a waiting area. In the U.S., there are 2 billion parking spaces for 275 million cars, or more than seven for every vehicle,[86] so doing away with parking areas will provide lots of flexibility to redesign public spaces.

We suspect that lots more people will live in cities because they're efficient and because they'll become much more attractive once you get rid of parking spaces and the noise and air pollution that come with vehicles using internal combustion engines. Still, others will take advantage of their newly free time and distance and live near that lake in the country, know-ing they can get to a city any time they want, with zero inconvenience.* Cars, buses, trolleys, and subways shaped the urban/suburban landscape a century ago, making cities more attractive by getting rid of the steaming piles of horse manure that built up on every corner and allowing for sub-urbs to thrive, too. Similarly, AVs will create forces that impel new shifts, including many that aren't immediately obvious but that will develop as AVs remove design constraints and as brilliant imaginations run free.

Yes, lots of people and businesses will have to adapt. Most notable are the 4.5 million professional drivers in the U.S.[†] (whom we firmly believe will have ample opportunities for new employment, though we acknowledge the transition will be painful for many). Autonomous vehicles will also change emergency rooms; they currently treat some 2.5 million people each year related to auto accidents and, based on cur-rent estimates, might treat only 10 percent as many once AVs become ubiquitous. Car insurance will essentially go away—why do you need insurance when there are almost no accidents, and you aren't driving, anyway? Police departments won't need patrols on the road watching for misdeeds by drivers. And so on.

On the other side of all that adaptation, we know that health, wealth, education, economic mobility, and more will all improve, because access to resources currently constrains so many people, and the Law of Zero for transportation means those limitations will disappear in the Future Perfect.

We also know that women won't have to worry about being attacked by a driver, as there won't be one, and that the vast majority of the roughly 40,000 people who die on U.S. roads every year will miss that appointment with death and will keep living full lives.

• • •

Drawing on all seven of the Laws of Zero will now let us start to design the future we want, pulling from both our research and from the think-ing of some awfully smart friends we've worked with over the years.

---

* Google's buses are already showing the possibilities. Googlers who live within even 2½ hours of the headquarters in Mountain View, CA, can board a bus right near their homes that's as functional as their office and can work all the way to HQ, spend a few hours available for face-to-face interaction, and then be driven back home, working all the while.

† 3.5 million truck drivers, 230,000 taxi drivers, and 750,000-plus drivers for Uber and Lyft.

Based on the Laws of Zero and other likely advances in technology, in the next section we'll explore key areas where we think we can collectively design wonderful—yet plausible—futures. We'll also introduce you to the key tool, called a future history, that we use and that we will, at the end of the book, turn over to you so you can start to fill in the many blanks.

As we've said, not all these Laws of Zero will kick in right away. The laws will all evolve within today's reality and will require time to supplant it. For instance, the fleet of cars on the road typically takes about 15 years to turn over, so, even if autonomous vehicle technology were perfect tomorrow, people wouldn't just throw away their current cars and switch over to AVs—and AVs certainly won't be perfect tomorrow.

But we still think the core question here is a fascinating and important one: How will these Laws of Zero (and assorted other developments) let us design as grand a world as possible for our kids and for their kids in 2050? What can removing today's actual and cognitive restraints let us realistically project for them?

The short answer is: a lot.

The longer answer follows.

PART TWO

THE FUTURE
HISTORIES

"History will be kind to me, for I intend to write it myself."
—*Winston Churchill**

C hurchill was right. History will be kinder to us if we take the time to write it ourselves —especially if we do so *before* it unfolds, not after.

Every desirable (and undesirable) future scenario in this book depends on a host of complex interactions, and realizing our Future Perfect will require getting everyone on the same page for the challenging transition to it. The best way we've found for doing this is by imagining an idealized version of a future that's years out. Then, from that vantage point in the future, we craft a "history" that lays out how we got there from here. Thus, our name for these narratives: "future histories."

Devices like our future histories show up in many settings as ways of helping people jointly construct a vision and start implementing it. When Amazon begins work with a potential partner, it often starts by jointly producing a mock press release "announcing" a deal. Only when the two sides establish the broad outlines of the desired future do they start negotiating the details and working toward it. Maybe our favorite example reaches back to 1296, when the Catholic church in Italy laid out plans for the glorious *Il Duomo* in Florence and began construction—without knowing how to build the dome that gives the *Cattedrale di Santa Maria del Fiore* its famous nickname, but confident that the expertise would be there when needed.

* This is a common paraphrase of the sort of thing that Churchill said many times. For instance, toward the end of World War II, a British admiral said that the verdict on an operation would depend on who wrote the history, and Churchill replied that "he intended to have a hand in that." [*Churchill: Walking With Destiny*, by Andrew Roberts, Viking, 2018, p. 835] In a debate on foreign affairs in 1948, Churchill suggested that all the parties "leave the past to history, especially as I propose to write that history myself." [*Churchill*, p. 908]

A competition to design the dome was eventually launched in 1418, by which point understanding of architecture had, in fact, advanced sufficiently, and Brunelleschi completed the magnificent cathedral in 1436.

As we've said, future histories aren't meant to predict the future. Rather, our future histories focus on the outcomes we want to achieve. They can't be untethered, pie-in-the-sky, wishful thinking. We all want our team to win the Super Bowl every year, but it simply won't happen. (Yes, we realize there may be a Tom Brady exception.) Instead, our future histories focus on the outcomes we believe are *achievable* within the allotted time.

We'll ask: What would it be crazy for society not to have in 30 years? What big problems can the exponentials help us solve in that sort of timeframe? We picked a 30-year timeframe because that's so far in the future we don't have to worry (yet) about how to get there. At the same time, 30 years is close enough we can realistically envision what might be technologically possible, with enough foresight and effort—the scientific and technological starting points for much of what can be applied at scale in 30 years already exist today. That vision can then guide estimates of how much progress needs to be made by the halfway point, which, can, in turn, allow for the sort of five- or 10-year plan that's a common way of informing long-range strategy. Typically, those early investments are small, but you have to take that initial step so you can be ready for the next one and the one after that... and can be prepared to take full advantage when the exponentials kick in 10, 20, or 30 years.

It's certainly fair to worry about how we can possibly take the huge steps by 2050 that we'll lay out as goals for the Future Perfect. But allowing those worries to enter the process too early can severely constrain imaginations, and we might end up with incremental strategies that completely miss out on the future. Thinking bigger is almost always better. Kodak, the company that invented digital photography, spent decades taking baby steps toward digital and eventually went bankrupt defending its film and paper-based business. Incrementalism is why the original AT&T, which drove progress in computing, communications, and information for decades, couldn't make a successful transition from analog, circuit-switched, and wired phones to the world of digital, packet-switched, and networked mobile communications in the 1990s and 2000s and has had an up-and-down record since. Incrementalism is why many of today's business giants won't make the transition to our more perfect future of 2050.

But *you* will!

Future histories aren't encyclopedic blueprints of a desired future state. As much as we'd love to have a concrete vision of 2050, there are simply too many variables to produce a fully realized projection of the world 30 years out. So, rather than a grand unified field theory of the future, we're going to sketch out some of the defining features. We'll illustrate with examples that, while they're already in use, are so far ahead of the game they may read like science fiction. (In our vignettes dated from 2035 and 2050, we'll use some names of companies and individuals that you'll recognize, but, obviously, any "quotes" from those companies and any individuals as well as the actions we describe in the future are figments of our imagination; assume any names you don't recognize are invented to make for a better story, but any events we describe as having occurred in the present day are real. You'll have to be a little careful, but we've tried hard to reduce confusion.)

Future histories fulfill our human need for narratives, taking abstract capabilities and visions and making them real in ways that let people internalize them and get excited. Future histories help people understand how they can contribute—how they will contribute. People can understand timing issues and see how efforts will build. People can also focus on the threats to their vision that, as a group, they must fend off. These threats may no longer be the saber-toothed tigers that stalked our distant ancestors, but they are still very real obstacles. We hope future histories can unite us as we face the inevitable challenges ahead.

In the next several chapters, as much as possible, we'll infuse the future histories with systems thinking. In other words, we won't just describe the technological breakthroughs that are coming but will do our best to show how they'll play out in much broader systems. For instance, while some proponents of electric vehicles tout the fact that no pollution comes out of tailpipes, our broader systems view will note that the electricity for the batteries largely comes from fossil fuel power plants; that the metals used in batteries and many electronic components are the product of a mining process that causes considerable damage to the environment and comes from countries many other countries would rather not support; and so on.

We're pleased to see that some industries are already starting to take more of a systems view. Historically, consumer products companies, for instance, have packaged their goods and then left it to consumers to figure out how to dispose of the debris. They're now realizing—under some pressure—that they need to consider the full life cycle of their products and come up with biodegradable packaging, a recycling process that goes far beyond what is happening today, or something so that we don't just keep adding landfills or expanding the 80,000-ton Great Pacific Garbage Patch. Nordstrom encourages customers to bring in beauty product packaging for recycling. MAC gives customers a free lipstick in return for a certain number of empties. But industry doesn't have a great track record on systems thinking. Companies optimize the performance and the cost of their piece of a system while not worrying about the whole.

The effect has been to create what Alan Kay calls "Myopialand" and to push to the future costs that are being incurred today.* Energy generation probably provides the best example, as the world has spent the past two centuries-plus producing "cheap" energy from fossil fuels and leaving future generations to deal with the costs of the environmental damage and to find a way to get the planet back on track. Swedish scientist Svante Arrhenius figured out 120 years ago how to calculate the effects of atmospheric carbon dioxide on the temperature of the planet and concluded humans were causing global warming, but warming was never assigned an economic cost, even as calculations of the cost have become increasingly precise over the past 60 years, so little was ever done. We'll try to be as careful as we can about weighing all the costs and all the prospective benefits in our future histories—though we acknowledge that experts in the areas we touch on will be far more precise than we are here and that, even for experts, it can be hard to predict all the interplay among forces in an ecosystem.

We won't write future histories for all the areas that we think are important and that will see massive change in the Future Perfect—we'd wear ourselves out, and we'd wear you out, too. But we'll cover several

---

* The intriguing sci-fi novel *The Ministry for the Future* by Kim Stanley Robinson builds on the idea of an international ministry set up to guard the interests of future generations against excessive climate change. While plenty of chaos ensues, Robinson describes the book as a hopeful "future history."

that we believe are key and hope we inspire others to use the model to tackle other critical issues, such as education, food, and shelter.

Like the Apple Knowledge Navigator video that helped produce the iPad some 25 years later, we'll include factors that should be revolutionary and will package them as neatly as possible. But, like that video, we won't presume to show all the changes that will ripple out from the breakthroughs. We'll count on you—and a host of other smart people—to figure out the rest.

Think of this part of the book as Future Perfect: Some Assembly Required.

Sound like a plan? Let's get started.

CHAPTER 8

The Future History
of Electricity

Fresh Water in the Desert

SAN PEDRO DE ATACAMA, CHILE, May 25, 2050—A water fountain sits in the middle of the Atacama Desert, a desolate, 600-mile long stretch along the coast of Chile. It has no pipes connecting it to a water source. The nearest power outlet isn't anywhere in sight. Yet the water fountain reliably produces purified water for anyone who wants a drink, day after day, week after week.

Credit: FreshWater

How is this possible? Some explanation may be in order.

The Atacama Desert is the driest place on Earth outside of the polar deserts. It averages 0.6 inch of rainfall annually, and some weather stations here have never registered a drop of rain. But the humidity is some 30 percent. That means there's a lot of water available in the air for anyone with a condenser and enough power to drive it.

That's why, 33 years ago, in 2017, Chilean engineer Héctor Pino and two colleagues at FreshWater, a Chilean startup, chose the middle of the Atacama Desert to dramatize their development of a free-standing water fountain.[87] The device ran on standard alternating current, on batteries, or on solar power—and the Atacama Desert, it won't surprise you to hear, has plenty of sun. Pino and his colleagues proclaimed that anyone setting up enough of their FreshWater devices and solar panels could have as much clean water as they wanted, anywhere they wanted it, without any connection to water pipes or electric grids. And they proved their point.

Circa 2020, about 40,000 Chilean communities, mostly in rural areas, had little or no access to surface or ground-water supplies and had to rely on transported water. Throughout Latin America, Pino estimated, 34 million people were living in the same situation. The World Health Organization (WHO) said that, globally, 500 million lacked sufficient water all year long and that four billion people spent at least one month a year without enough water.[88]

"We wanted to democratize access to this vital resource," Pino explained.

Earth's atmosphere contains 13 trillion tons of water in the form of clouds, fog, and water vapor, which is six times as much water as in the world's rivers. And, unlike rivers, the atmospheric moisture is everywhere—even in the Atacama Desert.

FreshWater's device was initially expensive (some $1,600 in 2020) and only produced nine liters of water a day. The WHO says a person needs 50 liters a day to meet basic needs for drinking, food preparation, personal hygiene, and sanitation. For good measure, the company ran into political and competitive obstacles. It turned out the companies that truck water to remote areas in Chile didn't exactly welcome the potential competition, and they held sway at various levels of government. FreshWater found its prospects limited.

Then, the Laws of Zero kicked in. Advances in computing and information drove the development of materials and designs to allow the company to more effectively and efficiently extract moisture. Some scientists, for example, took inspiration from plant structures, such as the fog-collecting needles of giant sequoia trees, to improve the surface structure design of collectors. Others, such as Professor Omar Yaghi at the University of California, Berkeley, developed much better water-absorbing materials.[89] Advances in 3-D printing allowed manufacturing to happen much closer to where the devices were needed and allowed for any replacement parts to be produced more quickly and cheaply. Increasingly advanced sensors alerted users when a device was about to fail, essentially eliminating downtime, and warned if water had been sitting so long in the device's reservoir that it had become fetid.

And, of course, the Law of Zero for energy kept driving down the cost for the solar capabilities that power these devices and make it easy for them to operate off the grid. The economics of water-from-air solutions overwhelmed all obstacles. It's now the de facto approach for bringing water to the thirstiest parts of the world, providing a wild boost to productivity—women in Africa used to spend 40 billion hours a year walking to and from wells to collect water;[90] now, in many places, they can just step outside their front door and collect all the water they need. Governments justify subsidizing the cost of the devices because the water is so pure it reduces health care spending, and many non-governmental organizations (NGOs) contribute funds because of the clear health benefits—circa 2020, more people died from water-borne illnesses than from all forms of violence, including war.[91] The old saying is that plumbers have saved more lives than doctors, and FreshWater became the plumber for developing countries.

In the 1920s and 1930s, Nikola Tesla worked on a plan to harness cosmic energy and broadcast electricity to everyone in the world without a need for wires. While the brilliant Serbian-American accomplished so many other things, including our system of alternating current and much of the early work on radio transmission, he never did manage to build what he called his World Power System. But today, in 2050, electricity is so cheap and widely available off the grid that even pulling water from the air is as natural as breathing in oxygen in many parts of the world.

Why, you could now have an orange grove in the middle of the Atacama Desert, if you wanted—perhaps to sell juice at the ice cream bar you're going to set up, using the abundant solar power at your fingertips to refrigerate the Ben and Jerry's Chunky Monkey you've had flown in to you by solar-powered drones.

The idea of water, water anywhere, and all the drops to drink (or to use however you want) is actually just the start of what the Law of Zero on energy delivers.

We think it'd be crazy not to have clean electricity available to everyone, everywhere, in abundant and affordable quantities in the Future Perfect.

Without breakthroughs, inertia will carry us to a future where we still rely heavily on fossil fuels and where many parts of the world have no or limited access to electricity, whether that's because costs are too high or because the grid doesn't reach them. But the exponentials in the Laws of Zero can deliver vast increases in carbon-free, renewable energy sources, together with either extensive batteries or nuclear energy that can fill the gaps the renewable sources can leave. The Laws of Zero will also allow more and more communities to cut loose from the grid and will extend access to power to parts of the world that currently aren't served.

Life doesn't exist without energy. With unlimited energy—free from the constraints that the dangers of greenhouse gases place on today's sources—life can be lush everywhere. The Law of Zero on energy will be the second coming of Prometheus, but no one will have to bear being chained to a rock and having his liver eaten and regrown every day as punishment from the heavens for this great gift to the human race.

Our goal is certainly formidable. Projections are that the world will need twice as much electricity in 2050 as is produced now. Even if the planet's population somehow doesn't increase, and even if energy efficiency improves massively, having billions of people climb out of poverty and into a middle-class existence means they'll consume far more electricity than they do now. And, even in most developed economies, clean energy still provides just a modest amount of the power—in the U.S., renewables supply only about 14 percent of the electricity. Do the math: A doubling of electricity consumption, while going from 14-100 percent reliance on clean sources, would mean we'd need about 14 times as much renewable energy in 2050 as what exists today.

It's not easy. But it's doable.

We've already explained how solar will have the potential to be everywhere and low-cost—it won't just be arranged as massive power plants or even as panels on your roof but as shingles on your roof, in your windows, even in the paint on your house or apartment building. You'll even get "solar" power at night, drawing on changes in temperature.

Wind power will be widespread, too, and, like solar, will be extremely inexpensive. Some countries, such as Denmark, which has access to the high winds on the North Sea, already get as much as half their electricity from wind and benefit from its zero marginal cost. Texas, while known as the home of oil and gas in the U.S., is also the state producing the most wind energy. The winds blow hard across west Texas. Wind power, which is strongest at night, complements solar power, and together they're expanding so quickly in Texas that they're expected to provide 59,000 megawatts of electricity by 2023.[92] That would be enough to power nearly 12 million homes in Texas, which has just 7.4 million households, meaning there'll be plenty of electricity left over for use by businesses or for export. Texas' black gold is turning green.

Yes, we all saw what happened in February 2021 when 10 days of cold weather caused a catastrophic loss of electricity in Texas. Many wind turbines iced up, and some Texas government officials, along with other critics of renewable energy, seized on the problem to argue that wind was too unreliable a source to play much of a role in the grid of the future. But the deep freeze hardly obviates a role for wind. Wind turbines work just fine in winter weather far harsher than Texas experienced—the issue in Texas is that officials didn't prepare for cold weather in the way that those operating in, say, Alaska and North Dakota do. The real issues, as the Texas crisis dramatized, are that we need to prepare better for extreme weather (which will happen more and more often) and that we need to modernize the grid. Texas operates almost entirely free of the rest of the national grid to avoid federal regulation, so only pockets of territory within the state's borders could draw on power from other states.

Critics of renewables are certainly correct in saying the sun isn't always shining and the wind isn't always blowing where you need electricity, but that doesn't mean there isn't plenty of shining and blowing somewhere within reach of a transmission line. You obviously don't have to have an oil well and refinery next to your garage to fill your car with gasoline; a massive, global system will ship it to you based on fracking in Pennsylvania or pumping in Saudi Arabia. And massive investments going into making transmission more efficient mean it'll be possible to deliver renewable power over great distances. Sunny North Africa, for instance, is exploring the possibility of powering cloudy Northern Europe.[93] China is building an ultrahigh-voltage "super grid" to carry electricity from the massive wind and solar farms in its rural Northwest regions to its megacities in the East and South. Last year, China brought a 2,046-mile-long transmission line online.[94]

Storage capability is moving the slowest of all the major factors in the Law of Zero on energy, but the magic of the markets should speed things up nicely. If you think about it, Tesla is basically a bet on a rapid improvement in batteries. Tesla needs the best batteries in its cars, because range is key in the competition among electric vehicles. So Elon Musk is investing in the area as fast as he can, including by building multibillion-dollar plants to generate economies of scale. Tesla's purchase of SolarCity also depends on improving in-home batteries to the point that they, in combination with the batteries in Tesla cars, can capture all the power generated by solar panels and produce a system that powers both the home and the car. The stock market is giving Musk all sorts of encouragement. As of this writing, Tesla is valued at $655 billion, more than all the other car companies in the world, even though the company commands just 1.6 percent share of the auto market in the U.S. So, Musk has access to all the capital he needs—and then some.

Markets aren't always trustworthy. In fact, they remind us of the famous line about the once closely watched index of leading economic indicators, the federal government measure that was said to have predicted "nine of the last five recessions"—but markets don't have to be trustworthy, at least for our purposes. While markets are providing all sorts of capital for Musk to drive innovation in batteries, they're also creating loads of incentives for others to emulate him and will provide tons of capital, whether wise or wasted, that will help others drive innovation in batteries and in a host of other areas that touch on our Future Perfect.* Basically, markets guess at what the future might be and then pull the benefits forward to today in the form of market value for those who are fortunate enough to make a compelling case about owning that future. We all benefit as a society from the resultant innovations, whether or not the investors do.

Global superpower competition will accelerate innovation in batteries, too. Other than the fight currently raging over which country will dominate 5G wireless technology, it's hard to imagine a more intense battle than the one over who will own the battery space. China, in particular, sees batteries as a route toward economic advantage,[95] but the U.S. and Europe won't give up without a fight.

There are concerns about the footprint that solar and wind power may require, particularly in a world where increasing food needs may claim dibs on usable land, but there are also alternatives for clean, inexpensive, ubiquitous electricity. Increasingly, many lean toward nuclear power, which provides so much more electricity for any given footprint. Supporters will have to overcome the continuing worries about radiation leaks and disposal of nuclear waste, but a host of small, modular designs for reactors show promise. So do new fuels, such as thorium, which costs much less than uranium, generates far less waste, and presents many fewer risks of a radioactive leak.[96]

Hydroelectric power, long the biggest provider of clean energy, will fade in importance but will likely remain a significant part of the renewable energy mix in 2050. Some utilities are even setting up solar farms that float on the water in the reservoirs; all that surface area is available,

---

* You can already see this phenomenon occurring in other climate-related technologies. The market cap of NextEra Energy, the world's largest producer of renewable energy, briefly surpassed that of ExxonMobil in 2020, and other renewable giants carry higher values than their fossil fuel peers. (https://www.bloomberg.com/graphics/2020 -renewable-energy-supermajors) Early-stage venture funding for climate tech companies rose to $16.1 billion in 2019, up 3,750 percent from 2013. (https://www.pwc.com/ gx/en/services/sustainability/assets/pwc-the-state-of-climate-tech-2020.pdf)

so why not use it? There are even synergies: Covering the water with panels reduces evaporation, and the water cools the solar panels, which makes them more efficient.[97]

Geothermal shows promise, too, at least in certain areas. Geothermal, which involves drilling deep into the Earth's crust to tap into pockets of heat that can then be turned into electricity, is of interest to the oil and gas industry. As fossil fuels fade in importance, the industry will be able to leverage its expertise and technology for such deep heat wells. Bob Metcalfe (who showed up as an early hero in our narrative, as the inventor of the Ethernet at Xerox PARC and as the eponym of the "law" on network effects) is leading a major effort at the University of Texas to innovate on geothermal.[98]

So, free(ish) sources of electricity will be abundant in the Future Perfect, even if we just maintain our current trajectory, and we'll be able to use the energy sources of 2050 to their absolute capacity without fear of generating greenhouse gases.* There are already so many sources and so many developing that you can assume, with great confidence, that energy simply doesn't have to be a constraint by 2050.

We as a society must face the issue of the loss of jobs in fossil fuels, which won't just hurt individuals but also whole communities and even regions. These effects are real concerns. But from the viewpoint of 30 years from now, the math is overwhelming. The price for building new solar and wind power will soon be lower than the cost JUST FOR THE FUEL in oil and gas plants in many areas, and the disparity will only grow as we approach 2050. So, all the growth will be in renewables—the International Renewable Energy Agency acknowledges that 7.4 million jobs in fossil fuels will likely be lost by 2050 worldwide but contends that 19 million jobs will be created in renewable energy, energy efficiency and grid enhancement, and energy flexibility, for a gain of 11.6 million

---

* There will be other types of pollution. Nuclear waste is an obvious concern. There are also issues related to the materials used in the devices that generate other types of carbon-free energy. Rare earth metals, for instance, are used in all sorts of electronics these days but are mined in a notoriously dirty way that can leave untreated heavy metals in rivers, soils, and aquifers. Even beyond the pollution itself, the sources of the materials can cause geopolitical concerns. The biggest miner of rare earth metals is China, with Myanmar and Russia also in the top six. (The U.S. is No. 2.) The largest producers of cobalt, used in electric cars, are the Democratic Republic of Congo, China, and Russia.

jobs.[99] We need to enable those new jobs, while doing everything possible to help today's workers, businesses, communities, and regions fit into that future.

The "everywhere" part of our what-would-it-be-crazy-not-to-have-in-the-Future-Perfect will be trickier, but not by a lot.

First, even though many sources of power will still run through the grid, solar can be anywhere. No grid required. Second, even with non-solar sources, batteries will give you much more flexibility in how much you'll have to rely on the grid. For instance, there'll be a huge number of community-sized "micro grids" that might not even connect to the central grid, instead drawing on some local source of solar, wind, etc. The key here will be having a massive battery at the heart of the micro grid to keep everything running smoothly (whatever form that battery takes, assuming technology delivers the hoped-for breakthrough). These micro grids could be communities that basically declare their independence from the existing grid structure or could be any sort of new community: a neighborhood, a factory, an office, or an apartment building, whatever.

Homes could even leave the grid, one at a time. They, too, will have exceptional battery capacity to store electricity from solar or any other source. They'll also have access to electric cars that will provide a buffer—you can use solar, say, to charge the car battery during the day and then have it power the house through the night.* Ford recently announced an electric version of its popular F-150 pickup that would provide exactly that sort of backup for days.

So, yes, you can count on clean, affordable electricity for everyone, everywhere in the Future Perfect.†

---

* There are lots of logistical details to work out here to ensure that homes don't lose power. The easiest solution would be to have central locations where people could recharge their car batteries, which would then power their homes during stretches when homes' solar generation didn't suffice. Other, better solutions could well evolve.

† If you want, you could say that electricity everywhere is already here, of the sort that one of your authors experienced nearly two decades ago, when his young daughters were part of a ballet recital in the auditorium at the local high school in Tahoe City, California. In the middle of a raging storm that dumped some four feet of snow, the power went out. To us city boys, that should have been the end. But residents of the mountains around Lake Tahoe are made of sterner stuff. The master of ceremonies asked if anyone had a generator. Half a dozen hands went up among the 75 or so parents there. The generator owners compared notes, and one gentleman drove off

The benefits will be enormous. For one thing, blackouts will almost entirely go away. If the grid goes down in a storm, the battery in your home or at the center of your micro grid should take less than a second to kick in. "Grid-scale batteries" will engage nearly as fast even for those who don't have a local battery backup. The grid will be far more wired than it is today, so it can sense and respond to problems instantly. As hard as it may be to believe, at the moment, a utility generally learns about outages when… customers call to complain. Managers map where the calls are coming from, guess where a line is down, and send a crew out to inspect it visually.

Blackouts cause around $150 billion of damage, including lost economic activity, just in the U.S. each year[100]—and the deep freeze in Texas will obviously make the figure for 2021 far higher. Now think about all the other countries where electricity is far less reliable and imagine the benefits that will come just from almost eliminating blackouts.

Health will also improve, especially in developing countries, where access to abundant clean electricity will let people stop burning wood, peat, cow dung, and kerosene (which is much cleaner than the others but is still quite bad). These fuels not only pollute the air but cause so many health problems for the folks who cluster around the fires for heat or to cook over, day in and day out, year in and year out.

Cutting way back on those fuels will, in turn, largely end the deforestation that results from the wood-burning in developing countries. When one of your authors visited Ethiopia in 1991, the magnificent forests in the highlands, fabled through the centuries, had been cut down for firewood and were almost wiped out. The denuded land had then seen vast amounts of topsoil washed down into the Nile by the summer monsoons. The problems have only worsened in the decades since. Trees don't grow overnight, and that topsoil will never flow back up the Nile, so the area will recover slowly, but it'll at least have some breathing room. The thousands of similarly deforested areas around the world will, too.

---

into the teeth of the storm in his four-wheel-drive pickup. Within half an hour, he had hooked up a diesel generator big enough to power the entire school. The performance by the little darlings went on. In the Future Perfect, we'll all have access to that same sort of power everywhere—just without the bulk of a diesel generator, without the noise, without the smell, without the cost, and without the delay.

A major cause of wildfires, which pose such a threat these days in much of the world, will largely disappear. Utilities spark many of the fires because long-distance, high-voltage lines arc in dry areas.* But batteries in the home and in micro grids will take much of the load off those dangerous trunk lines and thus reduce sparks from arcing. Climate change will increase the danger of wildfires in other ways, so we're not saying the risk will go away, but one of today's main drivers will. The sensors made possible by the Law of Zero on information will also let authorities learn of problems much sooner, likely—we hope—before they rage out of control.

Health problems associated with what's known as environmental racism will greatly diminish, too. Utilities tend not to build coal- and gas-fired power plants in wealthy areas. So, plants, which are still often built reasonably close to cities to reduce the distance for transmitting electricity, are generally built in poorer areas. That means the emissions disproportionately hurt BIPOC communities. Now, that pollution will go away. For good measure, while manufacturing facilities may still create pollution, the Law of Zero for transportation will make it easier for workers to live wherever they want, perhaps in cities, perhaps in rural areas far away.

The key issue is what to do about the grid. We already know we need to modernize it to increase reliability and ensure that, for instance, Texas has access to power in other states the next time weather takes down its grid. The bad news is that estimates for the cost of modernizing the grid just in the U.S. range as high as $5 trillion. The good news is that utilities are already projected to spend $1.5–2 trillion by 2030 to maintain reliability of the nation's electricity supply, so loads of money is already being allocated to the issue.[101] The question for the future will be how to best direct those funds.

This is where future histories and the idea of living in the future can help. Utilities and their regulators, buttressed by research in national labs, can imagine idealized futures now and can start to build versions of them. These prototypes will be far more expensive now than they would

---

* PG&E had to pay a $2.1 billion fine and set up a $13.5 billion fund to assist those injured in a series of wildfires it caused in California in 2017 and 2018. The utility also pleaded guilty to 84 counts of manslaughter. https://www.kqed.org/news/11804048/pge-fined-2-1-billion-for-wildfires-largest-amount-in-california-history.

be in 2050, because the technologies aren't ripe yet, but the experiments don't have to be that large and will do a lot to guide the expenditure of trillions of dollars.

We're intrigued by the potential of micro grids, about how reliable they'd be on their own, and about how they'd integrate—if at all—with the existing grid. If things go well, this is how the world might look in 2050:

Africa Rises Out of Energy Poverty

Addis Ababa, Ethiopia, February 14, 2050—Beniyam Tesfaye, a 45-year-old high school literature teacher, returned to his apartment in a town on the edge of this sprawling metropolis of nearly 5 million people after a long day with his students.

His apartment was cozy even at its elevation of nearly 8,000 feet during one of Ethiopia's two rainy seasons because of heaters driven by the small wind turbines on the roof of his 10-unit building. He went to his patio and collected the four liters of water his electricity-powered condenser had pulled out of the air during the day—a feat even easier than normal, given the current high humidity—and made himself and his wife some thick, black coffee. (He relies on the town's water system for use in his toilet and shower, but, for safety's sake, he uses the pure water from the condenser for drinking, cooking, and brushing his teeth. After all, the condenser only costs him pennies a day, and the economy in the capital is thriving.)

While his two teenaged children did their homework, Tesfaye plugged in his computer and connected to the internet via a low-Earth satellite. He decided to have his students read *Cutting for Stone*, by Abraham Verghese, both because Tesfaye loved the book and because he wanted to raise his students' sights. Verghese had been born just down the road in Addis Ababa, before earning a medical degree in India, working his way to a professorship at Stanford University, and then becoming an acclaimed novelist, so the book seemed fitting for the students. While *Cutting for Stone*, which was written in English, had long since been translated into Amharic, Tesfaye has been searching for material on Verghese in any and every language and was using Google Translate to produce a version in Amharic of Verghese's story to share with his students.

Thinking about Verghese's journey, which began when his family fled Ethiopia after Marxists staged a coup during the civil war that began in the mid-1970s, Tesfaye reflected on how he, too, had already made quite a journey—without having to go anywhere.

He'd grown up in the 2010s and 2020s, at a time when his town had no electricity—like half of the population in Africa at the time—and got its water from a well. While he was still quite young, his father had become sick and died, and, while his mother did whatever odd jobs she could, there wasn't much work to be had. Tesfaye, his mother, and his sister mostly lived on a modest amount of money funneled through an international relief agency—a 50-pound bag of rice was a big Christmas gift.

But Tesfaye persevered with his education through high school—and then the world began changing around him. As part of an economic development program, in a country that was the second most-populous in Africa and that had already begun modernizing, a wind turbine had been installed on the edge of his town in the early 2020s, and the government provided microloans for people who bought electric appliances. While the service wasn't reliable, it produced so much electricity that people could do some types of work more efficiently and, thus, produce more.

Before too long, some of the more successful entrepreneurs bought hot plates and mostly stopped burning wood to cook. The smoke that often hung over the town in the dry seasons diminished, and chronic illnesses declined. The creeping improvement in prosperity fed on itself, and, before too many years passed, the town was wired for electricity.

It then set up a small solar farm and installed some inexpensive batteries, drawing on low-interest loans from the government, to augment the wind turbine. The town began investing in services, including water and even education, the latter of which took a giant leap once the school bought a couple of tablet computers that connected to a satellite. Students suddenly had access to all the world's information.

The micro grid was quite reliable. The combination of wind at such altitude, on the edge of the Great Rift Valley, and sunshine just north of the Equator meant that power generation rarely lapsed for long. And electricity became almost totally reliable when a trunk line connected the town to a small thorium reactor that was set up to serve the far western suburbs of Addis Ababa. Africa had added 950 million people between 2020 and 2050, half the growth in world population during that period, and Ethiopia had been a leader in the new form of electrification—starting with micro grids and building up to a more national system rather than starting from the top down, building a massive grid and seeing how far out it could reach.

Pulling back from his reverie, Tesfaye moved on from his research on Verghese and began a new project: looking for videos from Addis Ababa. He and his mother had never been to the capital even though it was only 20 miles away, but a spur of the highway had finally reached their town, and autonomous buses now passed near them several times a day. He'd decided to surprise her with a trip to celebrate her 70th birthday—an age that would have sounded absurd to her when he was a child; so few lived even into their 50s in their small town.

The more Tesfaye searched, the more he realized how much Addis Ababa differed from the stories he'd heard his whole life. He'd grown up hearing that people piled, standing room only, into "blue donkeys" (minibus taxis) that traveled with their doors open to make it easier for people to jump on and off at corners. That the streets were full of beggars. That whole sections of the city could be a foot underwater during a hard rain. But all the videos Tesfaye saw showed him a city that looked more like New York than like the one in the stories he'd heard.

"Huh," he said to himself. "Maybe the whole country has changed."

CHAPTER 9

The Future History of Transportation

One Hundred Billionth Ride for Driverless Cars

MORGAN HILL, CA, July 17, 2035—Steve Mahan had a long and distinguished career, including as the executive director of a center that helped the visually impaired in Silicon Valley. He may be better-known, however, as Google's Self-Driving Car User #0000000001. Yes, Mahan was introduced as the "driver" in the very first demonstration video of Google's self-driving cars, back in 2012.[102]

Today, as the autonomous vehicle (AV) industry is poised to log its 100 billionth ride, let's look back at that first trip and the wild (but almost entirely safe) ride AVs have taken since then.

The world met Mahan as he slid into the driver's seat of a Toyota Prius with a strange, flower-pot-shaped contraption bolted onto a rack on top of the car. After some banter, he and his passengers decided to go get some tacos and burritos. But Mahan never touched the steering wheel or gear shift. He merely told the car the destination, and it took them to a Taco Bell drive thru. Next, Mahan "drove" to his dry cleaner. At that point, the voiceover narration noted that Mahan is blind.

Mahan was living in the future—which has now caught up.

According to a study by the Ruderman Foundation back in the 2010s, six million Americans with disabilities had difficulty getting the transportation they needed.[103] They struggled with the inability to drive themselves. They struggled with public transportation, too; there weren't enough accessible buses and trains, and many of the sidewalks and elevators that were needed to get to those buses and trains weren't accessible, either. People with disabilities struggled with the high cost of cars that could accommodate them. They struggled with human-driven paratransit services, which were far too expensive for most transit agencies to provide adequately and which were non-existent in rural areas, sometimes referred to as "transportation deserts."

But, thanks to the Laws of Zero, all the necessary retrofitting that cost hundreds of thousands of dollars on that 2012 Prius, including the flower-pot-shaped lidar on its top that used spinning lasers to track all nearby objects, now cost a tiny fraction of their 2012 prices and have been easily incorporated into all cars on the road. Every person, blind or otherwise, gets to "drive" an AV now.

By the time Mahan appeared in that 2012 introductory video, Google AVs had already safely driven 200,000 miles. By 2020, Google had spun out a subsidiary named Waymo to commercialize the technology, had a fleet of 600 test cars, and had logged more than 20 million road miles in more than two dozen cities, plus billions more miles in sophisticated computer simulations. Waymo had even launched its first commercial service in Phoenix.

The biggest challenge for the commercialization of these AVs turned out not to be having them learn how to drive. Throw any road, weather, or mechanical scenario at both a human and AV driver, and the AV will do better every time. The biggest challenge was getting AVs to learn to deal with humans, and vice versa. Pedestrians, cyclists, and other human drivers can do some really hard-to-predict (okay, crazy) things. Passengers—including the inebriated, the messy, and the overly amorous—proved to be quite a challenge, as well, as services scaled up.

So Waymo and early competitors like Amazon, General Motors, Aurora, and Uber spent a lot longer ramping up than any originally expected. But they all followed a mantra of "think big, start small, and learn fast" and developed a steadily larger set of services in a growing array of markets. This approach let service providers explore aggressively, learn constantly, and deploy as they were ready, but not before.

Meanwhile, service providers felt less pressure to rush to market because the massive investment in consumer-focused AV technology enabled a much narrower but quite profitable business model: trucking. Driving on highways doesn't typically involve passengers or pedestrians, and, on such roads, the driving and the other drivers are much more predictable. Developers and regulators had been wary of trucking in the early stages—"one video of an AV semi crushing a minivan, and we would have been done," one analyst commented at the time—but perception shifted by 2021. With so many safely driven miles already logged by its cars and with growing public and regulator acceptance, Waymo pivoted and soon dominated trucking, a $700 billion-a-year business at the time.

The market for autonomous trucking has now exploded. For safety reasons, drivers had been limited to 11 hours a day on the road in 2020, but the introduction of AVs in the trucking realm meant that rigs could now run 24/7—and without the expense of a driver. A cross-country trip that once took a human driver five days now requires only two. Trucking no longer has to be optimized to fill a full trailer to justify the expense of a driver. "Trucks" of all sizes can now be dispatched based on need, not on the size of a standard container. As a result, many shipments have eliminated the old, intermediate step, where they'd go to a warehouse and be repacked into other vehicles for local delivery. Businesses and people are happy to get their items much more quickly.

The supply chain for businesses was reinvented.* Oh, and that chronic shortage of truck drivers pre-2021? No one even remembers that problem existed.

---

* The reinvention of the supply chain will resemble what happened when businesses reorganized itself around the container in recent decades, as described in this article in the *New York Times*: https://www.nytimes.com/2006/03/23/business/the-container-that-changed-the-world.html The idea of batches will fade, because transportation will be so cheap and so automated. There will still be a long-haul transportation network, but far less effort will need to go into conforming to it. On the front end, trucks and trains will be organized more flexibly—rather than having to fill a standard container or assemble a long train, shippers will be able to dispatch much smaller loads, as soon as they're ready. On the back end, elaborate delivery routes will be less necessary; AVs and drones will be able to grab a delivery and take it straight to the recipient.

The profits from the burgeoning autonomous trucking business fed back into the consumer efforts and created a virtuous circle. Small, geo-fenced efforts like Waymo's service near Phoenix back in 2020 gradually expanded to cover whole metropolitan areas. AV offerings then moved beyond such weather-friendly areas to all major and even medium-sized markets, and urban redesigns have been integrating AVs into the fabric of life, making them even more valuable. We're now to the point where the federal government is debating whether to mandate universal access to AVs, akin to the universal access requirement for telephone service in the early 1900s.

Already, just 15 years after Waymo launched in Phoenix, it and the competitors it inspired are running AV transportation services in and are connecting more than 500 towns and cities in the U.S. Tens of millions of disabled, elderly, and economically disadvantaged persons now have access to cheap, fast, and accessible transportation services.

"The driverless car changed my life," Mahan said. "It gave me the independence and flexibility to go to places I both want to and need to go, when I need to do those things."

Without breakthroughs in transportation, we'll keep coasting along toward a polluted, congested future. While electric vehicles will grow as a percentage of cars on the road, the vast majority will still be powered by internal combustion engines. While we'll build lots more roads to try to alleviate congestion and limit the number of people sitting in rush hour traffic cursing their fates, they'll still be stuck in traffic, just in sleeker versions of the cars they sit in today.

We think it would be crazy not to have inexpensive, autonomous, electric vehicles widely available in 2050.

While AVs may seem to have come out of nowhere in recent years, they, like many innovations, actually have a long history that involved untold numbers of smart minds—and somehow trace back to Leonardo da Vinci. What didn't that man foresee? A sketch (see Figure 6) he drew circa 1478 of a gear-laden, three-wheel cart has been shown to be a workable, self-propelled cart with programmable steering.[104] (The cart bears a striking resemblance to the Spirit rover used by NASA on Mars.)

General Motors took up the AV cause at the 1939 New York World's Fair, unveiling a 20-year vision of radio-controlled electric cars powered by circuits embedded in the road. Almost on schedule, a 1956 *Saturday Evening Post* advertisement updated GM's vision. It depicted a family of four playing dominos in a car configured more like a living room than a car, with a caption that promised "no traffic jams... no collisions... no driver fatigue." The ad wasn't fantasy. Around the same time, a 400-mile stretch of highway was built outside Lincoln, Nebraska, that included electronic circuitry. Retrofitted cars had radio receivers that com-

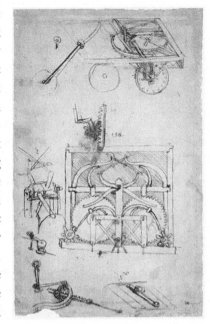

FIGURE 6

municated with that circuitry and controlled steering, acceleration, and braking. The system worked well enough that eminent researchers proposed building electronic superhighways.[105]

The complexity of the systems and the cost of revamping all roads killed the idea soon enough, but two major things happened in the decades since. First, the Laws of Zero made it possible to imagine putting intelligence in the cars, rather than having to rebuild all the roads. This prospect propelled steady, significant advances at universities and in research labs in multiple countries.

Second was the Iraq War.

The U.S. suffered such heavy casualties from ever-more-sophisticated roadside attacks on its vehicles that Congress funded an aggressive program for developing AVs that could move without putting people in harm's way. The goal was to make one-third of vehicles used by ground military forces autonomous by 2015.

DARPA, the U.S. Defense Advanced Research Project Agency, took up the challenge—literally. Rather than rely just on awarding typical Defense Department contracts (which were also done separately),

DARPA set up a Grand Challenge in 2004 where it offered a $1 million first prize for autonomous vehicles competing on a 150-mile course in the Mojave Desert near Barstow, California. Twenty-five groups entered, and 15 were invited to attempt the course. Most didn't make it out of sight of the starting line. One, a motorcycle, fell over right at the start. The farthest any vehicle went was 7.4 miles. Within a few hours, the challenge was shut down, and everybody went home. An article in *Science* referred to the contest as "DARPA's debacle in the desert."[106]

In fact, the challenge was a master stroke.

Importantly, DARPA had opened the competition beyond the defense contractors that were already working on the problem, and the competition stoked media attention. This helped capture the imagination and participation of a wide swath of corporate labs, university researchers and students, and even some bright high schoolers who had ideas about what they could do with a $1 million prize.

The attention grew when DARPA announced it would hold the competition again in 2005 and doubled the top prize to $2 million. This time, the field exploded to 198 applicants, with 23 finalists invited to attempt the course. Five vehicles (including an updated version of the motorcycle) completed it. A team from Stanford University won first place, while teams from Carnegie Mellon took second and third, winning a combined purse of $1.5 million.

In 2007, DARPA held another challenge on a 60-mile urban landscape course, complete with driving regulations, traffic signals, congestion, and merging traffic. This time, a Carnegie Mellon team took the $2 million first prize, while a Stanford team won the $1 million second prize.

The race was on. With just a few million dollars spent on prize money, DARPA had produced a proof of concept for autonomous vehicles and generated extraordinary interest in the idea.

Larry Page took the next big step. Page, co-founder of Google, had been a spectator at the Grand Challenges and, with roughly all the money in the world at his disposal, hired the leader of the Stanford team, Sebastian Thrun.* Thrun then recruited many of the best alumni of the

---

* Thrun says he was motivated to work on autonomous driving because his best friend as a teenager died in a car accident—the sort of harrowing personal story that has focused many on the work and that AVs should almost eliminate in the Future Perfect.

winning teams, including Chris Urmson,* who led the rival Carnegie Mellon teams, and launched a self-driving car project at Google.

The combination of unmatched Google assets and, arguably, the world's greatest collection of expertise produced amazing results. The Laws of Zero in computing, communications, and information helped, too. Just look at lidar—that distinctive device on the roof of the early Google cars that used a rotating laser to track everything around the car. Even after the experimental versions went into production, a single lidar sensor still cost $80,000 as recently as 2017. But new, solid-state sensors will cost $500 apiece—a price drop of more than 99 percent—and numerous suppliers think they can cut that price to under $100 before too long. Suddenly, all the equipment needed for autonomy becomes affordable. One might almost say "free."

Tie it all together—breakthroughs in sensors and artificial intelligence, tested through billions of miles of driving in simulators, millions of miles of driving on actual roads with safety drivers, and tens of thousands of miles in fully autonomous mode—and by 2019 Google's Waymo had 300 AVs operating in an approximately 100-square mile service area that includes the towns of Chandler, Gilbert, Mesa, and Tempe, Arizona. By early 2020, Waymo was operating an Uber-like car service handling 1,000 to 2,000 rides every week, five to 10 percent of which were without human drivers in the car as backup.

What's more is that tiny bit of initial seed money from DARPA, amplified by Google's moon shot and assisted by the Laws of Zero, created competition that has pushed the private sector to invest many tens of billions of dollars in AVs and the technologies that will support them. The next 30 years of AVs will surely make the last 15 look prehistoric.

---

* Urmson tells us he very much counted on the Laws of Zero in the early days of AVs. He incorporated all of what he considered to be the best technical approaches, including lidar, even though doing so meant that his early vehicles cost hundreds of thousands of dollars apiece. He was confident that the costs of all his electronics would head toward zero. Google's approach caused a sort of arms race, pushing GM, Ford, and many others to also invest in the most robust technology possible, despite the expense. Others—notably, Tesla—relied solely on cameras and radar, which were already inexpensive and which could thus be used quickly to enhance safety. The devices Tesla used were also already miniaturized, so they wouldn't interfere with its cars' sleek look, as a flower-pot-like device on the roof would. Tesla's approach, while effective in the short run, is now being exposed as timid: While Tesla claims self-driving capabilities, they don't and can't approach what lidar-based systems can do.

While AVs will drive, if you will, the vast majority of change in transportation in the Future Perfect, two other innovations will also provide a great deal of progress, and some others may contribute.

Personal mobility devices, such as the e-scooters that are starting to proliferate, will play a significant role. At the moment, they have a neither-fish-nor-fowl problem. They're too fast to integrate with pedestrian travel on sidewalks, but they're too slow for use among cars and expose riders to far too much danger on roads. In the Future Perfect, where the vast amount of space used for parking has been converted into other uses, safe lanes for scooters will be available, and the scooters themselves will incorporate the kinds of safety features that are built into AVs.

Transportation will also go three-dimensional. Why limit ourselves to roads and sidewalks when all that air space is available and when you don't have to pave the air to be able to use the space? Yes, crashes up in the sky could be catastrophic in ways that those on the ground are not. There's no such thing as a fender-bender at 1,000 feet, and congestion will become an issue in the skies at some point. But, remember, we have unlimited computing power and communication capabilities available to us in the Future Perfect, along with an extraordinary array of sensors, so we'll have an air traffic control system that will prevent almost all crashes. The move to 3-D will begin with delivery drones but will expand from there. By 2050, you might even have your very own flying car.

Hyperloops might also be available, based on Elon Musk's idea for vehicles moving so fast underground you could get from San Francisco to Los Angeles in half an hour. We're not sure whether we'll need to do all that digging and build all that track when AVs have removed almost all considerations of time and distance for travel on roads and when flying vehicles may be available, but we're happy test projects are under way. We'll see what happens.

We expect breakthroughs in fuels that will remove the pressure to reduce air travel, which contributes to climate change. Yes, fuels will still need to be burned to create power, but the Law of Zero for energy means we'll be able to go to extraordinary lengths to create fuels that can be burned without hurting the environment. Progress is being made on using hydrogen as jet fuel (and safely—plenty of people still remember the photos of the hydrogen-filled Hindenburg burning in 1937). Electrolysis can separate water into hydrogen and oxygen, and then the byproduct of burning hydrogen is water, so there's no problem there. (Many see this "green hydrogen" as a way to take advantage of any solar and wind power that exceeds the needs of the grid at that moment and even as a sort of battery to cover times when the grid needs more electricity—you let the solar panels and wind turbines generate all they can and turn anything the grid doesn't need into green fuel. We may also have access to hydrocarbons that are created, using renewable energy sources, based on carbon dioxide that's extracted from the air. So, while burning these fuels would create carbon dioxide, it'd be recycled into the next round of fuel that the planes would use.

Whatever the technologies that become available over the next 30 years, we're going to need to take out a clean sheet of paper and show considerable creativity in redesigning our environment—and history suggests the redesign will be hard, because our minds are typically so immersed in the present. Alexander Graham Bell imagined the telephone* as a way of broadcasting symphonies, not as a new form of two-way communication. Early TV shows were just radio shows conducted in front of a camera. Early airports resembled train stations. Unless we want to keep repeating those mistakes, we'll need to start with the assumption that what we'll have in the Future Perfect will be far more than a better version of today,

Think of all the constraints that will disappear by 2050. We've already talked about all the issues of time and distance that go away and about all the space that will open up in cities once street parking and garages can be repurposed. But those are just the beginning.

People will no longer have to buy cars, which are typically their second biggest purchase after a home—even though the car sits unused for more than 95 percent of the time. That switch from a fixed cost to a variable cost for transportation will be profound, freeing up all kinds of resources for people. That's especially true because AVs will provide all sorts of efficiencies. There's no need for insurance for cars that don't

---

* The telephone is a good example of how a big enough quantitative change can produce a qualitative shift. The work that led to the phone began as a way to multiplex telegraph lines. Initially, a line could carry just one string of dots and dashes at a time, but techniques were developed that allowed for two signals at a time, then four, then eight... until enough of those magic doublings had happened that inventors like Bell could imagine having enough capacity to carry a voice signal. *Et voilà!* iPhones for everyone!

hit anything. There's no need to insure your life or health against a car accident that won't happen. Now, cars will fit the task at hand—you can summon a big car when you need one but use a car for one or two people when that's all you require. And, if you think about it, the vast majority of trips truly are for one or two people, without cargo. The huge inefficiencies associated with today's car sales—mainly, the tens of billions of dollars of inventory sitting on dealers' lots—will go away because purchasing will be done by companies managing fleets. The car itself will look different. Without all the parts and weight of the driving mechanisms, and without having to worry about accidents, designers will be free to innovate on shape, size, and use case. Want a pink, bounce house on wheels? A Batmobile? Maybe we'll even end up with that living room of a car that GM envisioned in the 1950s, where a family of four was sitting around playing dominoes.

With all sorts of constraints gone, we can design ways to attack some of today's seemingly intractable problems. For one, the new world of transportation could greatly improve health, giving people better access to care, among many other benefits. Transportation could also tackle poverty: Today's public transport often doesn't get people close enough to their jobs, but tomorrow's will take people right to the doorstep—no more changing public buses twice and walking the last mile in the cold or the rain.

We'll also surely see some positives we can't currently predict, just as we did with the first iteration of cars in the early 1900s. The car revolutionized production, creating the need for a motorized assembly line and for standardized parts, while also rewiring supply chains worldwide. The car created all kinds of secondary markets, too. For instance, the car created the need for roadside motels and hotels and, of course, auto insurance. The driverless car, likewise, might produce whole new categories of jobs, such as long-haul "drivers" who oversee numerous trucks from their homes. AVs also might spur other gains, such as transformation of local electric grids to support all the electric vehicles.

There are certainly a lot of operational challenges when it comes to running what's essentially a fleet of hotel rooms on wheels, as we learned in detail during our work on a consulting project with a major player in the AV space. Infrastructure that's currently paid for by taxes on gasoline will have a problem because, in the Future Perfect, there will be no gasoline; those projects will need to find new sources of funding. To get the full benefits in the Future Perfect, the transportation system will have to be multi-modal, meaning there will need to be work on integrating AVs with public transport, scooters, bikers, and pedestrians, rather than just pushing everything but cars off the roads, as typically happens now. We'll also have to be sure to not become victims of our own success: Making transportation free(ish) could easily encourage people to use so much of it that roads are overwhelmed with traffic.

As we've said, just because we can imagine a Future Perfect doesn't mean we won't wind up with a Future Pathetic. Creativity and care are required.

To that end, here's the sort of future history those thinking about transportation and its implications might write to help them both envision an ideal future and then start building pieces of it to test and prepare for all the advances that will be available to us in 2050. This builds on a real event: Toyota's announcement in 2020 that it'll start building a prototype model city near Tokyo to explore how advances in transportation might enable radically new conceptions of what a city is.

A Living Laboratory for the Future of Transportation

WOVEN CITY, JAPAN, March 24, 2050—A drone dips over the rooftop of an apartment building, edges over to the four-foot square landing pad on the third-floor balcony, gently sets down a jar of gochujang, and then flies away. Paula Endo, who had forgotten to include the Korean hot pepper paste in her order that an AV dropped off earlier that day, steps outside to retrieve the jar, returns to her kitchen, and slips back on the virtual reality goggles she was using to watch a chef demonstrate how to prepare tteokbokki, a spicy, rice cake-based dish Endo was making for a Korean friend coming over for lunch.

With lunch under control, Endo calls her elderly mother and asks if she can "come visit." When her mother responds cheerfully, Endo engages her mother's service robot and "enters" it. Through the VR goggles, Endo can now see through the robot's "eyes" and, by walking around in her own apartment, moves the robot around in her mother's. Putting on special gloves, Endo takes control of the robot's "hands" and opens cupboards to check on medicines, then tidies up a bit for her 104-year-old mother, who is mentally very sharp but has lost some manual dexterity and tires more easily than she once did. The mother smiles at her daughter's face on the high-resolution screen on the front of the robot, and the two have their usual, daily, 10-minute chat.

Endo's friend Jimin Jeon arrives on the helipad on the roof of her building in the one-person mobility drone he took from the train station. After arriving by high-speed train from Tokyo, he spent an hour in the gym at the station, then showered and headed over to Endo's. (Free gyms are located at transportation handoff points throughout the Woven City to encourage people to exercise.) Endo and Jeon share the tteokbokki and head out into the crisp, clear winter afternoon to go for a walk through Woven City,[107] which was built for just such strolls.

The 175-acre site near Tokyo was designed back in the early 2020s to put people, not cars, first—even though it was the car maker Toyota that financed the project. Streets in the city were split into three zones: one for zero-emission AVs; one as a promenade shared by pedestrians and slower forms of personal mobility, such as scooters; and one as a tree-filled park for pedestrians only. As much cargo traffic as possible was routed underground, so trips such as for grocery deliveries wouldn't clog streets. The remaining traffic was designed to mesh seamlessly—hence the name Woven City.

"Toyota began as a loom manufacturer," said Daisuke Toyoda, president of Toyota Motors Corp. "We didn't begin by making cars. Now, we have woven all the threads, not just cars, into a beautiful design for a city of the future.

"Thirty years ago, when many of our colleagues in the automotive and technology sectors were focused on perfecting autonomous technology to reshape the car industry, my father [Akio Toyoda, who was himself president of Toyota] was more worried about how the technology would reshape society. That's why he built the Woven City as a living laboratory with residents rather than building a test track for robot cars. The question of how to best serve society as a whole has guided our work ever since."

Amal Kumar, an analyst with XYZ Research, agreed: "In the 2010s and 2020s, other companies like Waymo, General Motors, and Uber were focused on testing AVs in real-world environments, such as Phoenix, Arizona, and the interstate highways of Texas. Akio Toyoda recognized the real potential of AVs was in the context of everything connected to everything else. To understand the art of the possible, he decided to build a connected, sustainable city-wide laboratory from scratch. Everyone else was trying to change the present; he wanted to live in the future."

The Woven City's entire infrastructure is below-ground, including its hydrogen power storage (with energy fed from all the solar panels on roofs and in windows in the city) and water filtration systems, so Endo and Jeon are free to enjoy the ambience as they take in a spectacular view of Mt. Fuji and appreciate the accents from the all-wood buildings. (Wood was chosen because it's carbon-neutral and allows for artisans to showcase the traditional Japanese craft of wood-joinery, which is now augmented with robotic production techniques.)

"One of the biggest breakthroughs in the process was accepting that the city of the future doesn't have to look futuristic but rather that the opposite should hold true," said Leon Rost, one of the original designers of the city. "Technology at its best is invisible and is secondary to human interaction and its connection to nature."

Endo and Jeon bump into some friends—Woven City was designed to promote interaction via "chance" meetings—and they chat for a while about how the city is about to be designated as a historic district, given its pioneering role in urban design.

As the sun starts to drop off the shoulder of Mt. Fuji, Jeon realizes it's time to head back to Tokyo, so he summons an AV shuttle to take him to the train station. He'll be back in his apartment in an hour, after having another personal mobility drone carry him from the Tokyo station to the roof of his apartment building. He'll get some work done on a client presentation on the way.

Endo walks for a bit longer. She's felt a bit claustrophobic in her apartment during the winter, and she's enjoying the sunshine. Her health monitor has also been prodding her lately to walk more to get her blood pressure down. After 30 minutes, she walks over to the vehicular lane and catches a shuttle that drops her off in front of her apartment building.

She settles in on her couch. She considers ordering in for dinner but decides she'll have some leftovers from lunch. That tteokbokki had turned out rather well.

CHAPTER 10

The Future History of Health Care

No More Pandemics?

WASHINGTON, DC, July 7, 2050—The Department of Health and Human Services (HHS) announced today it had identified 27 cases of COVID-49, the disease caused by the novel coronavirus that first appeared three weeks ago. But, as has become the norm, HHS said it expects to extinguish the outbreak in less than a month.

The nationwide tracking system that lets HHS see where concentrations of illness are building found the 27 cases in three pockets, one at a Utah ski resort and two others on the Gulf Coast, one in Houston and one in New Orleans. Contact tracing has identified roughly 1,000 people who are most in danger of having been exposed to those who are infected, and all will be quarantined for the next week while the tiny sensors they'll ingest every day are monitored for any evidence of the virus in their bodies.

The department said the genome of the virus makes it a near-perfect match for Vaccine #284-B in the HHS' library of 2,122 "plug and play" vaccines it has developed for the viruses that are most likely to produce global outbreaks. All have been tested for safety and efficacy, so vaccines can be rolled out immediately.

"The vaccine went into production this afternoon," said HHS Secretary Dr. Zoe Jenkins in a two-minute holographic call. "We'll have enough doses to cover the areas around the afflicted areas by the end of the week and will make enough so we can react immediately if the virus appears elsewhere. With this outbreak, we expect a total of about 100 cases nationwide, and, we hope, zero deaths. This outbreak should be fully behind us in three weeks."

She added, "We almost shouldn't talk about pandemics any more. 'Pan-' means 'everywhere,' and, while these viruses certainly have the same potential for devastation that COVID-19 had back in 2020 and 2021, viruses these days barely get a foothold before we stomp them out."

Without a serious change in course, health care in 2050 will still be better than it is today. That will be thanks, in particular, to the Law of Zero on genomics but will also be because of the sorts of improvements in drugs and treatments that Big Pharma, medical researchers, and hospitals will deliver in any case. But the current course in the U.S. would likely lead to health care that would be even more crushingly expensive and still piecemeal, with a mishmash of public programs and group insurance covered by employers. Private insurance will be prone to higher and higher deductibles, with continued inequity between haves and have-nots, and with the public debate on health continuing to be more about who pays for the care than about improving the care and lowering the cost.

We think it'd be crazy not to have terrific health care available to everyone at an affordable cost by 2050, providing longer, more active lives.

The health care cost problem is especially thorny in the U.S., where historical anomalies have produced a system that costs twice as much per capita as in other major economies while providing average or below-average care. But the opportunities for improved care extend throughout the world—and they're enormous. The Laws of Zero and a series of related breakthroughs in medical technology can produce two paradigm shifts by 2050.

The first shift will be from sick care to health care. At the moment, people tend to spend roughly seven minutes with a doctor during an annual checkup, and they otherwise encounter the health system only when they're injured or sick. We're the subjects—the patients—being treated by a system we struggle to figure out. By 2050, not only will we understand the system, we'll largely control it. We'll encounter the health system continually, mostly through feedback generated by AI,* but also through easy access to quick consultations with doctors, nurses, and other appropriate members of integrated care teams. The system will resemble a turbocharged Fitbit or Apple Watch. We won't just get information on step counts and heart rate, because the Law of Zero on information means that the sensors on our wrists will be greatly upgraded, that we'll have contact lenses rimmed with sensors, and that we'll have sensors the size of a grain of salt that we can ingest. (All these options will be at our choosing; no one will be force-fed technology or be otherwise wired up without their permission.) These sensors can then report on vital signs such as blood pressure and glucose and cholesterol levels, and they can even monitor for disease.†‡ We'll also be able to analyze the profusion of data in real time and translate the results into actionable next steps for both provider and patient—something that isn't possible today with the far more limited data available at our disposal.

---

* AI will be tricky, because it can unintentionally incorporate bias. If the data used to train the AI reflects, say, racial bias, then recommendations about health behavior can be skewed. But there are techniques to correct for bias, and the benefits of AI are already obvious—for instance, in some work happening now, the Centers for Medicare and Medicaid Services (CMS) Artificial Intelligence Health Outcomes Challenge has funded research to use AI to predict health outcomes, including hospital readmissions, adverse events, and mortality for CMS beneficiaries, to help CMS create plans that improve outcomes equitably.

† Researchers at MIT, Draper, and Brigham and Women's Hospital have developed an ingestible capsule that can reside in the stomach for at least a month, not only taking sensor readings but dispensing medications, controlled by signals sent via Bluetooth. http://news.mit.edu/2018/ingestible-pill-controlled-wirelessly-bluetooth-1213?

‡ Therapy can be delivered in similar fashion. An Israeli startup named Bionaut Labs has developed robots the size of a grain of rice that can carry medicine to the exact spot in the body where it's needed. That precision should greatly reduce the side effects that come from, say, chemotherapy or radiation, which currently have to be applied to relatively broad areas. While the tiny robots are currently designed to deliver therapeutics, future versions could provide electrical stimulation, thermal ablation, or radioactive plaque to treat other diseases.

While people today marvel about the Internet of Things, in the Future Perfect these sensors will give us access to an Internet of Me. The data stream from all the sensors on and in our bodies will be controlled by the person hosting them but will typically be shared with the computer systems of care teams. While people today try to get to 10,000 steps, people in the future will have access to a series of more sophisticated and important goals on blood pressure, blood sugar levels, etc., and they'll be provided with advice on how to hit those goals. This advice will become increasingly personalized as the Law of Zero on genomics takes hold and we learn more about our individualized vulnerabilities, based on our unique genome and how it is being expressed via epigenetics.

If we want, we can be coached toward our goals using the best behavioral science, too. Americans have been described as the worst patients in the world because of all our bad habits.[108] But think about how successful Facebook has been at tweaking its algorithms to capture ever more of your attention; now think of what could happen if that same sort of constant testing and tweaking could be done by medical professionals to help us overcome our bad habits by providing information and nudges that would continually improve our health.* Done right, behavioral science could drive as much change as just about any of the coming breakthroughs in medical science. A prominent doctor friend of ours says, "I can tell people exactly what to do to decrease their risk and, individually, how to do so with high efficacy. But that knowledge doesn't get translated into action. Moving to action is where the gold is."

The second paradigm shift in health care will build on the same sorts of Laws of Zero capabilities to go beyond today's focus on individual care and allow for an overlay that manages public health in ways far more powerful than are possible today. In the U.S., in particular, the devastation from COVID-19 occurred because of a failure in the public health system. The U.S. system is designed around, "Call your doctor," and, "Work with your insurer to figure out how much you'll pay out of pocket." But that approach doesn't work so well when you need to

---

* We acknowledge that Facebook has an easier time of it because it steers us toward things we already want to do: "Here, watch this video from someone whose politics match yours." A message of, "Don't drink that Coca-Cola" is tougher to sell.

test whole populations (repeatedly) and need to institute contact-tracing programs. That "call your doctor" and "work with your insurer" approach also doesn't address the social determinants of health—such as income, education, neighborhood conditions, and access to transportation—which are often related to racial inequities and which are increasingly understood as crucial. Besides, many of those who suffer based on these social determinants of health don't even have insurance or a regular doctor to call.

Management guru Peter Drucker once wrote something commonly paraphrased as, "What gets measured gets managed." Well, in the Future Perfect, almost everything will be measurable, so almost everything will be manageable, both for the individual and for the public at large. AI will be able to flag areas where, for instance, groups of people's temperatures start rising and will alert public health authorities to investigate. AI will rapidly spot nascent pandemics* and other problems that affect a whole population, such as the epidemic of opioid use that was ignored for so long and the water problems that hit Flint, Michigan. AI already allows for early detection of heart attacks, influenza, and other conditions by examining the language used in tweets and in internet searches.

Health officials will be able to calibrate the value of tools that aren't typically thought of as part of the medical arsenal, such as transportation. Public health officials could blunt the scourge of suicides,† which claim more than 40,000 lives each year in the U.S., by seeing patterns that represent warning signs of depression and by letting them test what interventions work.[109] In general, while clinical trials have been expensive and have taken ages to conduct, in the Future Perfect it'll be possible to test and constantly learn about the effects of medicines and treatments. The whole world will be a natural experiment where researchers will be able to explore cause and effect and continually update the collective wisdom about best practices.

---

* While the first case of COVID-19 was diagnosed in the U.S. on Jan. 19, 2020, studies have since found the virus had infected people at least a month earlier; it was simply undetected at the time. https://fortune.com/2020/12/01/december-2019-covid-arrival-us/ In the future, AI will spot a new virus far faster.

† The Veterans Administration is doing some pioneering work on suicides, including pushing diagnostic and treatment capabilities out to kiosks and even individuals' laptops so that veterans have access to help at any time.

Becoming more wired-up and taking part in the public health monitoring will need to be voluntary. And we'll need to be careful. Nobody wants to create an opening for Big Brother. But the benefits of the sorts of breakthroughs we expect should attract more than enough willing participants to allow for the two paradigm shifts.

Those shifts will let us finally tackle the two stats that have long bedeviled health care: that five percent of people account for 50 percent of health care spending every year, and that 70 to 80 percent of spending relates to chronic diseases.

The five percent figure has always seemed to be an easy target: You just identify the five percent and focus on them, right? The problem is that the five percent change from year to year, as many recover or, sad to say, die. New people move into that five percent, but it's been difficult to predict who they'll be. That prediction, however, will become much easier with a huge chunk of the population essentially wired to identify health issues, and spotting illnesses like cancer in their early stages will make them far less expensive to treat.

The chronic disease issue will always be with us in at least some form. In some cases, the issue may expand because—happily—diseases like AIDS and many forms of cancer, once seen as death sentences, can now be managed as chronic conditions. But many chronic diseases, such as Type 2 diabetes, can be drastically reduced through new focus on prevention and population health and through the continual feedback that can help individuals manage their health better.

The Laws of Zero will also accelerate breakthroughs in the chemistry and biology of medicine. For Exhibit A, just look at the historic development of safe and effective COVID-19 vaccines. The success of Operation Warp Speed in the U.S. and similar vaccine development efforts around the world would have seemed impossible in early 2020. Now such vaccine development will become the norm, and there will be a long list of such amazing accomplishments between now and 2050. For instance, as we described in the chapter on the Law of Zero on genomics, insights from AI should let scientists target the gene-editing tool CRISPR and turn it into a full-fledged way to treat many chronic diseases, such as sickle-cell anemia and certain cancers. AI also recently contributed to a breakthrough in modeling proteins that is expected to allow for other life-changing drugs and treatments to be developed in months—not years—and at far lower cost.*

The Laws of Zero will solve some health and sickness problems on their own. In addition to what driverless cars do to improve health indirectly, they will, as we've noted, greatly reduce the traffic accidents that kill some 1.4 million people worldwide each year. The World Health Organization says 3.4 million people die every year of water-related illnesses. Give them abundant clean water, and watch what happens. Providing everyone with all the energy they need creates the potential to wipe out a huge percentage of the illnesses and deaths that now occur because of poverty.

The two paradigm shifts—reorienting around the patient, rather than the health care system, and adding a digital overlay focused on public health issues—will make the world look very different for individuals, providers, and government:

Individuals: The key development will be the emergence of an integrated data model that captures all the information on the health of those who'll choose to participate. Drawing on the Laws of Zero on computing, communication, and information, the single data base that will arise will always be up to date and available as the single source of truth when someone deals with the health care system. By contrast, doctors, hospitals, and insurers today each have their own snapshot of a patient's data and exert rigid control over what they know. Until very recently, some information couldn't even be sent directly to a patient; it had to go through a doctor first. The release in the U.S. in early 2021

---

* While it's been possible for going on 20 years to sequence the amino acids that make up a protein, knowing the sequence isn't as helpful as originally hoped. The key to understanding how proteins interact in our tissues and to predicting what drugs might bond with them is knowing what shape a protein folds itself into, and computing the shape based just on the genetic sequence turned out to be a wildly hard problem. Knowing the shape of a protein required a chemical process that typically took a year, required a device as big as a football stadium, and cost $120,000 for a single protein. As a result, only 170,000 of the hundreds of millions of proteins known to exist have been modeled. In 2020, however, Google's DeepMinds research arm demonstrated it could compute how proteins would fold themselves—and could do so more accurately than the messy, expensive chemical process. While the implications of the breakthrough in understanding proteins have yet to play out, they figure to be profound. https://fortune.com/2020/11/30/deepmind-protein-folding-breakthrough/

of long-awaited rules against information hoarding is already making a difference but is just the beginning of what will be a long process.

Advances in the Internet of Me will let everyone monitor their health, based on research-based evaluation of vital signs and real-time monitoring of diet, exercise, and sleep. Sleep's importance was always intuited but never really understood. We spend a third of our lives sleeping, and everyone always reports being tired. In the Future Perfect, we'll have figured out how to help people sleep better and will be able to show people the long-term effects on their health. The new health data model will include a growing amount of information based on genomics but also on income,[110] education, and other demographics not normally viewed as health factors—researchers have recently learned your nine-digit ZIP code may say more about your life expectancy than your genome does.

Health measurements will be used to fine-tune actions for best results for each individual. It's long been known that poverty correlates with poor health, and system administrators in the Future Perfect will understand the relationship. "Free" water and wide access to healthy food will enable administrators to direct resources to people in ways that could improve their diets and general health. "Free" transportation will be used by government agencies or doctors to send good food or other forms of help or to let people come in for any tests, consultations, or treatments.

Providers: Care providers will continually interact with individuals, drawing on the insights of behavioral economists and using methods that actually drive change—there will be no more reliance merely on annual suggestions about quitting smoking, losing weight, and exercising more. The interactions with care providers, most of them automated, will happen through texts, vibrations on the patient's smartwatch, or other digital communications and will incorporate continual feedback from the patient. Primary care doctors will operate as highly sophisticated advisers, working in care teams with other professionals such as nutritionists, health coaches, community health workers, and mental health professionals. Care will be longitudinal, not episodic. In other words, you'll feel like you're dealing with the same team for years or decades, rather than just bopping into a clinic and dealing with whoever happens to be there when you have a problem. Care teams will help people manage their health in every way, not just through the medical system.

A future consultation won't require you to sit in a doctor's office, where you've been waiting for 45 minutes after filling out reams of paper forms. The new consultation will mostly be between you and your wrist, as you use whatever device you've chosen to track your health status and to see what the AI is steering you toward doing in terms of diet or exercise. A more elaborate consultation with your provider will usually require nothing more than a video connection so you can confer with a doctor or nurse. The health care professional on the other end of the line will have access to all your health information in real time and will be able to gather nonverbal cues thanks to high-resolution images—say, a video of you walking and talking or perhaps via a picture you take of a rash or a mole.

The result of all these advancements might come to be known as lifestyle medicine, where the goal is just to keep people healthy. There will be plenty of hands-on care and access to miraculous drugs, but the focus will be on helping people be healthy through a better lifestyle. Gordon Bell, the developer of the first minicomputer back in the 1960s, used to say that "the most reliable part of the computer is the one you leave out," and that sort of idea will become a health care mantra: "The most effective treatment is the one you don't need."

The lifestyle medicine approach will draw on genomics and the profusion of other data and will be able to classify people according to those who need prevention, those who need occasional treatment, and those who require chronic care.

More generally, lifestyle medicine will mark a shift away from today's mindset of helping patients navigate the health care system. In the Future Perfect, everyone will be recognized simply as people, not as patients or prospective patients. People. People who want to live long and fulfilling lives. And why should people have to figure out the system? Why wouldn't the system adapt to fit the people?[*]

The shift in thinking will look a lot like the change that's occurred since the advent of personal computers 40 years ago. The techies kept telling everyone in the 1980s and 1990s that we all had to become

---

[*] The Department of Labor is attempting this sort of shift in thinking for government benefits. The DOL has produced an integrated portal for all benefits, and it uses AI to customize recommendations for each person by identifying benefits someone didn't ask about but might qualify for.

computer-literate. Computer literacy was supposed to be a matter of national importance that would help us better compete with other countries. The real issue turned out to be that computers were way too hard to use. Once Steve Jobs came along and showed everyone what good computer design looked like, using one became almost intuitive and the need for books and courses on computer literacy went away. Well, we haven't found the Steve Jobs of health care yet, but, regardless, in the next 30 years we'll finally kill the idea that people need to adapt to the system. In the Future Perfect, we will make the system adapt to us people.

Recommendations on how to achieve a healthy lifestyle will be backed by an enormously sophisticated system of data analysis—none of this diagnosis-by-infomercial we're encouraged to do today—and will be fine-tuned constantly, as we change and new insights are gained. Management guru Peter Drucker, in one of his crusty moments, once told us people don't change. They eventually die and are replaced by people who have more current ideas and information. Even with doctors, who must stay abreast of the latest research, it can take time for the whole medical community to catch up with a change in science. But, in the Future Perfect, the newest research will get pushed out instantly into databases and will be incorporated via AI into the computer-driven recommendations made to doctors on possible treatments. Doctors can be monitored, too, to be sure they're following the evidence, making something like the opioid epidemic of the 2010s much less likely to recur. Although some doctors may resist the monitoring part, we're confident, based on extensive work with the American Medical Association and other medical organizations over the years, that they and other caregivers will welcome the Future Perfect. For one, thanks to the far more sophisticated computing, communication, and information capabilities, they'll avoid much of the paperwork that bogs them down today. As a result, they'll be able to spend far more time with the individuals they're helping, and they'll get to see the sort of improvements in health that likely got them interested in medicine in the first place.

The more sophisticated approach provided by behavioral economics will help build a virtuous cycle, with continual communication through smartphone apps. In the Future Perfect, people will see they're becoming healthier, which could encourage them to continue on that trajectory, which would make them even healthier, which... you get the picture. Measures such as the Personal Activity Intelligence (PAI) will give those who want access to it a reasonably accurate real-time reading of their likely lifespan, which will motivate many to improve that number.

The new "hospital" will be your home, perhaps in the living room or a bedroom. In the vast majority of cases, the sort of equipment that's used in a hospital room can be set up in a home and monitored remotely, with a nurse or doctor providing most care via a telemedicine connection and with someone visiting occasionally. People actually tend to recover better when they're constantly around family or friends rather than when they're in a sterile hospital room, feeling cut off from the world.

Hospitals will still exist, sure, but they'll become more specialized. The key pieces of a hospital are the emergency care, the operating rooms, and perhaps the maternity department—though many women choose to give birth at home. But there's no particular reason the three entities need to all be together, and there's certainly no particular reason to have them in a huge building with every potential medical specialty, including psychiatry, physically present. Most elective surgeries, such as joint replacements, have much better results and are done far more cheaply in a facility that specializes in them, so more surgical procedures are moving out of the hospital and to ambulatory surgical centers. Even now, specialist facilities* known as "focused factories" draw patients from around the country. With the Law of Zero for transportation slashing transportation costs, elective surgeries will largely happen in specialist facilities because distance will be of no concern. Why rely on your local general surgeon, who last replaced a hip six months ago, when you can easily get to a doctor whose team has been doing three hip replacements a day for years?

Lots of health care organizations are already experimenting with ways to let people age in place as long as possible, which will reduce the number of elder care facilities in the Future Perfect. Much of the attraction for these facilities had been to help those who could no longer drive

---

* The Surgery Center of Oklahoma is a prime example of this sort of specialized facility operating today. So-called medical tourism also provides examples—though requiring much more than a car trip or short flight. You can go to India, have very high-quality open-heart surgery and be charged $2,100—versus a charge of $100,000 to $150,000 in the U.S. https://www.strategy-business.com/article/Physician-Disrupt-Thyself?gko=90272

and wanted their needs for food, medical care, and companionship to be met within walking distance. But autonomous vehicles remove travel constraints, and most people would prefer to stay near their friends and family rather than pull up roots and surround themselves with other old folks. Medical equipment, when needed, could be set up in homes.

Robotic assistants will increasingly be able to take on the role of nurses; they'll deliver medications, watch the patient take them, get people up and walking around, and let caregivers or relatives check in via video to see how the person is faring. Staffing with robots may seem impersonal, but their handling of mundane tasks will free the human caregivers to do the more meaningful and important work. And, as odd as it may sound, many elderly people form emotional connections with the robots. While a human caregiver can't spend all day with a person, a robot can, and it can alleviate some of the loneliness that can come with aging.*

Doctors will evolve into a sort of cyborg, gradually absorbing all the benefits technology can provide. They—and other caregivers—will bring all the skill and empathy that humans can provide and will also have constant access to data and the latest research that computer systems can provide. Again, we believe doctors will generally welcome the change, because it will reduce their need to memorize so much material and will let them focus instead on diagnostics and care.

Business models will change, both for hospitals and the health insurers that pay them on people's behalf. Many will likely resist, but the current models just aren't sustainable. Everybody has a hard time dealing with insurance, and few are wild about a hospital system that won't say in advance whether a common blood test will cost $10 or $10,000 and that may include a surprise bill in the tens of thousands of dollars because, even though the hospital is in-network, an out-of-network doctor briefly examined a patient. Bipartisan efforts to curb the excesses of "surprise billing" and to make drug and hospital pricing

---

* The team at NASA became very attached to the Mars rover known as Opportunity, which was supposed to last only 90 days but transmitted signals for 15 years from the surface of Mars. It signed off in 2018 by signaling, "My battery is low, and it's getting dark." The NASA team tried a number of "wake-up songs," including Gloria Gaynor's "I Will Survive." Without a response, the team finally played Billie Holiday's version of "I'll Be Seeing You" to the robot. Many on the NASA team teared up. Source: https://abc30.com/science/my-battery-is-low-and-its-getting-dark-opportunitys-last-message-to-scientists/5137455/

much more transparent are finally coming to fruition as of early 2021. So, in 30 years, you won't have to guess what you'll pay out of pocket, and you won't spend weeks fighting with your insurer about what is or isn't covered. We promise.

Government: Government policy will need to change to allow many of the benefits we're sure will be possible by 2050. While we're generally reluctant to prescribe policies, we think a few principles shouldn't be controversial. First, as a baseline, everyone should have access to good care when sick. Second, governmental policies should encourage and facilitate good health.

On sick care: In the U.S., the richest country in the history of the world, there isn't any excuse for not providing good care to everyone who is sick. Yet, at the moment, about 10 percent of Americans aren't covered by insurance, and deductibles are so high on many forms of insurance that people won't seek needed care. This needs to change. One possible model, prescribed by the late Uwe Reinhardt, a prominent health care economist, would work as much as possible within existing structures but would have the country define a base standard of care that would be covered through insurance with low deductibles. Anyone who could afford that insurance would pay for it (or any more expensive plan or care they wished to purchase). Anyone with no way to pay for the baseline insurance would have payments covered by the government. Those with modest means would be subsidized by the government on a sliding scale, with government support depending on their income that year. Germany roughly follows Reinhardt's approach and spends less than half per person what the U.S. spends on health care and also beats the U.S. on key metrics such as life expectancy, which is 81 years in Germany versus 78.5 years in the U.S.

On staying healthy: The role government should play in keeping its residents healthy is more politically sensitive. Few would argue government shouldn't keep poisonous chemicals out of the water supply and hazardous pollutants out of the air. But how far should that principle stretch? What role should government play in directing individuals away from smoking too many cigarettes or chugging too many sugary drinks, for example, even when it's scientifically proven that poor choices like these will dramatically increase the risk for cancer and diabetes? We don't have a simple ideological answer, but we do have a simple economic one: Policy should tilt toward encouraging health because the cost of not doing so is overwhelmingly high for society, including for the taxpayers who foot the bill for programs to treat those who fall ill.

While a 30-year glide path to the Future Perfect should allow for plenty of time to define a rational policy and let all parties prepare, and while all the progress in prospect would seem to demand considerable rethinking to design a system that takes full advantage, we realize the history of health care redesign has mostly been a disaster in the U.S. More than seven decades ago, President Truman tried to institute a national plan. President Nixon tried major reform again five decades ago. President Clinton tried three decades ago. President Obama tried a decade ago. You get the idea. But, as Germany shows, better care at lower cost is eminently possible, even today, and the Future Perfect health care system will slash away at two huge tranches of costs, freeing trillions of dollars to be deployed more productively.

The first tranche is the money currently wasted through administrative complexity, diagnostic errors, delayed diagnoses, undertreatment, overtreatment, and fraud. The complexity is actually a feature, not a bug, of the current system. Everybody pays a different price, negotiated by each provider with each payer, often with little connection to the actual cost—and providers and insurers profit mightily from the lack of transparency. (As of 2021, transparency into health care costs and charges became a reality, but a limited one with much more still to be done.) Electronic health records, often built onto platforms originally created to support medical billing, were conceived of as a way of standardizing and sharing information on those receiving care. Yet these records made it easier for providers to bill at higher levels for care delivered to patients. Even though providers benefit from the current system, when you add that complexity together with the errors and overtreatment, this tranche is an obvious target: It accounts for fully one-quarter to one-third of health care spending.[111] With U.S. health care spending headed toward $4 trillion a year, that means that $1 trillion to $1.33 trillion is wasted every year—which can cover a lot of cost in whatever new system is developed.

The waste and fraud ingrained in health care will be hard to identify and may be even harder to root out—after all, one person's waste is another person's revenue—but the Law of Zero related to information will give us access to (anonymous) information about every condition in every (participating) person in real time. The powerful network created by the Law of Zero on computing will monitor all this information and provide a feedback loop that will allow for constant learning about what works and what doesn't. After a few hundred billion cycles, that feedback will drive out an awful lot of bad decisions, including unneeded treatment and errors that produce expensive complications. For instance, it took years to realize how much unhelpful back surgery was being done, contributing to a $100 billion-a-year back pain industry that has been called "mostly a hoax,"[112] but, in the Future Perfect, correlations between treatments and poor results will be spotted far sooner. Constant feedback will make the system ever smarter about spotting fraud. Administrative complexity? That's easy. The computers will handle it all.

The second tranche is the money being spent to treat the late-stage manifestations of chronic diseases, like diabetes and cardiovascular disease. As we've noted, 70 to 80 percent of sick care dollars go to treat chronic diseases that often could have been better managed at earlier stages and that sometimes could even have prevented. For example, the CDC estimates that eliminating three risk factors—poor diet, inactivity, and smoking—would prevent 80 percent of heart disease and stroke, 80 percent of Type 2 diabetes, and 40 percent of cancer. The reduction in pain and suffering would be amazing; the cost savings would be spectacular.

Take diabetes, one of the fastest-growing diseases in the world. Thirty million adults in the U.S. suffer from it today. The American Diabetes Association estimates the total cost of diabetes in 2017 in the U.S. was $327 billion, made up of $237 billion in direct medical costs and $90 billion in decreased productivity. In the future, those costs could double or even triple. That's because another 84 million people have a milder condition, prediabetes, that puts them at high risk for developing Type 2 diabetes, and medical expenditures for people with diabetes are 2.3 times higher than for people without it—it is the leading cause of blindness and kidney failure, often leads to the loss of a leg or foot, significantly increases the risk of heart disease, and is one of the leading causes of death. Yet research and community experience show that diabetes is mostly treatable, and, in many cases, the progression from prediabetes to full-blown diabetes can be slowed or even prevented. Just taking a small amount of the money now being spent on dealing with later-stage diabetes and diverting it to prevention would pay back many times over in reduced cost and suffering.*

Imagine freeing trillions of dollars a year by eliminating waste and improving our handling of chronic diseases. Perhaps some of that money would even wind up in the pockets of workers in the U.S. who haven't seen much of a raise in decades because they and their employers have had to spend so much on health care. Many workers' salaries could be tens of thousands of dollars a year higher without the drag created by health insurance.

Cost control will take time. A long time. Americans don't pay twice as much for care per capita because they get twice as much care or care that's twice as good; they pay twice as much because prices of treatment, drugs, and everything else are twice as high in the U.S. But those setting the prices in the U.S. will defend them as hard as possible. No one will be shamed into easily giving up their share of the $4 trillion health care system.

But there is enormous pressure to fix the problem. Dave Chase has a chapter in his book *Relocalizing Health* titled, "Health Care Is Stealing Millennials' Future, But They Will Take It Back." He describes a hypothetical millennial who earns a steady salary, culminating in them making $180,000 a year at age 65. That millennial would earn $3.85 million in salary over their career—and would pay $1.9 million for health care. How does spending half your salary on health care make sense, especially when you know that so much is wasted? How much longer will people tolerate this kind of excess expense?

The federal government, spurred by employers and voters being bankrupted by the health care system, will have to do something. We believe in markets as much as anybody, but the lack of transparency in health care and insurance means what we have at the moment isn't a real market. Government has the power to set the rules for a market, and even a few conceptual changes—such as a requirement for far more transparency— would do a lot to get us from where we are today to the Future Perfect.

Based on all the likely progress, here's the type of future history the federal government or health care providers might write to guide their planning:

---

* Intermountain Healthcare and Trinity Health are two organizations doing a good job on prediabetes and, more generally, on focusing on prevention rather than just on sick care.

Healthier Health Care—and Why 90 Is the New 70

Williamsburg, Va., March 6, 2050—Jack and Jill went up the hill to fetch a pail of water. Jack fell down and broke his crown, and Jill came tumbling after.

The two 12-year-olds, who were participating in a reenactment of life in colonial times on a school field trip, immediately received text messages on their watches from a chatbot asking if they were okay or if they needed to speak with a doctor. Jill dusted herself off and was found to be fine, but sensors suggested Jack might have a concussion—the accelerometer in his watch showed a stop sudden enough that it might be dangerous. His parents had had him swallow a tiny sensor that morning because he seemed to be coming down with something, and that sensor, too, detected signs of a potential concussion. It relayed the data to his watch, which, based on the permissions he and his parents had established with their care provider, sent the information on to his doctor. The doctor's computer system analyzed the data, compared it against Jack's records and against relevant research, then notified the doctor's nurse practitioner that there was likely a problem.

This evaluation was more complicated than most, because Jack has a genetic disorder that requires monitoring, yet within 30 seconds of the tumble the nurse practitioner called the teacher in charge of the school trip. The nurse practitioner examined Jack via video call and decided he was likely concussed but didn't need to go to a nearby clinic for examination. The teacher called Jack's parents, summoned an autonomous car, and sent him home, along with one of the adult volunteers who had come along for the trip.

Total price: $25 for the quick consultation with the nurse practitioner, $15 for the auto ride, and, later, $5 for a pill. Total time elapsed for the diagnosis: two minutes.

There was no calling a health insurer and waiting on hold to be transferred yet again… and again to figure out what treatment was covered under Jack's plan and where to take him for treatment. There was no ambulance and no trip to the emergency room, so there were no bills trickling in for weeks from doctors who took a brief look at Jack and who all bill separately from the hospital. Instead, the bills, which were below the parents' deductible, were processed via block-chain and automatically paid by the parents within seconds, so there was no involvement of administrators, meaning no additional costs for the health care system. An insurance company never even got involved. There were no worries by the health care provider about nonpayment and, thus, no need for followup communications.

It was all administrative bliss; the system had worked exactly as designed, doing the right thing for the injured kid in the shortest time possible at a cost that made sense for all involved.

If a time traveler from the 2020s—when the U.S. health care system was mired in administrative complexity and seemed on the verge of bankrupting consumers, employers, and the U.S. government—had been there to see this all play out, they'd have been amazed at the quality and low cost of today's system. They'd have been even more amazed that most of our health care system's efforts were actually focused on health, rather than sickness.

Take Jack's father, Ray, who was recently diagnosed with predi-abetes; he has a long family history of high blood pressure and diabetes. Thirty years ago, Ray might have been resigned to the gradual progression to full-blown diabetes, as happened to both his parents. But, as is becoming the norm today, Ray is working with his doctor to delay—and even prevent—this progression. Ray is already a medical miracle. Even before his fight with diabetes, he benefited from the Law of Zero on genomics and had doctors use CRISPR to edit his genome and cure a debilitating disease. He now wears a watch that not only counts his steps and measures his heart rate but that also takes blood pressure readings and collects other vital signs. Ray's contact lenses contain sensors that measure the glucose level in his blood, among other things, and both he and Jack's mom swallow a sensor about the size of a grain of sand daily that tracks other vital signs. Once a month, they ingest a sensor that checks for blood disorders, including indicators of certain forms of cancer. Any anomalous data gets reported immediately to their doctors' AIs, via the wireless connection in their smartwatches. If the parents ever get sick or detect something abnormal (an odd stomachache, a mole, whatever) they can contact a doctor directly and quickly set up a telemedicine connection.

The parents have also opted to provide additional data via a miniature camera in a pendant they wear around their necks that's triggered every time they eat or drink something. As part of Ray's diet plan to ward off diabetes, the images the pendant takes are analyzed to estimate portion size and nutritional content. The system includes ways for people to deviate from the plan occasionally and remove items so the system won't feel draconian.

Over the last 12 months, Ray gradually reduced his body weight by seven percent and has been holding steady at his new weight. His doctors believe this weight loss will dramatically reduce Ray's chances of developing diabetes. His lower weight and increased physical activity have also lowered his blood pressure and decreased his risk for cardiovascular disease and strokes.

Based on all the daily inputs and the broader set of information that turns out to correlate so well to health (e.g., genetics, income level, ZIP code, and education level), the AI that monitors Ray calculates a health score, biological age, and life expectancy. Based on developments in behavioral economics that go well beyond the traditional appeals to reason, Jack's parents are connected to friends via social networks that help them encourage each other about health. The parents have also chosen to get pinged on their watches—on a carefully irregular basis, so the messages don't become routine and get tuned out—with messages that reinforce a healthy lifestyle. For instance, Jack's parents are occasionally asked to perform a nontraditional test of fitness, such as squeezing something that measures grip strength or seeing how many push-ups they can do, based on the growing realization that measures such as walking speed can tell more than an official vital sign like heart rate and certainly more than a mostly discredited measure like body mass index.*

All the data provided by Jack's parents and other voluntary participants in the health system gets rolled up with information from others into a sort of national health dashboard that not only registers progress but suggests where more effort could help. Everyone in this type of program gets to see where they are nationally, adjusted

---

* Experts estimate that perhaps 20-30 percent of Americans can do a single push-up. https://www.theatlantic.com/health/archive/2019/06/push-ups-body-weight-bmi/592834/

for age, genome, income, location, etc. The ranking has turned out to matter more than most anything in terms of motivating good behavior, as has been shown in other spheres.*

No one has been forced to do anything. But people become healthier because they want to be healthier, and now can be continually advised on how to get there. No, it's not everyone, but it's enough people to make a real difference. National dashboard results show millions of Americans are making significant improvements along three major risk factors—poor diet, inactivity, and smoking—and the health of the nation is improving.

• • •

As Jack arrived home from his school trip, his grandparents met him on the walk leading to the front door. This house, like so many these days, has a large vegetable garden where there once would have been a driveway or garage, both of which are no longer needed because of AVs. The grandparents lived across town but summoned an autonomous car as soon as Jack's mom asked them to help out, and the two-seater dispatched by the grandparents' subscription service dropped them off just ahead of Jack.

The grandparents, in sometimes-dodgy health, have managed to stay in their home for years longer than they would have in the past, when they would have had to move into an expensive, assisted-living facility. They have a robot that checks their vital signs daily, makes sure they're taking their various medications, and talks to them to detect any slurring of speech or other neurological issues. The robots can assist with many tasks, including some surprising ones, like finding an elusive piece to a jigsaw puzzle—machine vision turns out to be great for determining shapes and detecting slight differences in color. Jack's grandmother has palsy in her right hand, which is quite weak, but she has a flexible glove she can put on that serves as an exoskeleton, steadying her hand and strengthening her grip.[113]

---

* Opower has proved to be very effective at getting people to reduce their electricity use by letting them know how it compared with their neighbors', adjusted for factors such as size of dwelling and number of people living in it. Oracle bought the startup for $532 million in 2016, where Opower is now a product line.

While the aging grandparents need a fair number of tests, they can do most of them by themselves at home because of the great expansion in the DIY market for health.[114] These days, doctors are only pulled into the loop when there are anomalies or when advice is needed. Sensors, of course, sound an alarm if the people being monitored have a heart problem or fall. Cameras in the house can, with the grandparents' permission, be turned on so they can be monitored—or so they can talk with their children and grandchildren. Prepared food and medications are easily delivered by AV. And the grandparents retain access to friends (most of them still in the same old neighborhood) and family because the Laws of Zero have wiped out the time, distance, and other constraints that existed before AVs came along.

Jack's grandparents actually represent the biggest cost burden that has developed over the past three decades. They, and others of their generation, are living years longer than they used to, and older folks will always consume more care than younger ones. That's especially true now because diseases that would previously have been fatal can be treated as chronic diseases, meaning more doctor visits and medications. But those additional years in a person's life span are now much healthier and happier than they used to be.

"90 is the new 70," Jack's grandmother says.

So the cost burden of the older generation is—unlike the cost burden of the past—one families are delighted to carry.

CHAPTER 11

The Future History of Climate

The Model City That Shaped Climate Hope

BELMONT, ARIZ., December 15, 2050—Swedish Prime Minister Greta Thunberg addressed the crowd today at the 25-year anniversary of the opening of Belmont, the model city near Phoenix.

Speaking via VR conference to avoid air travel, Thunberg played off the title of the blistering speech on climate change she made as a teenager to the United Nations in 2019. In that speech, titled "How Dare You?", Thunberg reprimanded politicians. She said, "You have stolen my dreams and my childhood with your empty words" about reversing climate change while "entire ecosystems are collapsing. We are in the beginning of a mass extinction, and all you can talk about is money and fairy tales of eternal economic growth." Today's speech was titled, "Dare We Hope?", and singled out Belmont as an example of the enormous progress that has been made on climate issues in recent decades, because of cross-sector developments in energy, transportation, industry, real estate, agriculture, and consumption.

"There is much more we have to do," she said, "but today I want to celebrate the reemergence of hope."

Belmont, with its 200,000 inhabitants, roughly the size of nearby Tempe, has gone well beyond carbon-neutral to be carbon-negative, based on the profusion of power generated by clean sources. Belmont exports its excess power down a trunk line to Phoenix, reducing Belmont residents' energy bills while helping the nearby metropolis almost eliminate its own carbon footprint.

There is a large wind farm on the edge of the city, and solar is everywhere. Panels are on rooftops, carefully hidden from view. Even rooftops and windows are coated with photovoltaics. The wind and solar are complemented by a series of small nuclear reactors that provide a steady baseline of power. The molten-salt, thorium reactors, about the size of an old-fashioned water tower, are located near Belmont's manufacturing center, whose 3-D printing capabilities supply almost all of the city's requirements and whose peak power needs can stress the local solar and wind resources.

Bill Gates, the founder of Belmont, had made his second fortune—or is it his third?—when his early backing of small thorium reactors generated a return of more than $100 billion as they were adopted worldwide. The reactors not only power cities but provide so much energy that they are being used to extract carbon dioxide from the air, combine it with hydrogen, and produce carbon-neutral, renewable fuels, which have become another trillion-dollar industry worldwide.

All the cars are electric, and no one is burning anything to generate electricity in Belmont, so those deep blue desert skies are as clear and crisp as they were centuries ago.

Visitors eventually realize that another feature of older cities is missing, too: power lines. Homes generate so much power and have such battery storage that they're designed to be energy-independent. For backup—and to provide a way to contribute excess electricity for other homes or for export—a mesh network connects each house to its neighbors and eventually to a grid-scale battery at the center of each neighborhood's micro grid. (Although the grid-scale batteries were, for a long time, too expensive and lacked enough capacity to be economic, Gates subsidized them in the city's early days to simulate what micro grids could look like, and the batteries' capabilities eventually grew into the design.) The batteries also connect in a loose web to provide backup power to homes but carry little electricity, given the near-self-sufficiency of each house and each neighborhood, so it was easy to bury all wires underground.

The insides of homes in Belmont also feel different, mostly because of the exceptional focus on energy efficiency. The homes in Belmont use materials that allow for a radically different approach to air conditioning—they change chemical composition or shape as they absorb heat and cool a room, then are returned to their original state by applying electricity. The materials are built into the architecture in strategic spots, where they can take heat out of the air during the day and be "reset" each night. No need for loud AC units or for all the ductwork that homes used to use to distribute cool air. Ducts aren't needed for heating, either. A series of small, electric radiators take care of heating needs, so construction costs are much lower than they used to be.

Residents of Belmont—sometimes referred to locally as "Billmont," after the founder—have more money in their pockets because the exorbitant electricity bills they used to pay to run air conditioning in the summers near Phoenix (where highs can easily hit 115 degrees) have disappeared. The nearly limitless access to energy has also let Belmont solve one of the thorniest problems in the Southwest, water, which is simply pulled out of the air for most household needs.

Borrowing a concept proven in Japan's Woven City, the streets of Belmont are split into three zones: one for cars, which are mostly autonomous; one as a promenade shared by pedestrians and slower forms of personal mobility, such as bikes and scooters; and one as a tree-filled parkway for pedestrians only. This multimodal transportation system design alleviates several of the negative side effects of car-centered city planning: sedentary lifestyles and expensive transport. Just a few decades earlier, 40 percent of trips by car in the U.S. were for less than two miles, in large part because the streets were so inhospitable to pedestrians and cyclists. There are no such impediments in Belmont, and the residents are much healthier because of the increased physical activity. When residents don't want to walk or bike, they can hail an AV taxi service that's sized for their needs and that they can use at a much lower cost than owning their own car.

"As you look around your city," Thunberg said at the anniversary celebration, "you can see Winston Churchill was right when he said, 'You can always count on Americans to do the right thing—after they have tried everything else.'* America got off to a slow start on climate change and led the world in science deniers, but the country recognized the power of the Laws of Zero and has now led progress around the world for many years."

She ran through a list of achievements:

- Globally, the goal of reaching net-zero carbon emissions is within striking distance as the Laws of Zero continue to drive down the cost of clean energy and carbon removal.

- Economies have become so much more efficient that energy intensity—the amount of energy required to produce a dollar of GDP—has declined by between 50 and 75 percent in all countries around the globe. The drop reached 80 percent in India and China, mammoth economies where the most progress was needed.

- Traditional fossil fuel companies long ago realized their businesses had become unattractive. Large investors such as pension funds, insurance companies, endowments, and sovereign wealth funds pulled out of the companies because of concerns over climate change, and the companies saw better opportunities in adjacent areas. Many companies managed the transition risks and transformed into businesses focused on carbon capture, chemicals, renewable fuels, and geothermal drilling.

- As investors and fossil fuel companies shifted their focus toward opportunities in clean, sustainable energy, governments, especially in the U.S., yielded to public sentiment to pursue climate-friendly energy policies.

- The rapid infusion of new energy jobs has completely overwhelmed the loss of jobs in the old energy sector.

---

* Like many quotes attributed to Churchill, these words don't appear in any of his voluminous writings, and there's no evidence he actually said them. But, as Sen. Mark Warner, who is especially fond of Churchill and the quote, said, after being corrected about the attribution, "If Churchill didn't say it, he should have."

- Measures of equity in health, wealth, and happiness have improved globally, as the green transition provided a springboard to address poverty in developing countries and structural racism and social injustice in the developed ones.

As Thunberg ended her hopeful keynote, Gates, now 95 years old, said he hoped that she would soon visit Belmont in person, and with a clear conscience.

"We're making so much carbon-neutral fuel in Belmont that we don't know what to do with it all," he said. "I'll send you a jet, and you can have all the fuel you need."

Climate is the most dramatic illustration of how we're not trying to predict the future but invent it. We want to find a hopeful alternative. Sadly, if we were forecasting, the most likely future of our climate is a continuation of the long history of insufficient action in the face of ever-stronger scientific evidence of human-driven change and impending disaster. It's all the more critical, then, to articulate a less likely—but still achievable—future history of climate we can collectively work toward.

We think it would be crazy if we didn't significantly slow global warming and mitigate the worst effects of climate change by 2050.

The goal on climate change is stark. The federal government's recent, self-described "authoritative assessment of the science of climate change,"[115] the Climate Science Special Report (CSSR), said that, globally, we need to go from the roughly 51 billion tons of carbon emissions a year we're emitting today to net-zero emissions by 2050.* If we don't do so, the consequences will be disastrous for our kids and their kids—rising sea levels; extreme flooding and storms; heat waves; wildfires; droughts; devastated farming, fishing, and other food production; flooded cities and infrastructure; mass migration; resource wars; and

---

* The exact tonnage of global emissions is hard to measure; estimates range as high as 60 billion tons per year. When we refer to carbon emissions in this chapter, we use the estimates by Bill Gates in his recent book *How to Avoid a Climate Disaster*. The exact number is less important than the acceptance that the amount of carbon emissions is huge and that we have to eliminate all of it.

more. We're already seeing some effects. Try to think of the last time you managed to go on Twitter and didn't see an image of a wildfire, massive flooding, or even perhaps the ocean on fire.

To avoid climate disaster, we first need to start by getting to net-zero emissions in five types of human activities that contribute most of our carbon emissions: how we plug in, how we make things, how we grow things, how we get around, and how we keep warm and cool. (The relative contributions, as of 2019, are shown in Table 1.[116])

To make things all the more difficult, we have to hit a quickly growing target.

According to the World Bank,[117] about 74 percent of the world's population live in "middle income" countries. A further 9.2 percent live in poorer countries. All 6.3 billion of those people are working to share in the living standards enjoyed by the 1.2 billion people living in countries with "high income." And many more will join those aspirants: The UN estimates world population will grow by 1.9 billion between 2020 and 2050, with all of the growth happening in middle- and low-income countries.[118] That means more than 8 billion more people wanting more things.

That's a lot of people. And, as things stand, it'll result in carbon emissions dramatically rising, not falling. Growing food to feed all these people increases carbon emissions. Providing clean water and sanitation to them increases carbon emissions. Building homes for them increases carbon emissions. You get the idea. In effect, the world is building the equivalent of another New York City—every month. That means our planet will have added nearly 350 New York Cities between when we're writing this in 2021 and 2050. That's our goal date for slashing emissions

TABLE 1. Current Carbon Emissions

Current Emissions (2019)	CO_2 (Billion Tons)	Percentage of Total
Plugging in (electricity)	13.77	27%
Making things (industry)	15.81	31%
Growing things (agriculture)	9.69	19%
Getting around (transportation)	8.16	16%
Keeping warm and cool (shelter)	3.57	7%
	51.00	100%

to net-zero—and there's a lot of momentum taking us in the wrong direction.

The Laws of Zero are already enabling solutions that can bend the carbon-emissions curve. As we've seen, solar- and wind-generated electricity sources are becoming cheaper to build and operate than existing coal plants are to operate. And transportation is rapidly switching to electricity, which will increasingly come from clean sources. On their own, those Laws of Zero on energy and transportation won't get us to the answer, but the laws on computing, communication, and information give us a platform for innovation in an array of other areas. Those laws at least give us hope.

To succeed, the laws will need to enable a six-pronged strategy:

- Get all electricity from net-zero sources;
- Electrify everything possible—and develop clean fuels to do everything else;
- Introduce efficiencies that lower energy needs and emissions;
- Make scientific breakthroughs to address current gaps;
- Develop technologies that make it feasible to pull massive amounts of carbon from the air; and
- Do all the above… at a cost less than or equal to any carbon-emitting alternatives.

So you can see how close we can get to net-zero emissions based on current trajectories—and see just how sizable the gaps are that still need to be filled—we'll go through all six prongs in some detail. There's a cartoon we like where two professorial characters are standing in front of a chalkboard full of complicated equations. One points to a spot in the middle of the blackboard where the other has written, "Then a miracle occurs." The caption says, "'I think you should be more explicit here in step two.'" With climate change, we acknowledge a bunch of near-miracles need to occur. We're going to try to be as explicit as possible about where those need to happen so that all you future historians have a clearer picture on where you might want to get to work. Here's an incentive: Any one of these near-miracles would both help save the planet and generate a fortune the likes of which few have ever seen.

Net-Zero Electricity

Here's where the Laws of Zero really shine.*

As we discussed in the future history of electricity, we think it'd be crazy not to have clean electricity available to everyone, everywhere, in abundant and affordable quantities in the Future Perfect. Zero-carbon sources, mostly in the form of solar power, wind power, nuclear power, and hydropower, already account for 37 percent of all electricity generation. Getting those sources close to 100 percent by 2050 would eliminate a large chunk (27 percent) of the current problem for emissions and would mean clean sources would fulfill the many new demands for electricity.

But getting to total clean energy is far easier said than done. As we've noted, the current grid is a major problem. Zero-carbon electricity has to be reliably and affordably delivered where it's needed, when it's needed, and in the amounts that are needed, and the current grid isn't up to the task. We'll need to build long-distance transmission lines to take power from sunny and windy regions to other areas. We'll need major advances in batteries and other technologies to store enough electricity for use during nights and cloudy, windless days and to deal with the seasonal differences in sunshine and wind.

As drastic as these advances may seem now, there's a heated debate on whether they would even be enough. Two of the richest and most forward-thinking people in the world are on opposite sides of this debate: Elon Musk is among the optimists, and Bill Gates is among the skeptical. While Musk believes advances with solar, wind, and batteries will meet our needs, Gates (who supports the adoption of renewables as quickly as possible) argues breakthroughs may also be needed in nuclear fission and fusion to fill gaps in the service that renewables will be able to provide. (We think the stakes here are so high and the timing so urgent that we need to go full speed ahead on all fronts—just in case.)

Fortunately, tools enabled by Laws of Zero in computing, communications, and information will provide a platform for innovation at

---

* Tragically, technology to date has been a key enabler of global warming and impending climate disaster. The rise in atmospheric carbon and the resulting impact on the climate stem directly from the harnessing of fossil fuels that enabled the industrial revolution, warmed and cooled our homes, brought us the marvels enabled by fast and cheap transportation, fertilized our soil to grow things, and underpinned most aspects of the tremendous advances in standards of living over the past two-and-a-half centuries.

unprecedented speed. Tests of new materials, new approaches to building and managing the grid, and so on used to require painstaking work in the physical world. But those efforts can increasingly be done based on models and simulations, essentially becoming software problems that AI can tackle. The work can be done on computers over periods measured in seconds, minutes, and hours, not in months, years, and decades.

For example, multiple groups of researchers are now using sophisticated computer simulations to develop alternative strategies for transforming the U.S. grid. They're starting with detailed models of all existing power grids, along with detailed weather and usage patterns, and are then simulating different placements of generation and transmission capabilities. The researchers looked at current plans, including some considered ambitious, that would cut emissions by six percent by 2030 and have created more detailed options that could reduce emissions by 42 percent by the end of the decade.[119] The researchers have made their tools and models publicly available so others can stress-test the designs and explore alternatives.

Electricity Everywhere

Once we have all that net-zero electricity (we hope), we have to use it to replace fossil fuels in as many applications as possible.

Transportation

Transportation contributes about 16 percent of total global carbon emissions, so converting it, alone, to clean power sources would be a major advance. As we've explained, we're on the cusp of having electric vehicles that are cheap enough and have enough range that they'll initiate the phaseout of internal combustion engines. The challenge will be scaling: We'll have to adopt clean electric vehicles everywhere possible and do it fast enough to replace all existing dirty vehicles by 2050.

That will be hard. (Everything about climate seems to be.) At current rates, it takes about 15 years to turn over an entire fleet of vehicles.[120, 121] So, starting in 2035—15 years before our deadline of 2050—all new cars would need to be net-zero. Forecasters aren't optimistic, however. As we write this in 2021, analysts project electric vehicles will make up just one-quarter of new sales by 2035. By 2050, electric vehicles are projected to make up only 60 percent of sales, and projections are that most vehicles in use will still be powered by fossil fuels.[122]

Still, some major companies and governments suggest the forecasters may be too pessimistic. General Motors, for example, has announced it will launch 30 electric vehicles by 2025 and will phase out all its gas- and diesel-powered vehicles by 2035.[123] Volvo announced it will stop selling fossil fuel-powered cars by 2030.[124] Ford and Jaguar said they would move to all-electric in Europe by 2030.[125] On the regulatory side, California has set a net-zero target for new cars and trucks by 2035.[126] The UK plans to ban the sale of new gas and diesel vehicles by 2030, while Norway has set a 2025 target.[127]

The Laws of Zero also suggest we may get closer to the 2050 goal than those naysaying forecasters currently predict—even professionals have trouble seeing the effects of the exponentials at work in the Laws of Zero. But some other things will have to happen, too.

There will need to be a virtuous circle of shared, autonomous electric vehicles. As we wrote in the future history of transportation, AVs enable consumers to forego the huge fixed cost of owning a car and, instead, bear the variable cost of an autonomous car service that provides transportation on demand. The potential market here is enormous. Early business modeling shows such services can deliver handsome profits while charging consumers a lower cost per mile than the per-mile cost of car ownership. Such services would grow rapidly, given the economics for both providers and customers, and all AV platforms will be electric because of the requirements of all the sensors in the vehicles. At the moment, many individuals are reluctant to buy electric cars because their up-front cost is higher than for those with internal combustion engines,* but these car services will be operated by large commercial fleet owners (including the likes of Waymo and General Motors), and they won't suffer the same sort of sticker shock that might scare off individual

---

* Operating costs for electric vehicles are lower than for those with internal combustion engines, and the lifetime cost of an EV can be far lower, but the crossover point at which an EV becomes less expensive has tended to be at least a year after purchase, and possibly much longer. The actual calculations obviously depend on a host of variables, including any government incentives for buying an EV, the model purchased, the miles driven, and the costs for gasoline and electricity.

consumers. Thus, electric vehicle technology could be adopted earlier and at price points higher than might attract consumers.[128]

Autonomous electric vehicles will also need to evolve into dramatically new forms. As we've discussed, fleet-level car sharing will allow for matching vehicles to particular trips rather than vehicles being one-size-fits-all. Because most car trips are short ones involving one or two people, most cars in a shared fleet could be smaller, simpler, and cheaper than those most of us own now. Such simplicity in cars would also reduce the traditional competitive advantages that stem from automakers' ability to manage complex supply chains and integrate thousands of parts. Simpler cars would also reduce the necessary engineering expertise and capital costs, two barriers to entry that have protected automakers from new market entrants. All these factors would invite more competition and innovation, enlarging consumer choice and accelerating adoption.

Governments will need to speed the transition to electric vehicles. Nations can, for instance, provide investment incentives and production mandates for manufacturers, purchasing incentives for consumers, and investments for the electric grid and for charging infrastructure to support electric vehicles. Nations can also create disincentives for the use of fossil fuels. While interested parties always push back when governments try to pick winners and losers, there's an international competitive dynamic here. Governments want to make sure that their countries' automotive industries remain competitive as the market shifts to electric vehicles and AVs.

Markets will have to do their job—as they generally do. Investors are already betting on the rapid transition to electric vehicles and, as a result, are providing tremendous amounts of capital to the companies most likely to drive the transition. Investors will continue to reward pioneers with promising ideas, as they have Tesla, and that should drive us closer to electrifying transportation by 2050.

Pulling all the right levers for cars, SUVs, motorcycles, and light-duty commercial trucks and buses by 2050 covers about two-thirds to three-fourths of all transportation-related emissions. But long-distance trucks, cargo and cruise ships, and planes could prove difficult to shift to electricity because of the weight of the batteries. For these applications, we'll need price breakthroughs in net-zero fuels like biofuels or hydrogen for trucks and planes (which currently cost two and a half to six times more) and perhaps in nuclear power for ships. The good news for shipping is that 40 percent of all cargo ships are devoted to carrying fossil fuels today, and that tonnage will almost certainly no longer need to be transported.

Heating and Cooling

Another area ripe for clean electrification is in heating and cooling our buildings, which currently account for about seven percent of the global total of emissions.

Cooling is the easy part, as air conditioners already run on electric power. If we can't generate enough clean power by 2050, though, we're in trouble because the demand for air conditioners is growing so fast, and that pace will only quicken in a warming world.* There are about 1.6 billion air conditioning units in the world, and that number will more than triple to over 5 billion by 2050, according to the International Energy Agency.† At that point, just air conditioners will consume as much electricity as all of China and India do today.‡

Heating, in the form of furnaces and water heaters, are the fossil fuel burners in our homes and offices. Today, half of all furnaces sold in the U.S. run on natural gas. Worldwide, fossil fuels provide six times more energy for heating than electricity does. The good news is, for new construction, the cost of an electric heat pump (which both warms and cools) is less than the combined cost of a new gas furnace and electric air conditioner. But furnaces tend to last a decade or more, so it'll take a long time to move away from those already installed. To get to a goal of all-electric by 2050, we'll have to stop selling gas-powered furnaces and water heaters by 2035. For however many remain in operation after 2050, we'll still need alternative net-zero fuels.

---

* Lots of people in the Pacific Northwest and western Canada never thought they needed air conditioning but found themselves dealing with sustained temperatures well above 100°F because of the heat dome that formed repeatedly in the summer of 2021.
† The U.S. and Japan currently lead the world, with more than 90 percent of households already having some form of air conditioning, according to International Energy Association estimates. China is at 60 percent. By contrast, Mexico and Brazil are near 20 percent, and South Africa and Indonesia are below 10 percent penetration.
‡ In addition to carbon emissions because of electricity consumption, air conditioners also emit what are known as F-gases (because they contain fluorine), which cause 23,000 times the warming effect of carbon dioxide.

Industry

Industry and the general activity of making things account for about 31 percent of all carbon emissions today, so there's a huge opportunity here. Unfortunately, there isn't a straightforward transition to clean electricity.

Industrial emissions come from three sources: (1) the fossil fuels used to generate the electricity used by factories; (2) the fossil fuels used to generate the heat used in manufacturing processes, like melting iron ore to make steel; and (3) the emissions generated when the materials are made, such as the carbon dioxide released by the chemical process of making steel. We've already dealt with the generation of clean electricity. Greater challenges lie in the second and third sources of emissions.

Take cement and steel, which together account for 13 percent of annual global emissions. Their manufacture requires intense heat, about 2,000°F, to melt the limestone for cement and almost 3,000°F to melt the iron ore for steel. Using electricity to generate that sort of heat is far more complicated than just plugging into the electric grid. However, nuclear power or hydrogen might substitute for some of the fossil fuels that generate the enormous heat we use today.

Likewise, the chemical processes involved in making cement and steel emit carbon dioxide that has nothing to do with fossil fuels. Globally, we currently make about four billion tons of cement each year, and every ton results in a ton of carbon dioxide. We make about 1.8 billion tons of steel each year, and every ton results in 1.8 tons of carbon dioxide. Those emissions are on top of the ones produced while melting the limestone and iron ore; reducing or capturing these emissions will also require innovations beyond electrification.

Agriculture

Growing food accounts for about 19 percent of all global emissions, and clean electrification will only help a bit.

In agriculture, we're mostly concerned with methane and nitrous oxide, not with power sources. While the amounts of these greenhouse gases are small compared with carbon dioxide emissions, they're particularly dangerous. Methane causes, per molecule, 28 times more warming than carbon dioxide. Nitrous oxide causes 265 times more. Together, methane and nitrous oxide account for about 80 percent of the emissions due to agriculture.

Cows are the primary source of methane. Cows, goats, and other graz-
ers are ruminants, meaning they can digest grass and other plants and
grains most animals (including humans) cannot. But their digestive systems use a process called enteric fermentation that produces methane. Lots
and lots of methane. The cows then release the methane into the atmosphere through what scientists call eructation and flatulence, or what our
kids refer to as burping and farting. Each cow burps and farts between 160
and 320 liters of methane every day and, globally, there are about 1.5 billion
cows.[129] Cows, alone, account for about four percent of global emissions.
Cows contribute about half the nitrous oxide released into the atmosphere
as their feces decompose, while pig feces contribute the other half.

Other major sources of agricultural emissions include deforestation
and other land use, which together add up to three percent of global
emissions. Fertilizers are responsible for about two and a half percent.
And as much as one-third of all food produced globally is wasted.[130]

Electrification offers no simple solutions for any of these agricultural
emissions, though other innovations hold promise. Pilot projects putting additives in cows' feed, derived from seaweed, have reduced their
methane output by 50 to 90 percent.[131] Scientists are studying ways to
reduce methane production through genomics and selective breeding.
The many companies now developing artificial meat could also greatly
reduce the size of cattle herds.*

Efficiency, Efficiency, Efficiency

In the 1960s, cautioning that federal spending had a way of getting out
of control, Senator Everett Dirksen reportedly observed, "A billion here,
a billion there, and pretty soon you're talking real money." Well, as our
above cataloging of the vast and varied contributors of carbon emissions
should attest: A billion tons of carbon here, a billion tons there, and
pretty soon you're talking real climate change.

But the billions can be rolled back, too. Cyclists packing their pan-
niers for their first road trips are cautioned, "If you take care of the

---

* While talk of artificial meat has led to claims that governments will outlaw hamburg-
ers, there is also a growing eco-conscious food movement that could shrink the need
for cows. So-called reducetarians are switching to oat milk and protein sources such as
tofu to decrease their consumption of red meat.

ounces, the pounds will take care of themselves." If we make efficiency a key component of the Future Perfect, we can, bit by bit, drastically reduce the amount of carbon we either have to reduce or capture. The easiest ton of carbon to eliminate is the one you never produced.

Efficiencies must be gained in two key areas: energy and materials.

Energy Efficiency

A 2020 study found that energy efficiency policies and programs enacted over previous decades in the U.S. saved so much energy in 2017 that, without them, U.S. energy use would have been about 23 percent higher. These policies and programs included fuel economy standards, appliance and equipment standards, the Energy Star efficiency program, utility sector efficiency programs, and energy codes for buildings. For example, standards have reduced energy usage of appliances by 80 percent since 1980 (saving the average American household about $500 a year).[132]

A host of additional energy-efficiency options will be available by 2050.[133] For instance, efficient design of new homes and commercial buildings, including electrification and the use of renewable electricity, could cut their emissions by 80 percent.

Materials Efficiency

Although we'll need to make a lot more things by 2050, as the population increases and poorer countries race to improve their economies, we can use less material to make those things. We can also shift to using materials that involve fewer emissions.

For example, the International Resource Panel, an arm of the UN, has developed a number of efficiency strategies that could, by 2050, collectively reduce emissions by 80 percent for materials used in homes and 57 percent for materials used in cars.[134] These strategies can be deployed starting now, with existing technologies. Among them are: designing lighter buildings, to reduce the use of carbon-intensive materials such as steel, cement, and glass; using wood, a carbon-neutral source, instead of reinforced concrete and masonry; and improving the recycling of materials used in buildings and cars.

Scientific Breakthroughs
(Where the Near-Miracles Occur)

Some of these needed breakthroughs will seem far-fetched, even impossible. But, as we've tried to convince you over the course of this book, the progress that will come by 2050 by following the Laws of Zero will, in many cases, feel like magic from the vantage point of 2021. In 30 years, some of these technologies will be routine—remember that the term "genomics" didn't even exist 30 years before the invention of CRISPR.

The breakthroughs we need to have happen to invent the future history of climate in 2050 fall into two categories: those in energy and those in areas that could significantly reduce carbon emissions.

Energy Breakthroughs

- Pumped hydro (water is pumped uphill to a reservoir when energy is available, then released downhill to a lower reservoir, through a hydroelectric generator, when power is needed)
- Thermal storage (a substance is heated when energy is available, then the heat is used to produce electricity whenever it's needed)
- Alternative fuels, including biofuels and hydrogen produced without emitting carbon
- Grid-scale electricity storage that can last a full season
- Geothermal energy
- Safe, modular nuclear fission
- Nuclear fusion

Carbon Emission Breakthroughs

- Zero-carbon cement
- Zero-carbon steel
- Zero-carbon plastics
- Plant- and cell-based meat and dairy
- Zero-carbon fertilizer
- Coolants that don't contain F-gases
- Carbon capture

Why do we believe these breakthroughs are possible? There are three reasons for our optimism.

The first is science.

The scientific discovery and invention platform enabled by computing, communications, information, and genomics allows "unbelievable leverage on the universe," as Alan Kay has observed to us. In every field, including mechanical, electrical, and biological systems, the process of hypothesis, testing, and learning provides access to boundless insight and is accelerated by computer modeling, analysis, and simulation tools. Individual learnings can be shared, stress-tested, and evolved through global collaboration and competition that is enabled by rich and near-instantaneous communications.

Science is now the standard method for developing everything, and it'll be the platform for making all the breakthroughs. These days, physical objects won't even be built until after extensive testing and validation via computing. And when they are built, the work can be done through computer-guided fabrication and 3-D printing. Like the technologies for reading and editing genomes, the Future Perfect computing platform can be used to invent things that were recently unimaginable and put them on an exponential improvement path.

The second reason is the urgency of self-preservation.

As the COVID-19 vaccines show—being produced and mass-distributed in less than a year as opposed to the normal 10 to 25 years—mankind can move fast when it must. To this point, the dangers of climate change have been ephemeral enough for many that it's been possible to defer action, but hurricanes, wildfires, derechos, and other disasters, combined with steadily rising temperatures, have changed the tone. Science and industry are rallying, and the pace will accelerate as the problems become more obvious.

The third reason is economics: the defense of value and the allure of new wealth.

BlackRock, the world's largest money manager, says, "Climate risk is … a historic investment opportunity." BlackRock says, "With the world moving to net-zero [carbon emissions], BlackRock can best serve our clients by helping them be at the forefront of that transition."[135]

BlackRock estimates doing nothing about climate change would result in a 25 percent cumulative loss in economic output over the next two decades. An orderly "green transition" could avoid these losses. BlackRock also believes companies that react best to climate change will gain an advantage. For example, a chemical company that positions its product line for the massive adoption of electric vehicles could be a big winner, while an insurance company that doesn't adapt to the growing risk from physical climate damages will perform poorly.[136]

The investment firm has $8.7 trillion of assets under management that will back up its market assumptions, so BlackRock is sure to get the attention of CEOs and boards of directors. It's already asking companies to disclose their climate mitigation plans and provide data to track their progress. And markets always reward winners.

The top 10 steel companies in the world are collectively valued at (as of this writing) about $140 billion, and whoever develops the best way to make net-zero steel has a clear shot at much of that value. Net-zero steel might even expand the market, letting steel be used in ways it isn't now.

The same kind of opportunity holds true for companies leading in any of the other breakthroughs we've listed as being needed. We're in an age of transition where new ideas can uproot long-established businesses. Trillions are up for grabs.

Carbon Capture

You might have noticed we keep writing about getting to "net-zero" emissions rather than "zero" emissions. That's because even the most optimistic among us doesn't believe there will be some combination of scientific breakthroughs and societal fortitude that enables us to eliminate all carbon emissions by 2050. Some emissions will still happen, such as from the fossil fuels that still get burned and the carbon dioxide from the traditional cement recipes that still are used. Rather than letting those emissions stay in the atmosphere, we'll have to "capture" them. The emissions that we produce minus the carbon that we capture will net out to zero. Thus, "net-zero" rather than "zero."

Unfortunately, there might be a lot of carbon to "net" out. According to analysis by the UN, there is no plausible path to mitigating the worse effects of climate change without the successful capture of 100 billion to 1 trillion tons of carbon dioxide over the course of this century.[137] To put that in perspective, remember the world produces about 51 billion tons every year at the moment. Once we get to net-zero in terms of our new emissions, there's hope carbon-capture technologies can be used to get to net-negative emissions, i.e., to extract the excess carbon pollution of past years and lessen global warming. (Spoiler alert: That possibility is a long, long way off.)

There are two general ways to capture carbon dioxide. One is at the industrial source, like power plants and cement kilns, before carbon dioxide is released into the atmosphere. The other method is to pull the carbon dioxide out of the air. In both methods, the captured carbon dioxide is compressed, transported, and buried in geologic formations, such as oil and gas reservoirs, coal seams, and deep saline reservoirs. There are also efforts to use the captured carbon to make things such as plastics, liquid fuels, fertilizer, and even cement.

We won't go into the technical details of how each way works except to say that both are technically understood, and small-scale efforts are in place. Because of cost, complexity, and policy challenges, however, both approaches fall into the "near-miracle" category in terms of the work to be done to reach global scale by 2050.

It's possible, for example, for industrial facilities to scrub carbon dioxide from their flue gas and reduce their life-cycle emissions by 55 to 90 percent. Yet, according to the International Energy Agency, only 30 million tons of carbon dioxide is being captured each year—just 0.3 percent of a reasonable goal for 2050.

Direct air capture is even more nascent. Carbon Engineering, a high-profile, Canadian-based company doing this, operates a proof-of-concept facility that captures 365 tons a year. It anticipates its first commercial plant will capture one million tons per year at a cost of between $94 and $233 per ton[138]—meaning the cost would be at least $1 trillion a year to reach a reasonable 2050 target for carbon capture.

Elon Musk has funded an XPRIZE competition for carbon removal to inspire and help scale efficient solutions to pull carbon dioxide directly from the atmosphere or oceans. After 18 months, 15 teams will be selected to receive $1 million to build their demonstration systems. To win the four-year competition, teams must demonstrate a rigorous, validated scale model of their carbon removal solution and the ability of their solution to economically scale to gigaton levels. $50 million would go to the winner, with $20 million and $10 million going to the second- and third-place teams.

Likewise, NRG and Canada's Oil Sands Innovation Alliance have sponsored a $20 million XPRIZE for developing ways to more effectively turn captured carbon into valuable products, thus helping enhance market mechanisms to support significantly more carbon capture. The concept, known as the circular carbon economy, is essentially turning carbon into a reusable material for making things, rather than just leaving it as the waste product of the industrial revolution. That's because, in theory, any product made with carbon from fossil fuels could be made with carbon captured from the air. Imagine turning the carbon dioxide captured from the chemical process of making steel into fuel for heavy trucks and planes. In addition to fuels, the long list of carbon-based products being adapted for captured carbon include cement, concrete and other construction materials, industrial gas and fluids, polymers, chemicals, carbon fiber, animal feed, and fertilizer.

Few believe using captured carbon for making things will put a major dent in carbon emissions any time soon, but it might help make carbon capture more economically viable. Every advance along that cost curve helps. Someday, we may even look back on these XPRIZEs in the same way we do about DARPA's grand challenge for autonomous vehicles—both may have helped to engage a generation of scientists and entrepreneurs and launched the exponential improvements necessary for this prong of our climate change mitigation strategy.

Far Lower Cost

Carbon emissions anywhere on Earth affect our collective atmosphere. So, to achieve a hopeful future history of the climate, we have to get to net-zero carbon emissions not just in the U.S. or in other countries rich enough to afford it, but everywhere. Imagine you were very poor; which would you choose: to be richer or greener? We'd love for everyone to be greener, but we all have to provide for ourselves and our families. That means we need to find alternatives that get us to net-zero that are at least economically neutral, or the world will tilt toward cheaper fossil fuels—and a climate disaster.

The cost difference between a zero-carbon solution and its carbon-dirty alternatives is known as a "green premium."[139] For example, if a gallon of standard jet fuel costs $2 and a gallon of zero-carbon biofuel for jets costs $5, the green premium would be $3, or 150 percent. Some folks might be willing to pay that extra 150 percent for clean fuel, but the bulk of the global airline and air freight industries—which already operate on razor-thin margins—will have to stick with the $2 option. If someone could invent zero-carbon jet fuel for $2 or less, however, then there's no conflict in choosing it.

Green premiums currently hinder the adoption of most zero-carbon solutions. In addition to jet fuel, substantial green premiums exist for zero-carbon fuels for cars, trucks, ships, and heating. Plant-based meat substitutes cost a lot more than meat does. Direct carbon capture of industrial carbon emissions, like the making of cement, significantly increases manufacturing costs. And so on.

So we not only need science and technology breakthroughs, we have to make them much cheaper to drive global scaling and ubiquitous adoption.

• • •

Government policy will have to fit in the equation, too. As we've said repeatedly, we're not writing a policy book, but we as a society will need to cooperate to achieve a Future Perfect. Governments will need to facilitate that cooperation among different interest groups on climate policy—and policy can be even harder than science. Someone will have to live near that new, advanced nuclear reactor, and we'll need to sacrifice some habitat as we deploy more wind and solar. Communities are already battling over habitat—real estate developers want the land, as do advocates of renewables. In general, the dialogue in Washington, DC, suggests we're a long way from developing and implementing a thoughtful climate policy in the U.S.

If we can't get the policy measures right, economics may not save us. The idea that people will pay a "green premium" presupposes that people are eager to adopt a greener solution once it reaches cost parity. In fact, academic work and business history show that the diffusion of innovation happens fastest when the new solution provides a clear set of advantages, not just parity. Yes, climate change poses an existential threat, and concern is rising steadily, potentially pushing more of us to accept a "green premium," but it's hard to see why green jet fuel, for example, would appeal to airlines merely by reaching cost parity with conventional jet fuel. After all, there's a great deal of operational risk in switching to a new fuel, and someone will get fired if the new fuel disrupts flight operations.

This means progress depends not only on producing some audacious technology breakthroughs but on having governments provide the right framework for helping society to cooperate as it nurtures and then absorbs them.

Despite the challenges we're facing, here's an example of how exponentials offer some hope:

Saving Billions, Making Trillions With Climate Solutions

SEATTLE, May 18, 2050—The Gates Foundation announced today that its endowment has surpassed $1 trillion in assets, even though the foundation has been spending and donating some $3 billion a year since its inception in 2006.

While the foundation was initially known for its efforts mostly on health-related issues, such as combatting malaria and eradicating polio, and while founder Bill Gates earned a great deal of attention in the 2020s for his years of prescient warnings about the sort of pandemic disaster that COVID-19 caused, the recent surge in the foundation's assets has largely come because of his work on climate change.

In particular, the surge has occurred because Bill Gates and his ex-wife, Melinda, donated so much of the fortune they based on a series of investments beginning in the 2010s that attacked carbon emissions. Those donations then made the foundation a magnet for funding by others who were focused on the cause.

"The foundation has played a significant role in helping us get so close to net-zero carbon emissions, seemingly in time to prevent the most severe problems of climate change we all worried about so much 30 years ago," said Andrew Tyler, the lead researcher for the UN Council on Climate. "Governments obviously spent more money, but the foundation seeded several key ideas and helped unleash the market forces that accelerated so many solutions."

Gates said the foundation expanded beyond its initial work on global health and poverty because he and Melinda saw that those suffering the most would also be hit disproportionately by the effects of climate change. They took the long view on climate, rather than seeking the sorts of quick returns venture funds and other investors typically pursue. The foundation invested only in companies that had the potential to eliminate one percent of global carbon emissions. The two also convinced a group of other billionaires and countries to invest alongside them.

The biggest successful investments included an early one in modular nuclear reactors, whose new design and growing safety record allayed the decades of fears about nuclear power, exacerbated by a few high-profile failures. An innovative design for grid-scale storage also proved massively successful. Those two investments alone now have nuclear power providing clean, baseline energy around the world and mean that solar and wind power can be deployed essentially without limit, with huge batteries capturing all the electricity they can produce.

Beyond energy, the Gates Foundation also championed startups that sparked breakthroughs in other areas needed to address climate change, such as better, less expensive cement and steel without CO_2 emissions.

The returns for the former couple dwarfed what they earned from his first venture: Microsoft. While much of the potential from their more recent investments is still to be realized, the markets have assigned the companies valuations that mirror the sort of success that Elon Musk had in the early 2020s with Tesla.

The foundation has had a bunch of duds, too, of course. Few remember, for instance, some of the early investments in carbon capture. However, the duo parlayed these early learnings into smarter investments in the critical technology area, and direct air, carbon-capture facilities are scaling up fast because of their persistence.

"That's how investment portfolios work," Tyler said. "If they don't include a bunch of duds, then the aspirations aren't high enough to let the successes be so huge."

CHAPTER 12

The Future History of Trust

Cyber Threats? What Cyber Threats?

WASHINGTON, DC, January 19, 2050—Juan Luis Ojeda, the secretary of Homeland Security, issued the annual report on national cybersecurity today—and it was short. "We're in good shape," he said in an interview.

While cybercrime in the U.S. had been about $250 billion a year (roughly half of the global total) three decades ago in 2020, the latest report found there were less than $20 billion of losses in the U.S. this past year.

"Still, that number's way too high," Ojeda said. "The tools for spotting potential fraud are so much better than they were in decades past that we should be able to stamp out cybercrime entirely. The only reason we haven't is that there are still careless people in the world, and criminals will always find a way to target them."

As usual, the report found no foreign interference in the latest elections.

"Several state and non-state actors tried," Ojeda said, "but we stopped them cold, because we can now be certain about the identities of those who are trying to vote. Most countries respected the formal and informal agreements we've reached over the decades to leave each other's elections alone."

The annual index of consumer trust on privacy and security reached 94.2, inching up to a record for the 15th consecutive year, in the absence of any significant event that would undermine trust.

"People are using the privacy and security tools the government and private industry are giving them," Ojeda said, "and they're feeling the benefits."

Trust is an even more complicated topic than the ones we've already visited—and, as you've seen, getting the future of electricity, health care, transportation, and climate right will be plenty complicated. Trust is so hard because we don't just have to overcome the status quo and inertia, or even the inevitable bad ideas, as with the other topics. We have to overcome bad people—lots and lots of bad people. Many of these bad people deliberately sow mistrust as a way to gain money or power. Think of what the Russians have been doing in recent years to try to undercut Americans' faith in our electoral system. Think of all the scam artists who are trying to steal our identities or trick us into believing they're someone or something they're not. Even in the Future Perfect, these bad people aren't going away. In fact, the tools they'll be able to use will keep getting more powerful.

Left unaddressed, the problem of trust will only fester on our way to 2050. Social media and resulting misinformation campaigns will become more of a mess. News media will fragment the country further, with watchers/readers almost separating into different universes with different accepted sets of facts. Thefts of data and identities will be so rampant it'll be hard to be sure who and what is real when interacting with individuals or organizations.

We think it'd be crazy if by 2050 we couldn't (mostly) guarantee trust in our interactions with each other, with government, with organizations, and with devices/entities in the cloud.

No, trust won't be perfect in 2050, but we can do a lot better on many fronts than we are now—if we start to invent the future soon. While trust comes in many flavors and involves a host of actors in an array of relationships, four issues will be key for the smooth functioning of society:

1. We need security for our identities. People shouldn't be able to falsely pretend to be us.

2. We need to be able to authenticate our identities to others (the flip side of No. 1). You need to know we are who we say we are.

3. There needs to be truth. This will be the most intractable issue. Who gets to decide what's true? No one, obviously. We can set up fact-checkers, but then we'll have fact-checkers fact-checking the fact-checkers, and fact-checkers fact-checking the fact-checkers who are fact-checking the fact-checkers…. There's no end, no absolutely trusted source. In any case, we'll still face the problem that everyone seems to have their own version of the truth, no matter what the facts in front of all of us plainly show. The old line is that "Seeing is believing." But it's also true—and maybe more important—that believing is seeing. Once we believe something strongly, we see the world through that lens, and almost nothing will change our minds. But despite these complex problems, we can do a much better job by 2050 of providing people with information on the reputation and bias of a source and of generally dampening the spread of false claims. The solution is complicated (and, again, far from perfect), but it should allow for considerable improvement over today.

4. We need more control over our privacy. We shouldn't have to share any more information than we want to share.

Our hope may seem like a fantasy. Even the most sophisticated systems in government and business fell prey to the SolarWinds attack by the Russians in 2020, which led to all sorts of data breaches, and a group of Russian hackers shut off the gasoline supply for much of the East Coast through a ransomware attack on the Colonial Pipeline in 2021. We read about other cyberattacks, large and small, all the time. Meanwhile, social media is a cesspool of misinformation and disinformation, and privacy seems to be a mirage. In April 2021, Facebook acknowledged it had exposed 530 million users' personal information back in 2019 but was so unconcerned that it didn't even notify them. What hope do we have to protect ourselves?

But the Laws of Zero on computing, communication, and information (and perhaps even on genomics) will give us good guys some key new powers. The most important is the ability to triangulate.

You can see the power of triangulation in the GPS, which uses three satellites to pinpoint your location in 3-D space. Two satellites won't cut it—you could be in an infinite number of locations based on what two satellites learn about you. But three satellites? That's magic. They can glean exactly where you are, so your phone can then tell you, turn by turn, how to get to that new restaurant.

When it comes to authentication, the goal of triangulation is to combine something you have, something you are, and something you know so that you wind up with three different ways to point to the truth of your identity or someone else's.

Already, it's becoming routine to have a business send pictures of the person coming to fix your plumbing as an extra form of authentication, following the lead of ride-hailing platforms, which send information about the driver's car along with the license plate number and the name and a picture of the driver. Basically, businesses are adding information about something the plumber or driver is (the photo), to go with something he knows (where you are and what your need is), and possibly with something he has (some identification). Your watch and phone can pay at the grocery store, because they're something you have and can, if desired, be combined with something you know (a password or card number). At the airport, you can enter the country using your fingerprints and clear passport control using your iris (something you are).

How does authentication work if you're not physically there? Even if the bits coming across the wire match your iris scan, how do we know it's really you sending them, with your eye in front of the scanner, and not a fraud being committed by someone who's hacked into a record that contains your iris scan? And once someone has the data from your iris scan, what's a person to do? You can't get a new set of eyeballs.

Triangulation to the rescue.

Already, we're bombarded by websites to enable two-factor authentication (2FA) by adding a second "factor" to our passwords—typically providing a phone number so the app can text us a code we type in after entering our password. (This wouldn't be quite so important if people didn't use passwords such as, well, "password" or "123456," but we have to play the hand we're dealt). Next is multi-factor authentication (MFA), which adds more points of verification using biometrics or other "things you have." And MFA is just the beginning.

First, the number of "devices" we use will explode. Beyond watches and phones, we'll have glasses, earrings, contact lenses, and tiny machines all around us and even inside us. Triangulation then becomes an order of magnitude more powerful, as we can mix and match this multitude of devices to make it increasingly difficult for anyone else to pretend they're us—even if a bad actor somehow gets something like your iris scan. Mixing and matching makes it easy to keep changing our unique identifiers. Even today, a "stolen" identity is a misnomer. Your identity is copied, not stolen, because you still have your information. Now, in the Future Perfect, you'll be able to change enough of your identifiers to thwart a would-be thief.

Second, many of these tiny machines that will be inside us or on our bodies will be very difficult to remove. The sheer number of sensors will make it difficult to compromise any number of them simultaneously. And, with the computing power that will be available in three decades, it won't be a problem to use as many sensors as we want to create a unique "signature." While you can't replace eyeballs, these tiny sensors can be replaced or the number can be expanded at any time. Even if a bad actor compromises some number of these tiny helpers, we can just swallow a bunch more. Swallowing or "wearing" tiny bots may seem even spookier than the current identity verification schemes, but it's already happening, and the benefits to health sensors will be difficult to pass up. If we asked our predecessors how they'd feel about many things we take for granted (contact lenses we place on and peel off our eyes, medicinal skin patches, surgery), they'd have been spooked, as well.

While there are (and will be) issues around data control and privacy, the Laws of Zero are making possible decentralized approaches to securely storing and analyzing sensitive information such as biometrics. Already, for example, blockchain enables secure storage and use of sensitive information under the control of the individual rather than under some other institution or government.[140]

We'll need secure connections everywhere to transmit information back and forth without compromise. Fortunately, this is already a somewhat solved problem. Current encryption is very difficult to break, and it's getting better all the time. The commercialization of quantum computing could change the game because of the massive increase in power it will provide—but the benefits will go to both the good guys and the bad guys.

New government-private partnerships will surely arise that will help authenticate our identities and those of any we're considering trusting.

These institutions would provide physical identification as well as verifying remote "signatures"—the U.S. Postal Service is already providing 2FA identity verification services based on possession of a mobile phone and knowledge of a password. The work shows how other organizations could then work with these trusted institutions to use the immense computing power available to thwart attempts at impersonation as they occur. This approach to authentication would resemble what credit card companies do now, intervening in suspicious transactions before they are completed. And these new organizations would be backed up by the force of law, deterring violators.

A reasonable analogy as we try to put out the fires raging around authentication is, well, actual fires from a century-plus ago. The widespread deployment of electricity changed society dramatically and for the better, but with electricity comes the threat of fire—and there were lots of fires beginning in the late 1800s as buildings got larger and became wired for electricity. Insurance companies, which bore the brunt of the financial risk from these fires, eventually drove the adoption of uniform building codes and the creation of Underwriters Laboratories to certify the safety of electric appliances.[141] Note that issues of identity, authentication, and enforcement had to be addressed as part of this new framework via building contractors, permits, laws, and inspectors. Today, fires are so much less frequent that fire fighters spend the vast majority of their time as emergency medical technicians, dealing with health emergencies.

The Future Perfect will also allow for authentication that goes beyond our identities and gets at an issue near and dear to so many of us: our reputations. Triangulation will allow for a sort of Yelp writ large—very large. Such apps provide a consensus view based on perhaps thousands of reviews. Yes, there are ways to game the system by writing fake reviews or by getting others to praise your business or trash a competitor, but the algorithms for detecting fraudulent reviews are getting better all the time. Ultimately, the issue is: Can I trust that the entity on the other side of the transaction will deliver, whether it's in sending the product I paid for or by verifying the post on a social media platform is really from Taylor Swift? And the Law of Zero on information will make the world so much more transparent that it'll be much easier than it is now with Yelp et al. to develop a consensus view on the reputation and reliability of the party you're dealing with and for them to get a better sense of you.

As you can see, triangulation takes us a long way toward keeping our identities secure and authenticating ourselves to others, especially when triangulation becomes demi-cent-angulation—or whatever you call it when something like half a hundred points for identity verification become available.

Triangulation also helps a great deal with our desire: for all of us to have a better handle on what's true. We already triangulate to some extent. We decide which friends we trust to provide us with information and which we deem as suspect. We trust certain news sources and not others. With the advent of social media, though, many stories get amplified reflexively, in no time, because they play into biases, even though they may come from sources that have already proved unreliable or have almost no history—perhaps a Twitter account with an egg as a photo and two followers. As a result, misinformation and disinformation may be accepted as true. That sort of reflexive behavior might explain President Trump's June 2020 retweet of video by a Twitter user unknown to him. On initial glance, the original tweet seemed to show a parade of Trump supporters. But the parade also included a golf cart driver holding his fist up and yelling, "White power! White power!" The president soon undid his retweet, and a White House spokesman said the president hadn't heard the racist language when he retweeted it, but many of Trump's tens of millions of followers had already seen the retweet. Trump later said in an interview that "it's the retweets" that get him "in trouble."[142]

Some social media sites are trying to deal with disinformation manually—for instance, Facebook has people reviewing potentially objectionable posts and taking many down—but the Laws of Zero will make it easy to automate the process. In the Future Perfect, social media posts will carry a note such as, "This comes from a source that has been challenged X thousand times in the past month," or, "This comes from an anonymous source that matches the patterns of Russian bots." These notes would be based on real-time tracking of the provenance of posts and on sophisticated analysis of its content, and a Twitter user's reputation could be rated based on the number of their dubious retweets (or whatever such posts will look like in 30 years). You could still decide to post that video "showing" aliens built the pyramids. You could probably even tweak your settings so whatever sort of newsfeed you have in 2050 will assign extra credibility to those who share your views. But, however you manage your feed, at least you'll have access to real-time, AI-generated ratings that will help you assess the validity of your sources.

At the moment, it may seem daunting to think of continuously monitoring highly connected, distributed systems with thousands (to millions) of servers and millions (to billions) of users, but this'll be trivial in 2050 because of the exponential increase in computing power. In fact, many institutions, including the U.S. government, already maintain what's called continuous monitoring. Booz Allen and others currently provide these services to keep government systems as safe as possible.

Some sources are being developed that should provide a bedrock of facts, at least for anyone who trusts government data. For one, USAFacts, founded and personally financed by former Microsoft CEO Steve Ballmer, relies solely on official data but presents it in a friendlier way than most government sites do. As we write this, a big issue is the number of COVID vaccinations that have been performed in the U.S. We could go and try to find data state by state and search through the CDC and other federal websites, or we could go to USAFacts and ask, "How many COVID-19 vaccinations have been distributed and taken?" and get a consolidated answer. The U.S. government has built www.data .gov, which pulls data from across its many parts and makes consolidated information on government spending available to the public. The Laws of Zero will provide the processing power to make it even easier to let more, official data see the light of day.

They'll also allow for instant updates. If you've cited a number from a database, and that number has changed, your citation can automatically be updated. Business leaders complain about how the proliferation of spreadsheets and presentations keeps them from having a "single source of truth." Someone prepares a spreadsheet or a PowerPoint and uses a number from the corporate database, perhaps a forecast on the size of a market or on sales of a product. Then the number changes in the corporate database—but the spreadsheet or PowerPoint lives on, because it's being used by someone who doesn't know about the update. Multiply by the number of people using data in an organization and the number of data points they use, and you see how hard it can be to get everyone working off the same set of information. The Laws of Zero will not just solve that problem for businesses but will allow for instant updates everywhere: news articles, books, academic papers, you name it.

Basically, the Laws of Zero will let us apply a scientific mindset, in real time and to a vast array of information sources. We'll all start out skeptical but, aided by all that computing power, will keep gathering evidence, millisecond by millisecond, until we have enough of a consensus that we've achieved the best view of the truth that's possible—for now. And then we'll get updates as the consensus evolves.

But even getting much closer to the truth in the Future Perfect won't be enough. What if we're too late and only get to the truth after great damage has been done? Look at Twitter, where a clickbait tweet with false information gets orders of magnitude more views than any clarification or even retraction that may come out days or weeks later. Unlike commercial transactions, which can generally be unwound, it's harder to undo damage to a reputation. So we not only need tools that can greatly improve our ability to discern the truth but that do so instantly, as soon as someone tries to make a false claim.

In the same way new entities can watch for someone trying to impersonate you, reputation services could alert you when someone tries to say something negative about you and allow you to respond immediately. Whatever form social media takes in 2050 could even provide a brief buffer—perhaps measured in just milliseconds—so that bots acting on behalf of all parties could do a preliminary adjudication of whatever claim is being made, a sort of trust auction based on criteria decided through neutral institutions. Already, some sites delay posting. Look at the site Front Porch Forum, which asks users to consider "deep breath" time before posting a response to something that elicited a strong emotional reaction. Posts in the future might still be allowed on a public platform, but they'd carry qualifiers based on whatever evidence was, or wasn't, available. They might also include pointers about the credibility of both the person making the claim and of the target of it. Perhaps the social medium would ensure that anyone who saw the initial claim would see any future clarifications or retractions. There will undoubtedly also be room for entities to create services for repairing damaged reputations, to the extent possible.

All of this will be automated and will use AI that both identifies the problem and notifies you of a proposed fix that it's already installed before any more damage can be done. Disinformation campaigns will at least become much harder to launch.

We realize AI can carry its own biases, but titans like Google and Microsoft are investing heavily to try to create AI that recognizes and even corrects for various kinds of these biases, whether based on data used to create the system or some inherent part of the system itself. Booz Allen has also contributed to the movement toward what's known as responsible AI, pointing out that AI needs to create trust, that creators of AI must be accountable for the AI they produce, that all data used in developing and running the system should be auditable and transparent, and that all decisions made by the system should be explainable. Other companies have suggested similar ideas.

We also think people will become more discerning about the accuracy of what they see on social media. It's still a relatively new medium, and history shows that excesses with new media get curbed over time. Email brought us Nigerian princes who desperately wanted to send us big chunks of their fortunes, but we've pretty much all gathered that those emails are scams. We've learned to be savvy about evaluating the trustworthiness of sellers and buyers on eBay and Craigslist. Think about the classic "War of the Worlds" radio broadcast Orson Welles gave in 1938. The medium was new enough that, when Welles read his dramatical adaptation about a supposed invasion by Martians, masquerading as a news broadcast, lots of listeners thought an invasion was really happening. But people became more sophisticated about radio soon enough and can now distinguish plays and other sorts of programs from newscasts. The same sort of learning should make us all less vulnerable to media manipulation in the Future Perfect.

Social media institutions—whatever they look like in 30 years— will also behave more responsibly.[143] No, we're not expecting any sort of great awakening; they'll still focus on maximizing profits. But the days of operating without any restrictions will be long gone. The government may well impose some responsibility on companies for the posts they allow users to make. That would at least rein in the most extreme forms of disinformation, such as QAnon-level conspiracy theories. Even beyond whatever government does, there's a sort of public shaming forming that will create consequences for those who abuse the platforms. The platforms will likely at least tone down their algorithms that currently do the utmost to create controversy and drive engagement. If some claim is likely false, but not definitely so, the Facebook of 2050 (or its successor) might still publish it but wouldn't push it into billions of newsfeeds—so, an Alex Jones-type could still rant and rave all he wanted on *InfoWars*, but that person would get little or no pickup on social media. (If disinformation falls in the forest with no one around, does it make a sound?)

So, we've pretty much taken care of three of the four big concerns about trust we mentioned toward the start of the chapter. Triangulation will let us verify the identity of those who want to interact with us. It will let us authenticate ourselves to them. Triangulation, plus new information-based services, some education, perhaps a bit of government intervention, and some good, old-fashioned public shaming should provide the parameters for determining truth.

That just leaves us with the issue of privacy. "Just."

We actually think privacy becomes less of an issue when you can secure your identity and reliably authenticate yourself to others and store and share your data, under your control, via a decentralized, secure system.

Headway is already being made in areas like health care, where we want our devices to know enough about us to help but to not share information without our approval. New governmental approaches such as the General Data Protection Regulation (GDPR) and new efforts by platform companies are also starting to give us control over our privacy. Innovations that will accelerate with the effects of the Laws of Zero are already appearing in social media.

All these efforts will be greatly accelerated in the lead-up to the Future Perfect, based on the idea that we should own and control the data about us—no more saying something about cold weather and having your Google Home instantly arrange for you to start seeing ads for sweaters. Some of the improvement will come from just moving up the learning curve. Companies have learned, for instance, that just because they can connect certain dots doesn't mean they should connect all of them. We're thinking of the story several years ago about how Target inferred from various searches and purchases that someone was pregnant and started mailing her coupons for diapers and such—but she was a teenager living at home and hadn't yet told her parents about her pregnancy. In any case, apps are appearing that help people mask their actions. For instance, you can get an app that clicks in the background on every ad that a website tries to put in front of you—you won't actually see those ads, but any site trying to monitor your actions thinks you've clicked on every single one. More—and more sophisticated—apps will surely help us mask what we share about ourselves.

In the future, we think ownership of data will be much more explicit than it is today. For instance, we might all have "data trusts." Basically, any company like a Facebook that gathers information on you and your actions would have to keep that all together in a "you file" whose use only you could control—this is starting to happen but will be far more developed. You could make all or part of it available to companies you want to buy from or otherwise do business with—or not. You could also decide that you no longer want to keep that "you file" with Facebook and could take it away from Facebook and provide it to a competitor, much as you can now change cellular providers while taking your phone number with you.

Just because Facebook and other companies can currently gather data on us with impunity doesn't mean they (or their successors) will always be able to do so. We're still in the very early stages of deciding what the rules of the road on privacy should be, so there's loads of room to design a better future.

Even Zuckerberg Can Be Redeemed

MENLO PARK, CA, May 14, 2050—At today's retirement ceremony for Mark Zuckerberg, on his 66th birthday, he received holographic calls from leaders around the world, thanking him for fulfilling the vision he set out in the famous letter he and his wife, Priscilla Chan, wrote to their newborn daughter, Max, in 2015.

In that letter, Zuckerberg and Chan committed to making the world Max grew up in "dramatically better than the one into which she was born." The parents wrote, "We will do our part to make this happen, not only because we love you, but also because we have a moral responsibility to all children in the next generation."

Zuckerberg had gone through a stretch in the 2010s and 2020s when he was public enemy No. 1, because of the rapacious appetite for data that the founder and CEO of Facebook showed, unapologetically, and because the social media site amplified so much harmful disinformation. But, by 2030, he finally began to play by a new set of rules, reportedly after Max, razzed at school as the daughter of a monster, waved the letter in his face and called him a hypocrite.

Whatever the reason for his change of heart, Zuckerberg made it far easier for users to withhold data they wanted to keep private. He began respecting the growing use of data trusts, allowing members to take the data Facebook had amassed on them and share it with other sites or even move all the data to a Facebook competitor. Zuckerberg also backed away from his eyeballs-at-all-costs approach to engagement; he remodeled Facebook so it could quickly remove false information and mute other information that was likely false and harmful. Government intervention required some of the changes, and Zuckerberg made others "voluntarily," under threat of stiffer regulation.

In 2020, Facebook was known for sharing misinformation that discouraged people from taking common sense health measures that would have sharply reduced the death toll from the COVID-19 pandemic. The site also helped dangerous conspiracy theorists find and feed off each other, contributing to the rise of right-wing violence that culminated in the infamous assault on the U.S. Capitol on January 6, 2021.

But Zuckerberg has since returned Facebook to an earlier vision as a place where people can keep track of friends and families, share photos, videos and holograms, and converse—without being inundated with ads and posts seemingly designed to raise everyone's temperature.

The retirement ceremony ended with Max and her sister, August, reading an emotional letter to their parents that played off that 2015 letter to Max. The letter concluded:

"You did it, Mom and Dad. We love you, and we're proud of you."

CHAPTER 13

The Future History of Government Services

'Invisible' Government

CRYSTAL LAKE, IL, October 1, 2050—Connie Civis has just moved across the country and is getting her family settled into their new home in Illinois. As she unpacks boxes, she takes a moment to survey her new surroundings.

"A definite improvement already," she thinks. "And wait until we get settled."

As a veteran, Civis received a loan from the Veterans Administration to purchase her new residence. All she had to do to apply was indicate, via the Citizens.gov app on her phone, how much she wanted to borrow from the VA and provide the address of the property she hoped to buy. The app had already assembled, securely, her digital persona based on all the records the government had for her—including her service record from the Army and her income and number of dependents from her tax returns. To complete the application, she merely clicked a button on her phone that authenticated her identity. Citzens.gov queried the website of the broker who had the listing and instantly gathered all relevant information on the property. Within moments, Civis knew the size of the loan that had been approved.

She also recently applied, through Citizens.gov, for a VA grant to make some accessibility changes to her home, because she has a disability as a result of her service in the Army. Now that she has taken possession of the house, Civis gets an alert that her request for the grant has been approved and that the bank has received the funding.

Remembering she has some other transactions pending, she authenticates herself to her phone again and logs back in to Citizens.gov to be sure her driver's license has been transferred from California to Illinois, that her car is now registered in her new home state, and that she's registered to vote in Illinois. Sure enough, all the needed data handoffs have happened since she told the app the house she was buying would be her permanent residence.

She sees both the IRS and California's Franchise Tax Board have posted the drafts of her federal and state tax returns for her review. Her taxes are straightforward, and everything looks right, so she accepts both the IRS and California drafts and officially files her returns. Moments later, her bank notifies her the refunds have shown up in her account. She thinks she'll use the money to pay for new household items—maybe a new kitchen countertop. Civis makes a mental note to check back in a week or so to make sure that her tax withholdings are correct, given her new job in Illinois comes with an increase in salary.

Before she signs out of the app, she's prompted to see if she wants to file for federal student aid for her son, who turned 18 two months ago and is reviewing college admission offers. She clicks "yes" and receives confirmation that her son's application has been filed. She'll get details on the size of any loan once her son hears back from all the colleges he's applied to and tentatively commits to a school.

Later in the day, Civis receives a notification on her mobile device asking if she'd like her new address and her household size to be included in the next American Community Survey (ACS) that will be conducted by the Census Bureau. She opts in and is asked to complete some additional questions to verify other critical demographic data for her inclusion in the survey.

Realizing that, even before finishing opening her boxes, she's completed what not too many years ago would have been days' worth of frustrating interactions with government agencies, she decides to take a well-earned break and heads to the refrigerator for a beer.

With or without the future histories built on the Laws of Zero, governments will keep making progress, but this will likely happen slowly as they struggle to keep pace with improvements in the commercial world and with the sorts of new expectations by citizens who have been raised to expect instant access and response based on phone apps, texting, and whatever new forms of communication develop by 2050. Government agencies would also likely maintain the sort of siloed approach they take today, focusing on their own affairs and not much on working with other departments, agencies, and levels of government.

But great progress is possible if governments raise their sight lines and imagine how a Future Perfect could look—and then work backward to the sorts of measures they should be taking today to prepare. We'll illustrate by looking at three key areas: what we call invisible government, as well as elections and infrastructure resilience.

Invisible Government

We think it'd be crazy in 2050 not to be able to interact with government to receive critical services and benefits in a completely digital, self-serve manner.

The first three Laws of Zero—on computing, communication, and information—will make this goal possible. The basic capabilities are already there, and they'll become far easier to tap into with the exponential improvements we'll see by 2050. The key will be amalgamating and deploying the sort of digital identity that Connie Civis used so effectively.

At the moment, all the pieces of government data related to that identity exist... somewhere. Perhaps they're on paper in a file cabinet in an office. Perhaps they've even been updated all the way to a PDF (though that's basically just a picture of a piece of paper) on a hard drive. Perhaps the data even exists in some more advanced digital form—though good luck sharing that data across government agencies, which use a multitude of different formats for the data and may lack a secure way to share it. Those pieces can be accessed by the individual... if you stand in line at a government office or wait on hold long enough. Oh, and, of course, if you know in advance to fill out Form XYZ and have every bit of necessary documentation with you. Otherwise, you'll have to come back tomorrow and start the whole process again.

Even without a future history sort of approach, government will make considerable progress toward pulling all that data together seamlessly and reducing inefficiency. Laws—notably the Paperwork Reduction Act of 1980—have encouraged government to take a whack at bureaucratic complexity, and there's been steady progress. Various other laws and regulations have been aimed at smoothing interactions with citizen-customers. President Obama appointed a federal chief information officer in 2009 to take a more strategic view of how government can exploit digital technology, including on behalf of those who use its services and receive benefits. Initiatives such as Benefits.gov are masking government's complexity and are helping citizens get simple answers to questions.

But even with the progress already underway, there's still a benefit to stepping back and imagining a Future Perfect, because it can provide a unifying vision to aim at. We've shown the data compatibility and sharing issues can be resolved by 2050 and moved to the background, where the Laws of Zero will do the work. As you've also seen, we'll have a digital identity we can trust won't be hacked by criminals or be misused by government. This all means we can imagine a set of government services that should look pretty great—and we can start inventing them now.

Future interactions will be simpler and will be possible through voice queries via phone or computer. The bureaucracy of days past—the standing in lines, the filling out of forms, the long waits on the phone—will go away because, once you authenticate yourself, all your information is available in verified form to whatever arm of government needs it.* Government will save untold billions it's currently spending on gathering data that already exists elsewhere and shuffling that data around. Those savings could then be plowed back into providing better services—provided by the same people, who get to shed their clerk-like tasks and spend much more time interacting with and assisting citizen-customers.

The appreciation for a new, seamless approach to government services will be enormous. We can all imagine how much better government services would be with an Amazon-like interface. Just imagine. Go

---

* Data architecture will enhance the security of the information. The IRS won't have to send all of Connie Civis' tax information to authenticate her loan application, for example. It'll keep all her information within its walls, subject to all the security it can provide, and just answer questions that authorized institutions pose about income level, dependents, etc.

to the main federal government site and search for something specific, if you like. Perhaps type in a general query on a keyword or two and see what turns up. Want help? Here are recommendations based on your profile and on those of others like you. Need more help? Click on the icon in the lower right corner to initiate a chat, initially with a bot but with a human expert always within easy reach.

Yes, government will still be there and be enormous and powerful, but it can do an awful lot more without requiring so much time and effort from us citizens—as Connie Civis showed us with her tax returns and loan requests. Government won't be invisible, but it can get a lot closer than it is today.

Elections

We think it'd be crazy if you couldn't vote securely and anonymously, anywhere, at any time of day in 2050.

While elections today are tied to paper—and, thus, to all sorts of limitations of the physical world—think about this: Every day, we send trillions of dollars around the world, conduct hundreds of millions of dollars of transactions (on Amazon alone), and make innumerable withdrawals, deposits, and credit card purchases on- and offline without paper. Those transactions are secure, and we trust that they are secure.

We conduct business at ATMs without paper forms. In fact, we can almost all simply take a picture of a check on our phones and send that picture to the bank for deposit—no deposit slip or other paper required. Restaurants and stores routinely email receipts. Venmo, PayPal, and other direct transfer apps now send around tens of billions of dollars per year without any paper involved.

If the financial system can get all these complicated and super-important transactions right, what's so hard about conducting fraud-free elections? They're basically just a one-time survey of the population. And why do we need paper as a backup?

Now, there is significant, and reasonable, concern over the security of electronic voting. After all, there were attempts at electronic interference by Russia and other bad actors in the 2016 and 2020 elections.[144] The hanging chads and other issues in 2000 undermined trust in voting systems, in general. More recently, cybersecurity has become a big issue across all networked systems and added to the worry about using inter-net voting or electronic voting at the precinct. All this has led to concern that, without human-readable paper ballots, creating a verifiable audit trail for recounts would be challenging. So we've run backward to a sys-tem where around 95 percent of the vote is cast with paper ballots.[145]

But there's no evidence that the attempts at interference changed any votes in 2016 or that fraud of any sort had an effect on the 2020 results.[146] And, while internet voting is contentious, it has been in use since the 2000 election, when Booz Allen worked with the Foreign Voter Assistance Program in four U.S. counties on the U.S.'s first internet voting project.[147] Online voting is reliable, and we already know how to do it.

Getting to the Future Perfect goal of voting anywhere, anytime requires a baseline of trust, but we've already shown how trust can be much more robust, without paper. We'll be able to easily identify our-selves to the voting system, and the system will be fully up-to-date regarding who is eligible. At the moment, issues occur in updating voter rolls because it takes time for one government system to notify sys-tems involved in the electoral process that someone has died or moved. Confusion occurs because of people with the same or similar names or because of typos and other mistakes that are introduced as information gets transferred into government systems from the paper forms people fill out. But those errors and timing issues are gone in the Future Perfect, thanks to the profusion of computing and communication power and the unlimited access to accurate information.

Now, even a minor problem with online voting could be used to cast doubt on the whole enterprise. But the capabilities for secure online voting will be so strong as we move toward 2050 that heading in that direction is inevitable. Look at professional tennis, where super-fast, high-resolution cameras combined with super-fast computers have replaced humans and call the lines almost perfectly—there is currently a one-millimeter margin for error, but the computers are so much better that players accept the electronic calls.* When is the last time you saw

---

* One of your authors has called a side line in a match involving two soon-to-be Grand Slam champions and is more than confident that the machines are superior. Even assum-ing he got all the calls right when his view wasn't obstructed, you try looking through a player's legs while he's lunging for a 120mph serve that maybe clipped the outside of the line 50 feet away from you. The machines are more than welcome to that job.

a player pull a John McEnroe "You cannot be serious" with an umpire? Players needed a brief stretch to get comfortable with the technology, then the tantrums just disappeared.

In elections, three key phases need to be addressed to get us to the Future Perfect: registration, the voting itself, and the post-election auditing. Let's delve into them.

Voter registration

Political issues aside, registration needs to be accurate—and there's no reason it shouldn't be. Problems of identity can, as noted in the chapter on trust, be solved by triangulation, and we're already starting to see this happening with voter registration. For example, the Electronic Registration Information Center (ERIC) is already in use by 30 states and Washington, DC.[148] ERIC, a nonprofit formed by the states and the PEW Charitable Trusts, consolidates several sources of data, including state vehicle registration, USPS address information, and the Social Security records of deaths. ERIC then triangulates information to identify individuals who have moved or died. Thus, ERIC identifies eligible voters who aren't registered to vote, as well as the names of those who are no longer ineligible. As data formats standardize across government and as the Laws of Zero provide additional computing power, even more detailed and accurate triangulation will become possible.

We can already see glimmers of the prospects for this kind of public-private partnership, via automatic voter registration, which began in the late 2010s, often triggered when a vehicle is registered with the state.[149] Data from the registration can be checked and then used to register the owner to vote—if the owner isn't registered already and wants to be. Voter registration increases dramatically where an automatic system is implemented. (This approach is part of the growing movement to use behavioral economics to "help us help ourselves."[150])

The Future Perfect will thus resolve today's conflict, where some argue voting needs to be more secure, while others focus on making sure all those eligible to vote have their rights protected. In the Future Perfect, all those, and only those, entitled to vote will be authenticated as able to cast a ballot. In the language of the debate going on today: Everyone voting will be required to show voter-ID—and every eligible voter will be able to do so.

Casting the Vote

It's hard to imagine that our use of paper ballots won't become a source of late-night comedy. Having to get to a voting precinct within limited hours, wait in line, and correctly fill in a paper ballot will seem quaint.[151] And today's in-person voting tends to exacerbate disparities of access based on race and economics.[152]* For those with disabilities, the use of paper ballots is especially vexing, given disabled persons' difficulties getting to a voting place and, for some, challenges with marking paper ballots.[153] Remote voting is already supported in every state, because it's required for those in the armed services who are deployed out of state, and most states support early voting by mail for the entire population, so many of the mechanisms for online voting are already in place.

How would it work? Well, there are two parts to casting a vote: 1) authentication of the voter's ID and right to vote and 2) the actual casting of the vote. Authentication is already done in many in-person settings via electronic poll books combined with some sort of ID.[154] These poll books rely on multi-factor electronic authentication, which is far more reliable than a signature match, the standard used for most mail-in ballots today, and these systems are scalable over the internet. They're already much less costly than other current systems.

The big concern over the last few elections has been that electronic votes are more easily hacked than paper ballots—but an electronic audit trail can be created and secured via multiple backups. Those backups can be used to check the validity of internet voting systems, just as a paper trail was used to validate the counting of the unfairly maligned Dominion voting machines following the 2020 elections. Some complain that electronic voting makes it difficult for the voter to review the ballot and be assured it was counted—but that's just an interface issue of the sort that web-based designs solve all the time.

Online ballots can also be live, meaning you could click on, say, the titles of local offices and see what issues they have decision rights over. Voting on local offices and issues would surely increase, boosting civic involvement.

---

* The need for remote schooling during the pandemic showed how greatly race and economic status also affect access to computers and Wi-Fi, but that problem will disappear by 2050 because of the Laws of Zero that will deliver free(ish) computing and communication, so electronic access won't be an issue for voting.

An ever-improving form of online voting can accommodate those with disabilities much more easily, both directly in the interface and by making voting available where they are. The same goes for the elderly, minorities, those who have limited access to transportation, or those who have difficulty getting to the precinct within voting hours.

Counting and Recounting

Think about it: We use paper ballots now largely because they're hard to hack over the internet—but most are read by optical scanners, which can themselves be hacked or just not work. After the scanners register the votes electronically, we tabulate the totals... electronically. Why start with paper?

Yes, paper ballots can be recounted by humans, but paper copies of online votes are easy to print securely, if desired for backup. Banks, hospitals, governments, and all sorts of other institutions have stringent security, record retention, and regular audit requirements, which they manage by creating geographically separated electronic backups and even offsite backups of computer records, all of which can be audited. Voting can follow these well-trodden paths to verify results. In fact, with the Laws of Zero in our favor, every vote can be audited using several methods in real time to provide the most robust verification of results possible in the shortest time.

Easy voting anywhere, anytime, with airtight results. We'll vote for that!

Infrastructure resilience

We think it would be crazy if we didn't have robust infrastructure that is resilient in the face of man-made and natural threats in 2050.

Infrastructure resilience? Why should I worry that roads, electricity, water, or other key aspects of public infrastructure might suddenly be compromised or even unavailable? Two words: toilet paper.

In March 2020, the world changed overnight with the onset of the pandemic. Suddenly, almost everyone was asked to stay at home. Within a few weeks, shelves in stores were barren of the precious tissues. The supply chain for toilet paper simply couldn't respond to the surge in demand from all those trips to the bathroom at home that normally would have occurred at work, a restaurant, a concert, and so on.[155]

There were many reasons behind this lack of resilience for the supply of toilet paper. The profit margins are, to make a pun, paper thin, so there is little tolerance for any excess inventory in the supply chain. Demand is generally extremely stable, so there is no incentive to create the ability to respond quickly to changes—and the pandemic required a major change, given that the toilet paper purchased for home use is not the same product businesses and public authorities buy for use outside the home. Consumers went into panic buying mode, further exacerbating the demand increase.

Virtually everything in our lives is produced through coordinated activity in supply chains, and many can't withstand even a mild shock, let alone a pandemic. In addition to toilet paper, bicycles, appliances, and many other things were in short supply at various points during the pandemic. More ominously, automobile plants had to slow or shut down production, and Apple had to delay the release of a new phone due to a shortage of computer chips as demand for them surged when the pandemic began to recede. Shipping containers were in short supply; ports were clogged trying to get ships in and containers unloaded; restaurants couldn't find cooks; and trucking companies couldn't find drivers. These issues then cascaded into other effects—e.g., the lack of truck drivers reduced work in manufacturing and other industries because there weren't enough drivers available to deliver the resources they needed.

At the most serious level, lack of resilience for some infrastructure, such as the electric grid and national defense, can threaten life and security, as became so clear during the 2021 winter storm that pretty well shut down the electric grid in Texas. Climate change will continue to exacerbate infrastructure risk, including by producing more frequent and higher-intensity storms. Major flooding in the Midwest has already caused massive destruction of infrastructure, while causing crop shortages, and severely damaging military facilities in the Midwest that are vital to our national security.[156] Cyber security hacks happen daily and threaten our economic security through fraud and disruption of our financial infrastructure. A ransomware attack shut down the Colonial Pipeline for days in the spring of 2021 and cut off gasoline supplies to much of the East Coast. Then attacks shut down a major meat processor, JBS, in June. Even our essential water supply utility infrastructure has been the subject of cyber/industrial control system attacks.

The SolarWinds cyber breach demonstrated, too, the need for more attention to our communications infrastructure.[157] Communications infrastructure has already become embedded in virtually everything and will continue to become even more critical as we create connected vehicles and add sensors in the power generation and transmission infrastructure, water infrastructure, and national defense apparatus. Satellites in low Earth orbit will help create broadband access everywhere—but will require considerable monitoring for resilience. The sheer number—tens of thousands are planned—create the potential for collisions with each other or with cosmic debris that would damage the satellites and create even more debris.

And, of course, 2020 showed the need for infrastructure resilience to cope with pandemics. Everything from hospital and health care supply chain problems to the shortages of toilet paper and other items on stores shelves could be traced to the effects of the pandemic worldwide.

Resilience is a funny thing: We assume reliability for basic services like electricity, water, and broadband and may only think about the issue when disruption hits those services. We hope we've learned enough painful lessons, though, that we'll start to think about resilience ahead of time rather than just rue its absence when the sort of freeze that wouldn't even make anyone in the Dakotas blink shuts Texas down for a week.

Fortunately, the Laws of Zero are already helping and will continue to do so as computing, communications, and AI advance.

Heading off threats begins with planning and monitoring—and help is already on the way. The incredible proliferation of sensors and exponential growth in computing and communications power will mean that buildings, grid structures, and all sorts of digital assets can be monitored like never before. Augmented reality/virtual reality (AR/VR) will be commonplace and inexpensive, making it possible for humans to have holodeck-like visualizations with incredible detail. With advanced AI, we will be able to control even incredibly complex, critical infrastructure.

At the federal level today, the National Risk Management Center provides simulation tools, planning, and assessment for all stakeholders with critical infrastructure.[158] For instance, the center offers the Infrastructure Visualization Platform, an advanced, early AR/VR tool that uses information and imagery from across agencies to create an immersive planning environment—for instance, for special events such as the Super Bowl or a presidential inauguration. The tool is also used for infrastructure resilience planning at a regional level based on information and imagery that regional utilities and stakeholders provide.

As examples of what the Laws of Zero can do in the Future Perfect, let's look at two key aspects of infrastructure: the energy grid and our water supply.

Energy Grid

We take electricity for granted. You plug an appliance into a socket, and you get power. But there have, in fact, been major outages in the past decade, and there are many reasons to fear more. Here are just some of the major incidents:

- A derecho caused massive flooding in the Midwest in 2012 and left some five million homes without power, in some cases for weeks.

- That same year, Superstorm Sandy hit the East Coast and left around twice as many people without power, again for long periods even though utility workers were brought in from around the country to help with repairs. Lower Manhattan was completely flooded, threatening major financial institutions on Wall Street. More than 150 people perished.

- In 2013, a group fired high-powered rifles at 17 transformers in California, in an attempt to disrupt power to Silicon Valley.[159] Had the domestic terrorists succeeded, they would have disrupted Google, Cisco, and more that support a variety of critical communications and technology functions. Those problems would have cascaded into the broader economy, hitting firms that rely on those infrastructures.

All these examples make it clear that critical infrastructure faces significant threats on a regular basis, more so in this era of more extreme flooding and more powerful storms.

Now we have to add the threat of cyber-attacks. Many critical parts of our energy grid are controlled by devices that were designed well before there was extensive digital communications and connectivity to the internet. As a result, these devices are ripe targets for cyber-attack. Often, they were installed without any thought about security, as they were physically isolated and not wired to any communications infrastructure. While there's yet to be an acknowledged cyber-attack on the U.S. electric grid, Russian hackers took down a portion of Ukraine's electric grid in 2015, leaving over 200,000 people without power,[160] and U.S. utilities privately estimate they are directly threatened hundreds of times every day.[161]

In response, government agencies such as the North American Electric Reliability Corporation are working with utilities on many aspects of grid resilience. A host of startups, such as Grid Assurance,[162] have arisen to attack the problem. Grid Assurance aims to help by offering a subscription service that gives utilities quick access to equipment such as transformers, which are too expensive for utilities to keep on hand in any quantity and which have long lead times for purchase. This would help electric utilities replace equipment much faster following a disruption.

More broadly, utilities are investing in areas such as "smart grids." This involves installing new forms of the IoT that will help more accurately monitor critical infrastructure, which enables more rapid response to avoid problems. The smart grid capabilities will improve as the Laws of Zero accelerate and will result in a totally different design by 2050.[163] Over the past century, the grid has developed largely based on economies of scale, beginning at the top and cascading down. A company would produce an ever-increasing amount of coal, gas, or oil and ship it to a utility, which also would aim at the most efficient scale.[164] The result was a sort of broadcast system à la television from the 1960s, which had three national networks covering the country. Smart grids will turn that '60s-era broadcast model into one more like the internet, with essentially unlimited sources coordinating with each other in an everybody-to-everybody mode rather than three-to-everybody.

There will be sensors everywhere, monitoring who is producing how much and who is consuming how much, in real time. Appliances will, with the permission of their owners, cede some control to the network so that air conditioners, dishwashers, water heaters, and other major appliances can be taken offline briefly to maximize the efficiency of the whole system.* Individuals and businesses will receive feedback—in real time, if they want—on their energy consumption, using behavioral economics to encourage efficiency. AI will monitor the whole system for problems and reroute electricity as needed, creating a self-healing, self-balancing, self-optimizing grid.

Water and Wastewater Systems

There's little more important to human life than water. And the infrastructure that carries away our wastewater and processes it is crucial to public health, as well as to the efficient reuse of water, especially where it is in short supply.

The problems of the current system are obvious. For instance, London's pipes leak half a billion liters of water a day, and leaks cost the U.S. more than one trillion gallons of water a year.[165]

Invisible government is already helping through the Creating Resilient Water Utilities (CRWU) program at the Environmental Protection Agency (EPA), which provides planning assistance, tools, and more to water sector utilities to help them create infrastructure that is resistant to climate change.[166] CRWU also enables information sharing to accelerate learning across the community from the many different efforts at local and regional levels. The city of San Diego's Public Utilities Department, for instance, used a CRWU tool to assess impacts from climate change, which are important to the city given its reliance on distant water supplies and the prevalence of wildfires and storm surges.[167]

As with the electric grid, the Laws of Zero will take today's efforts and improve them exponentially by 2050. Sensors that feed into far more sophisticated management systems will, again, play a key role. Water utilities will be able to visualize the entire water system, measuring flow, usage, leakage, and more. Utilities will be able to see which leaks to fix— sometimes by sending tiny robots down pipes—and to identify bigger

---

* This control of major appliances may be more complicated than utilities hoped. When the Texas grid struggled during a heat wave in the summer of 2021—the Texas grid had a rough year—many customers expressed surprise that they had given the grid managers permission to turn down their air conditioning.

infrastructure issues to address.[168] A whole host of companies that are startups today but will be established companies in 2050, in the case of those that succeed, are tackling related issues, such as watching for arsenic and other contaminants and removing them from water sources before they ever reach our lips.[169, 170]

The Future Perfect for water, like for the electric grid, will be far more efficient, and resilient, than the haphazard system we have today.

Texas Freezes—and Nobody Notices

LUBBOCK, TEXAS, March 12, 2050—Connie Civis, having recently settled into her new home in Illinois, decided to take a well-earned vacation to visit family in Lubbock, Texas, and landed right in the teeth of a record winter storm.

It caused a far worse freeze than the one that essentially shut Texas down way back in 2021—yet nothing troubled her vacation.

Having long ago learned about the need to prepare for surprise weather events, Texas utilities winterized their electricity generation. In 2021, natural gas pipes and even piles of coal froze and were unusable. But, today, sensor-driven AI reallocated power to keep the grid working, drawing both on local sources of power (individuals' and businesses' batteries, charged by solar and wind) and on connections with surrounding states.

With so much power available, heating never became a problem in the state. Nor did access to water, as it had in 2021. Yes, this time around the roads were still icy for a few days, but the automated vehicles that used them had seen that problem before, not just in Texas but around the world, and had no trouble navigating. Civis took an AV from the airport to her parents' home and gave them both a big hug.

What If the Future
Isn't Perfect?

Our brief histories of the Future Perfect are just a few morsels from the bountiful future feast we hope our kids and their kids will experience by 2050, and we hope we've sparked your imaginations about the wealth of things that are possible. Whatever futures we actually build by 2050 will set the foundation for humanity's collective future in the decades beyond—no pressure. But our Future Perfect is hardly guaranteed. As we've said repeatedly, we aren't predicting the future; we're just offering a way to invent a great one.

So, before moving on to how individuals, corporations, and governments can do their part to advance the Future Perfect, we'll step back for a moment and offer a reality check, in two forms. First is a look at inertia: What might happen if the course of history just continues along current trajectories? The second is what we've called the Future Pathetic: What if technology, instead of amplifying upward trajectories, pulled us down toward the abyss?

Future Perfect or Business as Usual?

Many current trends offer worrisome future scenarios—the rise in atmospheric carbon, growing inequities between rich and poor, threats to our infrastructure, inadequate educational systems, the continued entrenchment of structural racism and social injustice, and the rising cost of health care, just to name a few. Table 2 summarizes where our hopeful future histories could take us and compares those results with where we might expect to get based on just incremental changes.

The one "business as usual" possibility that really, really scares us is climate change. There are many bright minds who argue we're already too late to escape the worst effects.[171, 172, 173] If we haven't made enormous progress by 2050, all bets are off.

The rest don't sound so awful—but they could be, in any of a number of Future Pathetics.

Future Pathetics

While it took us 175-odd pages just to scratch the surface of a few pieces of the Future Perfect, we bet we can ignite vivid and pathetic scenarios in most of our readers' minds with just a few words: *1984, Brave New World, Dr. Strangelove,* and *A Tale of Two Cities.*

Here's how technology might take us down a very different path, toward one of those four dystopias:

1984

In George Orwell's *1984,* a future history published in 1949, the instrument of totalitarian surveillance was a pervasive two-way telescreen and a society where everyone spies on everyone else. Hello, Big Brother. Today, the Laws of Zero already enable pervasive surveillance through a multitude of channels, ranging from ubiquitous public and private closed-circuit television cameras to the easy-to-hijack ones on Nest cams, dashcams, bodycams, webcams, and phones. Even baby monitors aren't safe. Now, add billions of pictures, videos, and self- and friend-revealing posts on social media. Process all of the above through the latest AI face-recognition algorithms and crowdsourced human spotters. Cross-reference the results with numerous personal information sources. Magnify all that by a factor of one million times better computing power, communications speed, and information density under the control of unchecked totalitarian ambitions. Welcome to 2050, *1984* style.

TABLE 2: Future Perfect vs. Future Pathetic

We think it would be ridiculous if, by 2050, we didn't have...	Unchanged, current trends might lead us to:
• **clean** electricity available to **everyone, everywhere,** in **abundant** and **affordable** quantities	• cleaner but still quite **carbon-dirty mixes** of abundant and affordable electricity for those who live in **upper-income countries,** with billions of people remaining in energy poverty
• widely **accessible** and **affordable** transportation, enabled by **clean** electric **autonomous** vehicles	• widely accessible transportation, but **mostly human-driven** and burning fossil fuels, with autonomous vehicles serving **premium markets** in rich countries
• **terrific** health care available to **everyone** at an **affordable** cost, providing **longer, more active** lives	• **expensive health care** with lots of **waste** eating up an ever-larger portion of GDP, **rationed** by ability to pay and mostly focused on **sick care,** with too few resources devoted to prevention or public health
• **significantly slowed global warming** and the mitigation of the worst effects of climate change	• **unabated global warming** and worsening climate change effects, perhaps passing the point of no return
• **trust** in the verifiability, privacy, and security of information and **technology markedly improved**	• **trust continuing to erode,** producing innumerable problems, including **civil unrest**
• **easy-to-use, self-serve digital interaction** that provides critical services and benefits via an **invisible government**	• government services continuing to be **fractured** across agencies and departments and demanding **too much time, cost, and effort from citizens**
• elections that are conducted **accurately** and anonymously, **anywhere** and **any time**	• **muddled,** mostly paper-based elections that are **subject to frequent challenges** related to manipulation
• government that **builds resilience into infrastructure**—the electric grid, communications networks, information platform, water systems, and more	• **haphazardly improved infrastructure,** addressed as time and money allow, hampering safety, growth, and innovation

Brave New World

Aldous Huxley's 1932 novel, *Brave New World,* was set in a numbed world, where drugs kept the populace under control and where factory-hatched, designer babies enforced a rigid social caste system. Huxley set his novel some 500 years into the future, but the Laws of Zero will likely deliver the genomic engineering, designer pharmaceuticals, and other technologies he envisioned by 2050, if not sooner. A rogue scientist in China has already modified the genomes of human babies using the CRIPSR technology we described in the Law of Zero on genomics. He was thrown in jail but not before the babies' lives were forever altered, and the episode shows how easy it is for safeguards to be evaded. What's more, in our future, technological distractions could take the place of Huxley's drugs. Think about how much time we spend doing idle things on our devices—often more than one at a time, as we scroll on our phones, in front of our laptops, while a television plays in the background. Technology companies have realized the most precious thing they can get from a consumer is attention. So they want all of it. And they're really smart about how to get it. They've fine-tuned algorithms to keep people on Facebook, to keep them scrolling through Twitter, to keep them perusing TikTok—and sharing videos so other people get hooked, too. No, the technology companies aren't using drugs, and they aren't forcing anyone to do anything, but it's easy to imagine how we might slide down the slippery slope to a Pathetic New World by 2050.[174, 175]

Dr. Strangelove

Then, there is the march to doomsday envisioned in the classic 1964 movie, *Dr. Strangelove or: How I Learned to Stop Worrying and Love the Bomb,* which is relevant today and will be even more so in 2050, when the mechanisms for doomsday machines and mutually assured destruction will be well within the reach of many. The dangers won't just be the nuclear weapons featured in that movie but will include a wide array of possible attacks: human-engineered viruses; poisoning of water supplies; use of cyber-attacks to take down communications networks, banking systems, electric grids, or transportation networks; and more. The human race has avoided catastrophe thus far because state actors have always stepped back from the brink, but success is by no means guaranteed, and tensions will surely heat up at least as the U.S., the E.U., China, Russia, and others vie for supremacy in numerous areas. What's more, the Laws of Zero will put weapons of mass destruction into the hands of non-state actors, who are becoming more important because of the growth of numerous movements worldwide, as humanity fractures into as many factions as there are grievances. We won't be learning to stop worrying or to love the bomb any time soon, that's for sure.

A Tale of Two Cities

Just to ruin whatever is left of your happy mood, let's look at possible analogies to one of the great novels of all time, Charles Dickens' *A Tale of Two Cities*. Our previous trifecta of dystopias doesn't mention heightened inequity (let alone climate change, which we've covered elsewhere). Yet rising inequality, as in the Dickens classic, is affecting more than two-thirds of the globe.[176] UN chief António Guterres writes that the world is confronting "the harsh realities of a deeply unequal global landscape," in which economic woes, inequalities, and job insecurity have led to mass protests. "Income disparities and a lack of opportunities are creating a vicious cycle of inequality, frustration, and discontent across generations."[177]

While technological innovation can support economic growth, offering new possibilities in fields such as health care, education, communication, and productivity, there's also evidence it can lead to increased inequality in wealth and wages and can displace workers. For now, highly skilled workers are reaping the benefits of the so-called fourth industrial revolution, while low- and middle-skilled workers engaged in routine manual and cognitive tasks are seeing their opportunities shrink. The near-magical capabilities delivered by the Laws of Zero over the next three decades could amplify this disparity.

Inequality has been found to hurt economic growth—for everyone. In 2014, the Organization for Economic Co-operation and Development (OECD), a collective of the world's 35 wealthiest countries, found that rising inequality in the U.S. from 1990 to 2010 knocked about five percentage points off cumulative GDP per capita over that period. Similar effects were seen in other rich countries. "Inequality affects growth… by undermining education opportunities for children from poor socio-economic backgrounds, lowering social mobility, and hampering skills development," the OECD found. Employees become less productive, which means lower wages, which means lower overall participation in the economy.[178]

Inequality could accentuate crime, too. A 2002 World Bank paper, for instance, found data strongly suggesting high levels of inequality create a permanent underclass forced to compete, sometimes violently, either with itself or with other classes for scarce resources.[179] A 2016 London School of Economics study found that "income differences create an incentive for those relatively poor to steal from richer households."[180]

And history shows inequity can cause societal upheaval, à la *A Tale of Two Cities*, if allowed to grow too big or fester too long. Pervasive economic inequity is the common thread tying together the most disruptive revolutions of human history, and it already has some scientists worried about the U.S. Not only does history repeat itself, but it may do so again sooner than we think.[181]

2050 could easily be the best of times and the worst of times, to paraphrase Charles Dickens. It will be an age of wisdom. Will it also be an age of foolishness, where inequities stretch beyond a breaking point?

• • •

We're not lacking for other dystopian futures (and iconic movies that bring them to dreary life), including a world overrun by garbage *(WALL-E)*, technology-enabled governmental intrusion *(Minority Report)*, and AI run amok *(The Terminator)*.

As we've said, we see no need to settle for the "business as usual" case in 2050, let alone the dystopias—but they're out there, and they're all too possible. That's why we hope you'll pay special attention to the final part of the book, where we lay out how individuals, corporations, and governments can move us toward our best possible future.

PART THREE

JUMPSTARTING THE FUTURE

Did you enjoy watching the U.S. women's national team (USWNT) run through soccer's World Cup in the summer of 2019 as much as we did? If so, you can thank a conceptually simple change in federal law known as Title IX. Passed as part of the Education Amendments of 1972, Title IX simply said there could be no discrimination based on gender "under any education program or activity receiving federal financial assistance." Given sports are an "activity," girls' sports were funded to a degree never before seen (after the requisite legal wrangling, of course, initiated by some who argued competition was only good for boys). Among the many ripple effects, the number of girls playing high school soccer in the U.S. went from a grand total of 700 in 1972 to nearly 400,000 in 2018[182]—and the UWSNT now has four World Cup trophies for us to admire.

The USWNT shows the important roles that must be played by all three types of actors who will have to work together to invent the future: government, organizations, and individuals. Government set the rules for how schools had to treat girls' sports. Organizations innovated within those rules. High schools began competing for dominance, and then youth soccer clubs popped up all over the country, providing a level of early developmental training seen in few sports to that point. Individuals saw an opportunity and worked like crazy to seize it, so much so that, in 2019, the U.S. had four of the world's very best midfielders on the same team—with only room for three of them on the field at one time. That's a nice problem to have, and it's one we think the Future Perfect can create elsewhere if we all fulfill our roles.

While the tendency is to think government, as the 800-pound gorilla, should be the focus, we believe individuals will need to take responsibility to drive the change we want, so we'll start with us, then turn to the organizations we form and lead, and leave government for last.

CHAPTER 14

What Individuals Can Do
(Starting Now)

You've likely never heard of Stanislav Petrov. But you may be alive because of him. We all may be.

When he was the duty officer in charge of the Soviet Union's nuclear early-warning system one day in late September 1983, satellite signals indicated the U.S. had launched a nuclear missile at the Soviet Union. Satellites quickly reported five more missiles had followed. Protocols required that Lieutenant Colonel Petrov report the warnings to his superiors immediately. That requirement was even more pressing because of heightened concerns related to the Soviets' shooting down of a Korean passenger jet that strayed into Soviet airspace weeks earlier, killing 269 passengers and crew; there was fear the U.S. would retaliate.

But something didn't sit right with Petrov. He reasoned that, in the unlikely event the U.S. launched a strike against the Soviet Union, it wouldn't just launch six missiles. It would launch hundreds. So, breaking protocol, the lieutenant colonel withheld information from the generals, knowing he had taken his career—and perhaps his life—in his hands.

Soon enough, a malfunction in the Soviet satellite system was discovered. The U.S. had launched zero missiles. Petrov's caution and rational thinking saved the world from what could have been a massive Soviet "counterattack" that would have produced a nuclear holocaust.*

---

* He never received a commendation from the Soviet Union. His reward was merely that he wasn't imprisoned or executed.

You likely haven't heard of Leó Szilárd, either, but the Manhattan Project wouldn't have happened without him, meaning the conflict in the Pacific in World War II might have lasted years longer. Szilárd was known in the pre-war community of physicists for his eccentricities—he typically began his day by soaking in a bathtub for two or three hours, thinking. But he saw the potential for nuclear fission before anyone, in 1933.* An immigrant to the U.S. from Hungary, he wanted to warn President Roosevelt about the potential of an atomic bomb but didn't have the cachet to get through to the president. However, Szilárd did have a friend named Albert Einstein. Szilárd drafted a letter to President Roosevelt in 1939 and showed it to Einstein, who, being Einstein, immediately saw Szilárd was right. Einstein signed the letter, which got through to President Roosevelt, who launched the Manhattan Project that produced the first atomic bomb.†

How about Hedy Lamarr? You may well remember her as an actress from the 1930s and 1940s, when she was sometimes described as the most beautiful woman in the world. But what do you know about her work on the side as an inventor? At the outset of World War II, she co-developed a predecessor of spread-spectrum technology by engineering a way (based on the rolls used in player pianos) to have a radio signal hop around within a range of assigned bandwidth; the idea was to keep Axis powers from jamming signals that controlled Allied torpedoes. Spread-spectrum technology, essentially taking a concentrated signal and spreading it across the available bandwidth, appeared in early versions of Wi-Fi and survives in Bluetooth to this day.

We aren't suggesting everyone can be a brilliant inventor like Lamarr, a physicist the likes of Szilárd, or a level-headed hero like Petrov. But we do want to dramatize the effects that individuals can have, well out of the public eye, even in ways that couldn't reasonably be expected.

Rosa Parks was a seamstress on her way home from work when she

---

* Szilárd received patents on the atomic bomb and on the nuclear reactor. He was also the first to file patents and to publish on the electron microscope, the linear accelerator, and the cyclotron. His reputation has aged well.
† Szilárd argued that an atomic bomb should be detonated in a remote location, to demonstrate its power, but that the bomb should never be used in warfare. He favored sharing the technology broadly, to deter any nation from thinking it could gain an advantage by using such a weapon.

set off a social revolution by refusing to move to the back of a racially segregated bus. Greta Thunberg had no idea her local activism in Sweden at age 15 would vault her to international fame and make her a leader of the movement to counter climate change. A friend of ours had no reason to expect a book he wrote with his daughter, called *The Power of Half*, would catch Melinda French Gates' eye and help her formulate the idea of the Giving Pledge. That pledge has encouraged more than 200 wealthy individuals to promise to donate half their fortunes to charity; pledges currently total more than $600 billion.

Surprises are out there. Individuals can do a lot, often more than we think we can.

• • •

We see five main ways we can all drive change as individuals: as citizens, as consumers, as employees, as investors, and as influencers. Not all roles will fit each of us. Some will make us more uncomfortable than others. Even when we try a role, we may fail at it. So, we leave the right approach to you. We'll just lay out the possibilities.

As a Citizen

We've seen the potential of activism through figures such as Greta Thunberg, Howard Jarvis, and Stacey Abrams. When Abrams lost the race for governor of Georgia in 2018, she took the lessons from that loss and built a voting rights organization that likely tipped the state to Joe Biden in 2020. Her work was also considered crucial in the victories by two Democrats in Georgia for seats in the U.S. Senate, giving the Democrats control of both houses of Congress, as well as the White House. Jarvis drove the anti-tax revolt in California in the 1970s that culminated in the collection of more than 1.5 million signatures and the passage of Proposition 13, which dramatically capped property taxes.[183] His legacy endures: California voters in 2020 defeated Proposition 15, which would have undone some of the earlier limits.[184]

We realize plenty of people wish that Thunberg hadn't achieved fame and that Abrams and Jarvis had failed. We're not making statements here about the merit of their causes. We're merely underscoring the power of their activism as citizens.

So, what can you do?

You can make calls, write letters, and attend town halls. You can march in the streets or launch a movement and make clear to those in power that an issue affects our votes. Look at the Million Man March, the Women's March, Occupy Wall Street, the Tea Party. We, your authors, are old enough to remember some of the demonstrations against the Vietnam War and know how powerfully they shaped public opinion. Public demonstrations provide political encouragement and support for those willing to take on big problems and drain support from those who aren't.

Don't just look at national politics, either. Yes, our national representatives have more leverage than their local counterparts do, but lots of key decisions happen at the local level. Mayors and city/town councils will have a huge amount to say about building codes and other issues that will determine how municipalities prepare—or don't prepare—for higher sea levels, stronger winds, fiercer wildfires, and other effects of climate change. Local utility boards, while even more obscure than town/city councils, will play a major role in determining whether the grid prepares for the Law of Zero for energy and allows for all the potential benefits we described in the chapter on electricity. Local school boards tend to wind up in the news as battlegrounds where people fight over what version of history our kids will learn, but there's another, maybe even bigger issue at play: Will children be taught strong enough critical thinking skills? Will they be able to separate truth from disinformation and comprehend the kind of exponential growth that the Laws of Zero describe (and that, unaided, the human mind really isn't designed to process and plan for)? Without the right local leadership, huge opportunities will fall by the wayside.

You can do a lot of good by working to persuade local officials to move in the right direction and prepare the way for a Future Perfect. Heck, you could even run for office yourself.

As a Consumer

When you look throughout history, you see innovators celebrated. Rightly so. Without the Alan Kays and Steve Jobses of the world, we wouldn't have our iPhones and a host of other technologies and products we value. But innovators are only one side of the equation. They're the supply side of innovation. There's also a demand side. Consumers. We consumers buy innovations and give them the momentum to expand and shape our worlds—or we don't. Our decisions to buy or not buy shape what innovations catch on and, thus, will play a key role as we collectively invent the Future Perfect.

Most of the time, we place the onus on the innovators: They have to find ways to entice us buyers to purchase their products. Loads of books have been written on how, for instance, to help innovations "cross the chasm," which means jumping from a small market of early adopters to a group of customers who, in time, could be shaped into a mass market. The responsibility is, in general, placed correctly. Markets sort out winners and losers. But we consumers have agency. We can decide what criteria we use to make our purchases. We don't just have to be driven by how cool or useful something seems and by what it costs. We can be early adopters. We can incorporate Future Perfect considerations into our purchases.

In particular, we can decide how much extra we'd pay for zero-carbon alternatives to what we buy today. That may mean looking at electricity, where we can see what premium (if any) our local utility charges for participating in a "green" electricity program. That may mean looking at what it would cost to retrofit a home to reduce greenhouse emissions. That may mean buying an electric vehicle, even though the up-front price is higher than for a car with an internal combustion engine.

More generally, consumers can pay attention to externalities related to the environmental regulations, labor practices, human rights, and other social implications of the manufacturing processes that produce the goods we buy. We're already seeing these sorts of decisions in the beauty and clothing industries. A small but growing number of consumers are committed to buying sustainable clothing that's made by people making a living wage in safe conditions, using ethical, natural fabrics that are non-pollutants. Brands are reframing the question from, "How can I afford a $50 T-shirt?" to, "How can we not afford a $50 T-shirt?"

As an Investor

Investing is another way of essentially voting with our dollars; it just focuses on stocks and other securities, rather than consumer goods. If investors shun, say, companies that have poor equity track records or no net-zero strategies, companies will get the message almost as quickly as entertainment networks see that few are watching their shows or movies. And companies don't stick with duds for long. Likewise, companies that invest in, perhaps, grid-scale batteries, may see, based on market performance, they have a blockbuster on their hands and will keep pouring money into it.

On reading an early draft of this book, a friend started to assemble what he dubbed a "Laws of Zero portfolio," where he'd invest in companies that were making smart choices and avoid those that weren't. Way at the other end of the net-worth continuum are the billionaire members of the Breakthrough Energy initiative, but their strategy is the same: Take a long-term (rather than a quick-win) view of investing to finance companies working on problems that'll take a long time to scale up but can make a big difference (and can make you a lot of money) if investors are willing to wait.

You might wonder how any one investor can make a difference, but you'd be joining a tidal shift. A survey by financial services giant Allianz found a growing number of investors are making decisions based on environmental, social, and governance (ESG) issues.[185] This holds true across age groups—64 percent of millennials, 54 percent of Gen Xers, and 42 percent of baby boomers said they want to participate in socially responsible investing. Another survey found 77 percent of investors globally upped their sustainable investments in 2020.[186] This broad interest has already captured Wall Street's attention, and a competition has ensued to create more ESG funds and to push corporations to be more socially responsible to be included in such funds.[187] In the spring of 2021, *The Wall Street Journal* reported that investing in environmentally friendly businesses appeared to have passed a tipping point. Global funds investing in such businesses reported $2 trillion in assets in the first quarter, and investors were adding $3 billion a day. Meanwhile, $5 billion of loans and bonds were being issued each day, meaning trillions of additional dollars for green initiatives even if the trends just continued through the end of 2021.[188]

Money talks—and companies listen.

As an Employee

While individual employees might feel powerless, they are, in many ways, citizens of a corporation who can apply leverage on executive leadership in much the same way voters can pressure government. Employees actually have many more tools for exerting pressure than they've ever had, via social media and corporate review sites like Glassdoor. A longtime colleague of ours who came out of retirement to help lead a revival of *The Los Angeles Times* said he learned he had to court "the consent of the governed" in ways he'd never seen in a newsroom before. In 2018, Google employees successfully pressured the company to drop a contract with the U.S. military that troubled them.*

We've been around the halls of business and government enough to know most big ideas and breakthrough changes stem from three key groups within those massive organizations. There are the individuals willing to think big—they could be great researchers or someone on the front lines who sees a big problem and has the insights and tenacity to imagine how to fix it. There are the great managers, the ones who recognize the value of the big idea and organize the resources and processes required to make it happen. And there are the sponsors, usually higher up in the organization, who champion the effort and guide it through the labyrinth of organizational hurdles that always rise up against such ideas.

Alan Kay, summarizing his experience on how breakthrough invention happens, tells us: "Great managers are scarcer than genius researchers, and the rarest birds are the executives who have the foresight and courage to give the funds to great managers and genius researchers." You could be any one of those.

As employees, we can also all vote with our feet (and our brains) and gravitate toward working for companies that support Future Perfect values. Companies know they're in a war for talent, so they have to pay attention to what employees are thinking. Even many oil companies are starting to promise a carbon-free future. Businesses don't last very long if the talent walks out the door.

---

* Again, we're taking no position on whether the employees or Google were correct. We're just noting the effect that individual pressure can have.

As an Influencer

This is the most nebulous of the roles, but it highlights how, often, it's the individual outside the walls of corporations and governments who can push massive organizations to use the tools at their disposal.

Take Alexander Sachs, a Russian-born economist, student of world affairs and, importantly, the friend of President Roosevelt who delivered the famous Einstein-Szilárd letter to the president. With war beginning in Europe, President Roosevelt had no time to entertain letters from even the world's most famous scientist, but Sachs, who had met Szilárd through a mutual friend, was able to get a personal meeting with the president to deliver the letter and press the issue. At the end of a follow-up meeting the next day, President Roosevelt declared, "This requires action."

Continuing on the World War II theme, Vannevar Bush was a former MIT professor and president of the Carnegie Institute when he presented a single-sheet-of-paper plan to President Roosevelt in 1940 to reorganize and coordinate the country's military research. The president approved the plan within 15 minutes. Bush went on to establish and lead the Office of Scientific Research and Development and directed the research and development of key technologies for the war, including radar, antibiotics, better artillery and explosives, blood substitutes, and, yes, the atomic bomb.

You could even write a book. Rachel Carson was a scientist and writer for the U.S. Fish and Wildlife Service who was well-known for her work on conservation and natural resources. As she grew increasingly concerned about the wide use of synthetic pesticides, she changed her focus to writing about the long-term effects of misusing them. Her 1962 book, *Silent Spring*, captured public attention, ignited the environmental movement, and spurred congressional and regulatory action.

You don't have to be a friend of the president, an MIT professor, or a best-selling author to be an influencer, especially in the age of social media. Ten or 15 years ago, the notion of a social media influencer barely existed, but, today, influencers in the lifestyle realm can earn $10 million in a year via social media, and those numbers are just from the early days of TikTok and Instagram. But for every Aimee Song or Emma Chamberlain at the high end of the numbers for influencers, there are thousands of would-be influencers who have given up. Our recommendation is that we all start out thinking we'll be Song or Chamberlain and then see what happens. We should look for every opportunity to spread our Future Perfect ideas via posts on Twitter, Facebook, and LinkedIn. We should get creative—if we're remotely creative—on TikTok and other, newer video-based media. We can even get creative about where we're creative, like how the Biden presidential campaign bought "yard signs" in a multi-player video game in 2020.

The worst that happens is that we educate a few friends. The best that happens is that we develop the sort of following that Greta Thunberg has.

Basically, we recommend coming up with and living by a "third list." The first list is filled with any urgent, attention-needing items for that day. That sort of to-do list is pretty common. The second list is a weekly list, filled with crucial things to do that week. That list is as far as most people go. The third list—the key one—contains the biggest, most ambitious 20 or 30 long-term goals. This list isn't just for wishful thinking; it focuses on the things that must be accomplished to materially advance the big goals.

We hope that we all as individuals will carry at least a metaphorical third list with us, so that we're always looking for ways to push toward the Future Perfect in our varied roles as citizens, consumers, investors, employees, and influencers.

CHAPTER 15

What Companies Can Do (Starting Now)

After doing charity work in Sub-Saharan Africa, including with a UN initiative in Kenya, and teaching kids in multiple African countries as a Fulbright scholar, Josh Tetrick decided the real way to channel his idealism into change was through business.[189] So he and friend Josh Balk founded a company—Eat Just—that aimed at a more sustainable approach to producing food. They started with liquid "eggs" made from mung beans and have sold more than 100 million of their egg-equivalents, JUST Egg. The company has now moved on to chicken. This time, the company, under the brand name GOOD Meat, produces actual chicken meat—but grown in a lab from animal cells, not via live chickens. Eat Just received approval in December 2020 to begin selling the chicken meat in Singapore and plans rapid expansion.*

Investors are flocking to the idea: The 10-year-old company has raised $800 million, partly based on forecasts that the market for lab-grown meat will reach $140 billion by 2030.[190]

There are loads of reasons to like Eat Just as a Future Perfect sort of solution. Producing a single egg uses 53 gallons of water. A pound of chicken meat requires 518 gallons. And growing a pound of beef requires 1,800 gallons of water. If you worry about making sure water is

---

* While the concept of growing meat in bioreactors takes some getting used to, early tasters have had favorable reactions.

plentiful in our future—as we do—then growing beef and chicken in a lab, with a much smaller amount of water used, is extremely appealing, as is substituting efficiently grown legumes for eggs.*

There'd be plenty of cascading benefits from the change, too. As we've mentioned, cows are major producers of methane, so growing beef in bioreactors would slash emissions that harm the climate. There'd be a whole lot less waste from cows and chickens handled. Labs for growing the meat could be distributed around the country, close to consumers, rather than having ranches raise cattle in the South and West and then transport the meat to markets as much as thousands of miles away. Labs would be able to replace slaughterhouses, where things are brutal under the best of conditions. (As it happens, the facilities turned out to be Petri dishes for COVID-19, leading to many thousands of deaths.)

Pulling the levers available to business is letting Tetrick do a lot more good than he ever could have even through his commendable work with kids in Africa.

These levers will be available to businesses of all shapes and sizes, and many will have to pull them if we're to meet our ambitious goals for 2050. We've already laid out a list of the near-miracles we hope companies can produce, driven by the enormous rewards the markets will provide to anyone who can produce carbon-neutral cement, low-carbon steel, and other needed breakthroughs. Such market forces are already reorienting some industries toward Future Perfect goals. For instance, some fossil fuels giants, including Enel, Iberdrola, NextEra Energy, and Ørsted, have shifted so heavily toward renewables and have been rewarded so much by investors that they've been lumped together as a class: the clean supermajors.[191]

The major players will extend well beyond the usual industrial giants. Insurance companies will have a big role on issues such as climate change because they'll price the risk clients will face and will provide incentives to those that can limit those risks. Already, the industry is working with the UN, through the Insurance Development Forum, to

---

* Progress hasn't always been smooth. Early on, the company attracted high-profile investors, including Salesforce CEO Marc Benioff, but questions surfaced about the quality of products in 2017, and the company was accused of buying its products off store shelves to inflate sales and buttress its valuation. The board resigned, but Tetrick stayed and has rebuilt momentum.

help member nations quantify risk and develop strategies that improve resilience. A few years ago, a corporate risk manager stood in front of an International Insurance Society global gathering of industry executives to offer a withering criticism: He was responsible for managing a broad range of enterprise risks, but the insurance products available to him covered only about a third of them. He complained of being left vulnerable to climate change, cyberattacks, natural catastrophes, pandemics, business interruption, and so on.[192] Increasingly, the industry will fill those gaps. Swiss Re, the world's biggest reinsurer, has forecasted that climate change will reduce global GDP by $23 trillion in 2050 if action isn't taken,[193] so insurance companies should hope they can change a lot of behavior for the good of the planet (while they also profit handsomely from taking on risk and from offering wise advice).

Technology companies will also obviously play a role by buttressing efforts in transportation, electricity, health care, and a host of other areas.

We aren't even suggesting there needs to be much change in corporate behavior as we head toward the Future Perfect. We're not expecting companies to give up on profits and shareholder value and to become a bunch of do-gooders. We're saying smart companies will see the potential profit pools available in the sort of change that's possible by 2050 and will go after them—hard. Imagine you're Foster Farms and the projection of a $140 billion market for lab-grown meat by 2030 is even close to plausible. Does your executive team: A) focus on getting slightly more shelf space in grocery stores while wringing a little more efficiency out of the supply chain, or B) move heaven and earth to try to develop that market before Eat Just and others do?

What we're expecting from businesses is them mostly raising their sights and looking at the future we can invent together. The biggest change in their thinking will involve timeframes. It's hard to see 2050 opportunities when your three main priorities are this quarter, next quarter, and the quarter after that. But some visionary companies are showing the way.

For instance, as we described in the chapter on climate change, BlackRock—the giant private-equity firm that's not known for mushy, do-gooder tendencies—has said it's orienting all its investments toward net-zero. BlackRock sees great risks for companies that are caught unprepared for climate change, while expecting that many of its companies can capture new markets and generate huge profits by helping the world move toward net-zero.

We realize it's hard for companies to reorient themselves away from businesses that have been profit engines for decades and toward new ones that, while promising, are still speculative. We've read all the books on the problems with corporate inertia, à la Clayton Christensen's *The Innovator's Dilemma*—we've even written a couple of those books. But we've still seen smart companies address the problem.

At General Motors, for instance, there has to be frustration about Tesla. As of this writing, GM's price/earnings ratio is roughly 9.6, while Tesla's is 685. Those numbers are not typos. Tesla's P/E ratio is more than 70 times that of GM's. If GM spends money on a visionary product like electric vehicles, that's treated as a normal expense as part of R&D and reduces the company's stock price by lowering earnings. If Tesla spends money on something like another Gigafactory for batteries, that expense is seen as part of a vision and can send the stock price soaring. But GM has still managed to be a leader in autonomous vehicles. It bought an AV startup, Cruise, but kept it separate and raised money from outsiders—including Honda, Microsoft, and Walmart—that put a clear valuation on the money GM was pouring into the startup. While GM hasn't said what its current stake is in Cruise, the giant automaker owned 83 percent at the end of 2019, and Walmart's April 2021 investment put a valuation of more than $30 billion on Cruise, so it's a major contributor to GM's $85 billion market cap, not a drag. (GM has continued investing in its core business while shifting fast to electric vehicles, which the company says will make up its entire product line by 2035. Carveouts aren't the only way to make the investments needed to prepare for the Future Perfect.)

Likewise, other companies can figure out a way to invest in the future without doing any particular harm to their plans today.

This is actually a golden time for companies to reset both their plans and their investors' expectations. Climate change—which was treated as a political issue for a long time but has clearly taken hold as a focus for businesses—creates an umbrella for change. Customers, employees, boards, and investors all expect to see companies adapt their products, services, supply chains, and many internal processes, so the groundwork has already been laid, and there's an opportunity to think big. When

Mike Hammer, a well-known consultant, pioneered the idea of business process reengineering (which used digital technology to transform workflows and business processes), he cautioned against paving the "cow paths" worn in by prior assumptions and workflows.* He argued in 1990 that "instead of embedding outdated processes in silicon and software, we should obliterate them and start over... to achieve dramatic improvements in their performance."[194] When you have the kind of paradigm shift that reengineering delivered back then and that climate change is delivering now, you can build a whole new set of (metaphorical) paths and roads—and even superhighways. Companies have great latitude to reset investor priorities based on their plans to reduce their effect on the climate or on their plans to profit by helping others do so.

As we mentioned, there's already a huge movement toward ESG (environmental, social, and corporate governance) that includes a push for companies to respond to climate threats and to attend to other constituents beyond shareholders and customers; companies are encouraged to focus much more on employees, suppliers, and the communities the companies serve.

Even the venerable Business Roundtable, an association made up of the CEOs of hundreds of the largest U.S. companies, recently announced a redefinition of the purpose of business:† "Major employers are investing in their workers and communities because they know it is the only way to be successful over the long term. These modernized principles reflect the business community's unwavering commitment to continue to push for an economy that serves all Americans." Instead of shareholder value, the group has embraced what's becoming known as "stakeholder value," which the Business Roundtable says focuses on "generating good jobs, a strong and sustainable economy, innovation, a healthy environment, and economic opportunity for all."

Yes, at the moment, the benefits of ESG are squishy and hard to measure. But demonstrating progress toward a higher purpose is important, especially to consumers and employees. Look at the success TOMS

---

* Hammer, an MIT professor and long-time Bostonian, was alluding to the notion that the meandering streets of Boston were just paved-over cow paths.

† Prior to this, the Business Roundtable's "Principles of Corporate Governance" explicitly endorsed shareholder primacy (the idea that corporations exist principally to serve shareholders).

had with its One for One model. Founded in 2006, TOMS pledged to give away a pair of shoes to needy people in countries around the world for every pair of shoes a customer bought. Young people, in particular, flocked to the company. It grew so fast that Bain Capital bought 50 percent of TOMS in 2014 at a valuation of $625 million.* Over time, the benefits of ESG will become more apparent and measurable as the perils of climate change and the long-term impact of social inequities on economic and societal stability and on growth become more obvious.

In the meantime, it's clear investors are insisting on ESG. One late 2020 survey of big investors representing approximately $18 trillion in assets found 73 percent plan to increase their ESG investment either significantly or moderately by the end of 2021.[195] Family offices, where older relatives are transferring control to younger generations, are especially forceful; two-thirds of a large group surveyed regarded sustainable investing as necessary for their family legacy.[196]

According to BlackRock, investors are being rewarded for their focus on ESG. During 2020, 81 percent of a globally representative selection of sustainable indexes outperformed their parent benchmarks. BlackRock also reports that companies with better ESG profiles are outperforming their peers in their industries, enjoying a "sustainability premium."[197]

This suggests companies have license to do the sort of thing we've recommended to individuals: Focus on creating demand for helpful innovations, not just supply. In other words, companies can buy products that don't have much of a market yet as a way of supporting their development for the Future Perfect.

An obvious example is jet fuel. Companies often catch grief for having private planes, but what if they committed to paying what's currently a hefty green premium for biofuel and to stopping their use of fossil fuels? Yes, the cost of the flights would increase quite a bit, but it's not like companies are operating a private airline. They have few enough jets and take few enough trips there wouldn't be a noticeable hit to the bottom line. In the meantime, companies could brag about being environmentally responsible.

---

* TOMS struggled under the debt load Bain placed on it, competitors began undercutting prices, and consumer interest in the philanthropic model waned, so creditors took over the company in 2019 to restructure its debt. But the company had a great run, coming from nowhere, and shows how purpose can rally customers.

A number of companies, such as LanzaJet and World Energy, sell sustainable aviation fuels but are stuck in a chicken-and-egg situation. Unless they build large-scale plants, they can't lower the cost of their fuels. And unless their fuels cost a lot less than they do now, not many companies will be willing to buy them. Goldman Sachs says merely getting companies to commit to buying a certain volume of the clean fuel at a future date would let LanzaJet or World Energy go to a lender and raise low-interest capital to fund a large plant.

So, for modest cost, companies with private jets could create demand for green fuels that might position them for an important role in the Future Perfect, while gaining some ESG bragging rights in the present.

The prospects for major innovation don't all have to hang off climate change, either. We've shown at length the sorts of opportunities available based on all seven of our Laws of Zero, and we seem to be in a moment where markets are receptive to innovation of all kinds. Venture firms have reported returns unlike any they've seen since the late 1990s,[198] and, with the pandemic winding down, the global economy seems to be set for a surge of growth.

Think Big, Really Big

It shouldn't surprise you that we recommend companies start their thinking about their role in the Future Perfect by writing a future history for their business in 2050. Having done many of these exercises with corporate clients, we can assure you people enjoy having the chance to get together for a day to imagine the future. Those involved get to be smart and creative, play off each other, and even challenge the bosses in the room. And these exercises always produce at least one surprising insight. We've seen whole corporate strategies launched based on a future history, while other strategies fall apart under the stiff scrutiny.

These future histories should certainly include the "E" (environmental) in ESG. What's your net-zero strategy, both for 2050 and for the risks on the path that'll take you there? Still, this exercise needs to be far broader. Think in terms of the Laws of Zero, the additional sorts of breakthroughs that'll be particular to your industry and company (such as those we've described for health care and transportation companies), and the sorts of scenarios we've laid out (and that you'll expand on) for how all the gains might fit together to support new lifestyles and consumption habits.

Then pull all the thoughts together into a single story that explains how you get there from here and that will stick with people. The CEO of a major company took a future history we wrote for him based on a session with his top team and referred back to it each year in his speech to the top 500 people at the company to remind them of their goal and of how they were doing.

You should also write the flip side, the Future Pathetic. Imagine all the doomsday scenarios based on customer behavior, on competitors, on technology, etc., being sure to include how rapid changes in government/investor/consumer emphasis on net-zero and green products might heighten the transition risk for your core products and business models. Think about how your 2050 future might intersect with other aspects of ESG and other stakeholders beyond shareholders, such as employees, surrounding communities, and supply chains.

Doomsday scenarios make for painful reading, but they can be at least as instructive as the sunshine-and-rainbows ones.

Start Small

Thirty years is a long way off, so, first, you need to pull the 30-year future histories back to more concrete, 10- to 15-year visions. These medium-term visions are critical. The early versions of the potential tools and capabilities needed to explore and build these futures likely exist, though in expensive and rudimentary forms, so you can start experimenting now with the tools and capabilities that would be needed for your 10- to 15-year scenario, on the path to your 30-year goals. The early versions of AVs, for example, were little more than golf carts with computers and sensors bolted or strapped onto them. Today, 17 years later, sleek minivans and sedans are autonomously navigating public roads.

Look for opportunities to connect with government innovation programs. You'll spot opportunities to partner with and commercialize government work. You will also get early introductions to new talent because young scientists and engineers drawn to such efforts often drive vast new opportunities.

Much of this type of work we're recommending costs very little.

While companies historically have tended to do lots of planning and have then built extensive prototypes, we're recommending a sort of lab approach—lots of little experiments where the goal is to learn and fine-tune your vision for 10, 15, or 30 years out.

If you think big but start small, you can learn fast through a steady stream of tests and can then continually course-correct.

Maybe Roll the Dice...

In its heyday in the mid-1900s, Bell Labs produced a remarkable array of scientific breakthroughs, including the transistor, the solar cell, and the laser. But the company's influence gradually faded, especially after the breakup of the Bell System in the early 1980s and a reduction in funding. In the 1970s and 1980s, IBM Research won three Nobel Prizes for Physics for work on semiconductors, for the scanning tunneling microscope, and for work on superconductivity, but funding was reduced in the 1990s, after IBM flubbed the transition from mainframes to more distributed forms of computing. Similarly, Xerox PARC made astonishing progress on personal computing in the 1970s, as we've described at length, but was tied more tightly to product development in the 1980s and lowered its ambitions.

In the last 40 years, few companies have launched anything as ambitious as Bell Labs, IBM Research, or Xerox PARC. While R&D funded by large corporations has grown from less than one percent to more than two percent between 1975 and 2017,[199] more of it has been focused on applied development rather than on the sort of basic research that happened at PARC. Venture capital and private equity investors reinforced this tendency to avoid basic research by disproportionately focusing on fast-payoff opportunities and industries, such as information technology, rather than on longer-term and capital-intensive investments, such as clean energy. The tendency is to harvest the fruits of past breakthroughs while not developing new frontiers of knowledge.

To us, this smells like opportunity. While it seems unlikely we'll see companies doing the sort of research Bell Labs and IBM Research did, supported by the massive earnings from the Bell monopoly and the IBM near-monopoly, there could well be room for a new version of Xerox's spectacular success with PARC.

Toyota is heading in a PARC-like direction with its Toyota Research Institute and its Woven City, which we mentioned in the future history of transportation. Alphabet, the parent of Google, has set up Google X, its moon shot factory. But we'd love to see several other companies step up and try their hand at a PARC for every one of the areas where we've laid out scenarios—transportation, electricity, health care, climate, trust, and government services—plus other critical pillars of the Future Perfect, including food, shelter, and education.

The good news is a PARC doesn't cost nearly as much as you might imagine, and the needed talent is out there, eager to do this sort of work. The budget for the parts of Xerox PARC that built the many wonders in early computing totaled about $10 million in the early 1970s (about $54 million in 2021.)[200] According to Alan Kay, a PARC-like effort requires "two dozen absolute geniuses" in a field or subfield related to a company's future, but he says this is "always doable." There are geniuses out there, and you can find them if you're selective enough.

The trickier part, Alan says, is developing the proper management perspective. Xerox management assembled the best people in the field and gave them license to build "the office of the future" (including the license to define what that meant). PARC managers, especially Robert Taylor,* had the wisdom to retain responsibility but cede control. He never presumed to direct the invention, even though he was the boss. Instead, Taylor focused on creating an environment safe from meddling and a culture that promoted cooperation when appropriate.

So what we're suggesting is hardly easy, but—if you feel like you have enough foresight and courage and can imagine finding and molding a Robert Taylor—there's huge opportunity in a creative era like the next 30 years to do something memorable.

Here's hoping at least a few of you try.

---

* Prior to joining Xerox, Taylor directed ARPA's computer research program, which funded most of the U.S. computer systems research at the time. This put him in a unique position to know most and hire many of the young geniuses in the field. In 1999, Taylor received the National Medal of Technology and Innovation. In 2004, the National Academy of Engineering gave him (along with three other PARC colleagues, including Alan Kay) its highest award, the Draper Prize. https://www.internethalloffame.org/inductees/robert-taylor

CHAPTER 16

What Government Can Do (Starting Now)

President Reagan once joked, "The nine most terrifying words in the English language are: "I'm from the government, and I'm here to help." He said in his first inaugural address that "government is not the solution to our problem; government IS the problem." Maybe sometimes, but not always. Actually, the federal government has consistently driven the kind of innovation that will be needed to get us to the Future Perfect. And governments at all levels have had more than four decades to up their game since President Reagan's memorable lines.

The U.S. government initiated the internet and GPS and nurtured them until they were ready to be turned over for commercial use. The federal government runs national labs and finances research that provide many of the breakthroughs in energy and medicine, including those that led to the sequencing of the human genome and to the remarkably rapid development of vaccines for COVID-19. The Department of Defense's DARPA arm's Grand Challenge sparked work on autonomous vehicles that's transforming transportation. The CIA financed a satellite mapping effort that was eventually sold to Google that became the core for Google Earth and contributed capabilities to Google Maps, where you may get most of your directions these days. The CIA's World Factbook was the core set of data that got Wikipedia launched. A Navy project provided the basis for 3-D printing. And so on.

In fact—sorry, President Reagan—the federal government has to drive the Future Perfect. The sheer scale of the problem and of the resources that have to be applied against it will absolutely demand the government does so. The Bill & Melinda Gates Foundation has the biggest endowment in the history of the world, but drawing down the entire $50 billion endowment would cover the education budget of California for about six months. One state. One budget item. Half a year. For the biggest foundation ever.

Businesses have far greater resources than foundations do, and they're the engine of our economy, but businesses are looking for returns for themselves, not necessarily for society. Why would a business ever have invented the internet or GPS, given that the benefits accrued to everyone and couldn't be captured just by the company that made the heavy initial investment?

As we've said repeatedly, we see businesses developing new modes of transportation, breakthrough sources of energy, and so on that will enable the Future Perfect, but we see government seeding many of the efforts and shaping them—before businesses take over. No, we're not advocating central planning. What we're saying is that government can: define a direction (on, say, climate change); supply a key tool (as it did with the internet and GPS); or even state a goal and attach a prize to it (à la the $1 million that generated so much early work on AVs); and then turn the work over to the many businesses that will see ways to make boatloads of money and will compete like crazy to get there first. A lot of smart people love going after interesting problems, and who wouldn't want $1 million? Or, perhaps, trillions of dollars, if you total up the market value of companies spawned just by the internet?

To get us headed toward the Future Perfect fast enough that we can hit our goals by 2050, we imagine governments at all levels, from federal down to the tiniest localities, taking a broad variety of actions. Not all of these actions cost any appreciable amount of money. Government can do a lot by setting smarter rules—for instance, for our health care system. It can also stop doing some things, including regulation, that get in the way of progress. But the federal government, in particular, will have to pony up some big bucks—as long as the Gates Foundation ran out of money paying for those six months of education in California.

Let's start with the federal government before working our way down to how state and local governments can contribute.

Historically, the federal government has played a lead role in the supply side of innovation. Government finances so much basic scientific research that, for instance, pretty much every medical breakthrough these days began in a government lab or through a government grant. (Big Pharma then commercializes the medicines and therapies.) Government also plays a growing role in what we might call the demand side of innovation. For instance, federal tax credits for purchasing electric vehicles let Tesla create initial demand even though its vehicles cost far more than comparable ones with internal combustion engines. Then, as economies of scale let Tesla narrow the price gap, the company became not only self-sustaining but a runaway success.

The federal government will need to begin with a plan—or, rather, given its scope, a whole series of plans. These can range from a broad effort (such as on health care) to an agency-specific effort (such as perhaps a long-term vision by the IRS to greatly reduce fraud or to radically simplify how citizens file their taxes and then interact with the agency). Every governmental department and agency should be asking, given the context of its mission and given the Laws of Zero: What would it be ridiculous not to have by 2050? Like businesses, these departments and agencies should turn those 30-year ideas into intermediate visions and then into very specific projects covering the next one to three years.

Starting far enough in the future is especially important for government efforts because it helps to avoid the tyranny of the current politics and interests. It also avoids the tendency to fixate on future scenarios that deliver incremental solutions for existing problems. To reach beyond the incremental, open the window of time wide enough for the exponential advances enabled by the Laws of Zero to overwhelm current impediments and radically alter the range of possible approaches. Remember, for example, our future history where the cost of water-from-air technology overwhelms the political power of the water-hauling truckers in the Chilean desert.

There will need to be loads of structure connecting these plans, many of which will interact with each other at the federal level and with state and local efforts. Some will require international cooperation, such as on research agendas or global-scale deployments. The plans will need to have champions at high levels—it's encouraging that President Biden has elevated the position of director of the Office of Science and Technology

Policy to cabinet-level—and will need to have built-in staying power, given that priorities obviously change as different administrations take charge. There are many successful governmental models and tools to leverage and to learn from, including the National Academies, the National Science Foundation, the Defense Science Board, the National Institute of Standards and Technology, DARPA, ARPA-E, and strategic foresight groups in multiple agencies.

In general, following the innovation mantra of "think big, start small, learn fast" will allow projects to keep going. They generally won't be too expensive to start with, and they'll quickly either prove their worth… or they won't.

A big issue will be the traditional budget process in Washington, DC, but that's starting to show some flexibility and can adapt further. In the past, government contracts tended to be highly detailed about how work was to be done and were put out for competition among multiple vendors. This limited the ability for favoritism to influence the awarding of massive contracts and reduced the possibilities for fraud. But you don't innovate via highly detailed specs. If you already know what the answer looks like, down to the kinds of minutiae that goes into government contracts, then what's to innovate?* Contracts can now have some flexibility built in. Agile contracts allow for statements of objectives rather statements of work, so government procurements center on outcomes instead of process—what needs to be done instead of how to do it.[201] Other Transaction Authorities (OTAs) allow for engaging industry and academia for a broad range of research and prototyping, with greater speed and flexibility than traditional contracts.[202] Collaborative research grants now enable substantive involvement and engagement between the awarding agency and the recipient.[203]

ARPA-E, the innovation arm of the Department of Energy, provides a good example of how visionary ideas can have staying power across administrations and of how even government budgeting processes can fit with an ambitious innovation agenda. ARPA-E, modeled on DARPA, was established in 2007 under President George W. Bush. No funds were initially appropriated for it, but President Obama provided a one-time

---

* One government procurement officer described the practice as like telling a doctor what surgery you wanted before there's even a diagnosis.

appropriation as part of the 2009 Stimulus Act and then won permanent funding. President Trump tried to kill funding for ARPA-E in the first budget he sent to Congress in 2017, but ARPA-E had enough of a success record that the Republican-led Congress voted for the funds anyway, which were signed into law by President Trump. President Biden is now reemphasizing ARPA-E's work as part of his push to combat climate change and to bolster our infrastructure. So, ARPA-E has now survived, and even thrived, across four presidencies with some radically different energy policies.*

ARPA-E has taken a very different approach to funding and collaboration. At the heart of its success are program directors recruited from academia and industry. Recognized experts in their fields, program directors define high-potential research areas, identify world-class potential contributors, and manage all stages of procurement and management and collaboration with funding recipients. Rather than providing research grants, which are quite hands-off, ARPA-E typically uses agreements that position it as an active participant in the work. This includes regular site visits, engagement in technical issues, and program reviews.[204] Its role as a potential conduit to the massive Department of Energy and to industry makes ARPE-E a valuable champion when it comes to commercialization, adding to its allure.

To date, the results have been huge. Since 2009, ARPA-E has provided $2.6 billion in R&D funding to more than 1,000 projects. Based on these projects, 88 companies have been formed, 237 companies have partnered with another government agency, and 177 teams have together raised more than $4.9 billion in private-sector follow-on funding. ARPA-E projects published 4,614 peer-reviewed journal articles, and 716 U.S. patents were issued to them.[205]

The model is catching on. As we write, the Biden administration has proposed ARPA-H, to focus on health care, and ARPA-C, to focus on climate. There could be room for many more.

---

* We're intimately familiar with ARPA-E because Booz Allen has been involved there since its inception. ARPA-E's success has been validated by an independent assessment by the National Academy of Sciences.

The Supply Side of Innovation

ARPA-E and its lookalikes can do a lot to buttress the already enormous amount of basic and applied R&D the government finances before unleashing businesses on scaling the opportunities. The government can invest based on time horizons beyond what businesses can tolerate and "de-risk" core technologies to get them to the point where companies can be reasonably certain they work. At that point, companies can begin the usual process of commercializing the technologies.

For instance, no business would have touched mRNA back in 1990; there was zero prospect of it being useful in medicine. Prospects were so iffy even the government-backed scientific community would barely look at it. Still, a Hungarian research assistant professor at the University of Pennsylvania named Katalin Karikó managed to scrape together some grant money and began experimenting with how mRNA might be used for disease therapies. After numerous setbacks in obtaining grants, in 1997 she began collaborating with Drew Weissman, a professor of immunology at Penn, on how mRNA might be used in vaccines. They met while standing in line for a Xerox machine, if you can believe it—the two started talking one day as they were waiting to copy articles out of scientific journals. Karikó mentioned her work on mRNA, and Weissman mentioned his on vaccines, and it was a lightbulb moment for them both. The pair's work went relatively unheralded, but the technology was developed enough by roughly a decade ago that it attracted early-stage venture funding. Two soon-to-be famous startups, Moderna and BioNTech, began working on using the approach to develop disease therapies. Karikó left academia to join BioNTech.

By the time COVID-19 arrived, the technology—while hardly proven—was ready to be deployed after three decades of curiosity-driven research and applied development largely financed by government grants and then picked up by the commercial world through early venture investment. Both BioNTech (in partnership with Pfizer) and Moderna quickly pivoted from developing mRNA-based immunotherapies to using mRNA for a COVID-19 vaccine. Hundreds of millions of vaccinations later, the pandemic is in retreat in the U.S. and should be beaten back broadly once those jabs get into billions more arms. The vaccine was a near-miracle, seemingly out of the blue, that was actually decades in the making, based on the sort of government-industry partnership that we think can be applied far more broadly.*

The federal government will continue to invest in a host of areas, including in the science that would be needed for the list of breakthroughs needed to get to net-zero carbon emissions by 2050. The government also has some other major tools it can use to move us toward the Future Perfect: Grand Challenges, Moon Shots, and Manhattan Projects.

Grand Challenges

These, like the DARPA Grand Challenges that spawned so much early work on AVs, would target areas where there needs to be the sort of engineering breakthrough that can be achieved by pointing a lot of smart people at a problem.

The idea of a Grand Challenge can be traced back at least to 1919, when a New York hotel owner offered $25,000† to the first person who could fly from New York to Paris (or vice versa). Numerous teams lined up to win the prize; one team even committed $100,000 for a prize a quarter of the size. At least six died in the attempt. Then Charles Lindbergh succeeded in May 1927 and helped usher in the era of long-distance plane flights.

The DARPA Grand Challenges for AVs were even more successful and came at a crucial time. While the race among pilots to fly across the ocean was already on in the 1910s and 1920s, the AV prizes came at a time when the prospects for driverless vehicles weren't at all clear. The prizes not only led to technology breakthroughs but created a community that has fostered the work ever since. As we explained in the future history of transportation, $4 million in prizes led to $80 billion—yes, "billion," with a "b"—of investment in autonomous technology between 2014 and 2017, according to the Brookings Institution.[206] That's just the investments announced publicly and, of course, doesn't count the prior investments or the money that has flooded into the field since 2017. All the investment has us well down the road, if you will, to full autonomy

---

* We'd happily place a large bet that Karikó and Weissman will win the Nobel Prize for Medicine—and soon.

† $361,000 in 2018 dollars.

and, in the meantime, has spun off all sorts of "driver assist" technologies that are making cars safer. (Now, if drivers would just get off their stinking phones.)

It's easy to imagine all sorts of additional Grand Challenges that could be set by government that would spur breakthroughs in engineering or even basic technology, which could either lead directly to profit-driven investments in the private sector or which could be nurtured by government until private industry is ready to take over and commercialize the advances.

Already, Princeton University sponsors Grand Challenges in areas such as urban sustainability and global health.[207] Booz Allen and Kaggle sponsor the annual Data Science Bowl, which brings together data scientists, technologists, and domain experts across industries in a competition that has advanced the state of the art in areas as diverse as assessing ocean health and screening for lung cancer.[208] The World Resources Institute and the World Economic Forum have set Grand Challenges in fields such as global food security.[209, 210] The U.S. Office of Science and Technology Policy has focused on topics such as the cost of solar power and potential cures for pernicious diseases such as Alzheimer's.[211] The National Academy of Engineering has laid out challenges in personalized learning, health informatics, and more.[212]

The Bill & Melinda Gates Foundation has handed out hundreds of millions of dollars in grants to tackle problems in the huge health challenges it has identified that don't attract profit-making enterprises.[213] The big money is in treatment, so businesses naturally look there, and they focus on the deep pockets in the developed world. By contrast, the foundation looks to prevent diseases in the first place or even wipe them out, and it focuses on the sick people, wherever they are, not on the money. The foundation has, for instance, donated heavily to efforts to develop vaccines for malaria—more than 200 million people contract the disease each year and more than 400,000 die of it, the vast majority children under the age of five, but 80 percent of the cases are in Africa,[214] and drug companies didn't see the economic case for all the work that would have to go into a vaccine. In April 2019, a five-year vaccination pilot program was rolled out in Malawi, Ghana, and Kenya.[215] Clinical trials found the vaccine to only be effective in 40 percent of people, but even 40 percent of 200 million is a ton of people who would be saved from the disease, and an awful lot of little kids would get to go on to lead happy, healthy lives.

Government could define its own Grand Challenges or could build on the many that have already begun.

Moon Shots

Moon Shots are all about getting to a proven solution where the scaling can be left to do later, perhaps through a Manhattan Project (which we'll explain in a minute) or through less urgent mechanisms.

Moon Shots would still spec out an audacious goal, as President Kennedy did in 1961 when he vowed to put an American on the moon by the end of the decade. At the time, Americans had spent a combined total of 15 minutes in space, and the total amount of computing power available to NASA was about what you'd find in a microwave today. President Kennedy described his literal Moon Shot as "long-range goals on an urgent time schedule" that would "serve to organize and measure the best of our energies and skills, because that challenge is one we are willing to accept, one we are unwilling to postpone."[216] When the president pointed the way and provided the necessary funding, the science community rallied and took us to the moon.

The U.S. never took moon landings to scale—or we'd have booked our tickets by now—but it solved the problem of how to do so and could have if the need had been there.

For the Future Perfect, there could be a Moon Shot in health care to develop the kind of digital overlay that would let health be measured at the population level—incorporating issues that aren't typically considered part of medical care, such as sanitation, gun violence and other crimes, income, and access to refrigeration and transportation. The basic technologies required are well-understood, but the health care effort would still be a massive effort to combine all the information in ways that can be measured and managed and communicated to us citizen patients and to caregivers so we can all start to change our behavior.

There could be a Moon Shot in education, too. There are loads of intriguing ideas that could lead to a far better educational system. At the moment, some argue for more pre-K and for changes in elementary education, including the use of more charter schools. Others advocate for more access to community college and to technical training post-high school. Still others focus on ways to revolutionize higher education—through massive open online courses (or MOOCs, which let thousands or tens of thousands take courses remotely) or through a so-called flipped classroom (where, essentially, the basic instruction is broadcast and then followed by interaction in small groups).

We see other areas in education that deserve focus, too. A large part of a kid's educational trajectory depends on the kind of support they get at home and what kind of expectations are set there, so we'd argue an evaluation of the educational system shouldn't focus narrowly on what happens between 9 a.m. and 3 p.m., five days a week, nine months of the year. A Moon Shot could formally test combinations of ideas to see what works and help design a system, in the broadest possible sense, that makes for better-educated people and better-prepared workers in the Future Perfect.

Still another Moon Shot could cover energy efficiency. Amory Lovins argues some efficiencies pay for themselves so fast that bonds could be issued to cover the cost and then repaid quickly based on the reduction in expenses—an energy-efficiency retrofit of the Empire State Building paid for itself in less than two years for the owners and in less than one year if you add in the savings for tenants.[217] Some attempts to issue energy-efficiency bonds (to be repaid from savings) have been tried, notably by the city of Chicago, and results have been modest.[218] But a Moon Shot sort of effort could very well identify an approach that could be deployed widely, saving energy while driving a huge amount of energy-efficiency business.

Manhattan Projects

Manhattan Projects would be used when the problem that needs to be solved is critical, when timing is incredibly pressing, and when basic technologies aren't fully mature, as was the case with the actual Manhattan Project during World War II. Manhattan Projects are about getting to scale urgently.

In WWII, the U.S. needed to develop an atomic bomb before the Germans or Japanese could and desperately hoped to have one in time to bring the war to a close. But much of the basic science still needed to be discovered and developed. When the war began, for instance, it wasn't clear that any kind of nuclear chain reaction was even possible. And the science turned out to be the easy part. The hard part was a manufacturing problem—particularly how to produce enough of the right kind of uranium for the bombs.* Separation of the right type from the wrong type was an excruciating problem (and is a major reason nuclear proliferation isn't worse than it is today). The scientists identified four methods that might be feasible in time but couldn't tell which would work at scale. So the managers took the approach that distinguished the Manhattan Project: They went full speed ahead on everything.

They built huge manufacturing facilities, knowing that, even in the best of circumstances, they'd have to rip out sections and rebuild them as scientists and manufacturing experts refined their methods. They hired 130,000 people. They built whole cities to house these people.[219] And they took the world from what was basically a hunch about chain reactions in 1939 into the nuclear age by 1945.†

The Manhattan Project was expensive, and the ones we envision will be, too, but it wasn't *that* expensive. It cost $22 billion in 2016 dollars. The project brought the war with Japan to a close earlier than would likely have been the case, greatly expanded U.S. military capabilities,‡ contributed numerous advances in science and medicine, and ushered in the nuclear power industry. That was $22 billion well-spent.

Operation Warp Speed, begun in May 2020 during the Trump administration, was a sort of Manhattan Project that was also a spectacular success. While it cost $10 billion, that was money very much worth it, given how much the project accelerated the availability of a vaccine that has turned the tide against COVID-19.

For the Future Perfect, a Manhattan Project could be set up, for instance, to tackle climate change. The technologies necessary for heading off the cataclysmic effects are far better understood than the physics

---

* 90 percent of the cost of the Manhattan Project was for building factories and producing the fissile material.

† The speed did lead to some problems that might have been spotted if time hadn't been so pressing, in particular with radioactive waste that is still being cleaned up at sites such as Oak Ridge, Tenn.

‡ Through atomic weapons, sure, but also through nuclear submarines, which can stay underwater indefinitely and are, thus, far harder to track.

of chain reactions were understood in 1939, but a huge number of ideas still need to be pursued at once, because we're running out of time. In addition to determining how to reduce greenhouse gas emissions at scale and as cost-effectively as possible, we need to develop more accurate and better-integrated models that project the effects of climate change. This would help track progress against the dangers and overcome skepticism— at the moment, a lot of chaff is being thrown in the air by skeptics, who argue the undeniable up-front costs will have an uncertain effect on the future. Finally, given the destructive forces already unleashed by climate change, we need to encourage innovation that will continually improve the technology for hardening our homes, offices, and other assets.

Designing the Portfolio

The portfolio of Grand Challenges, Moon Shots, and Manhattan Projects would function like a normal innovation portfolio—just on a ginormous scale. Because not every idea will pan out, no matter how great, lots of ideas will explored through research that will be integrated and tested at the Grand Challenge level and, to a lesser extent, the Moon Shot one. They'll have to be validated in the real world so the market can provide feedback about what works and what doesn't. Ideas will have to be financed at every stage, because hurdles aren't just hard to clear at the startup phase. Ideas may need to be nurtured through the pilot phase and then the rollout, which present new challenges and may require much more money than the initial test of an approach's feasibility.

If some astronomer announced tomorrow that their radio telescope had spotted an enormous asteroid that was on a course to collide with Earth in a decade and end all life, the odds are high we could figure out a way to divert the asteroid or blow it up. If that kind of focus can be brought to bear on Future Perfect issues, then the many tools at the disposal of the federal government can take us a very long way.

The Demand Side for Innovation

Driving the demand side of innovation is more controversial that driving the supply side. Innovation breakthroughs are generally available to everybody. But if the government is providing a subsidy for the purchase of something, it isn't providing a subsidy for something else. In the vernacular, government is picking winners and losers, and that sets people's teeth on edge.

Still, the federal government certainly has the power to provide tax incentives that would reduce the green premium for biofuels, grid-scale batteries, low-carbon concrete, and much more, boosting demand. On the flip side, the government could put a price on carbon to depress the demand for fossil fuels and the products that rely on them. Government could also eliminate the many tax breaks that still exist for fossil fuel companies and utilities that burn coal and gas. In addition, the government has the power to regulate standards that could require cleaner fuels, cement, steel, plastics, and so on. The federal government obviously does a massive amount of purchasing on its own and can also choose to steer its dollars toward, say, low-carbon concrete and steel and clean fuels.*

If you want to really get controversial, think about health care for a moment. It's clear the U.S. system is a mess—we pay twice as much per capita as other major economies for roughly comparable care. Much of the problem stems from an historical anomaly. The U.S. health care system, unique in the world, arose during World War II when the federal government froze wages and when businesses saw offering health benefits as a prime way to compete for employees. The federal government supported the move by making those benefits tax-free, and that was that: Businesses became the primary conduit for health insurance. All sorts of distortions have developed based on that one wartime decision 80 years ago. Today, people don't actually shop for health care. Few, including doctors, even know what a drug or treatment will cost—certainly not ahead of time—and insurance is designed so we likely don't care about the cost. We care only about what the portion we have to cover. Quality is hard to measure, too. So, we're left with a "market" where there's no sensitivity to price or quality. How's that a market? Instead of

---

* As we write this, the Biden administration has issued a number of executive orders to create federal government purchasing emphasis on green supply chain. For example: Executive Order 14008, Sec. 204: "It is the policy of my Administration to lead the Nation's effort to combat the climate crisis by example—specifically, by aligning the management of Federal procurement ... to support robust climate action"; Sec. 210: "The heads of agencies shall identify opportunities for Federal funding to spur innovation, commercialization, and deployment of clean energy technologies and infrastructure"; and Sec. 213: "...ensure that Federal infrastructure investment reduces climate pollution."

shopping for health care, we shop for insurance, which acts as an opaque intermediary between us and our health care.

We take solace from Stein's law, which says, "If something cannot go on forever, it will stop." And the health care system in the U.S. at the moment is unsustainable. But the inevitable changes could happen faster and work better if government provides guardrails that encourage great care at lower cost.

As Title IX showed when it revolutionized women's soccer, the government can do a lot to change the dynamics of a market. We've already seen how government incentives helped electric vehicles accomplish what tech entrepreneurs refer to as crossing the chasm—going from a viable product with a few early adopters, to the other side of the great divide, where a true mass market becomes possible. The federal government has the power to do many similar things that would, in particular, push us toward net-zero but that could also advance the Future Perfect in many other ways.

We realize some of the options we've laid out stray close to what would be considered industrial policy, traditionally a third rail in the U.S., given the decades when we defined ourselves in opposition to the Soviet Union and its disastrous central planning. But the international situation has changed. Rather than competing with a military power with a weak economy—Russia's GDP is about one-sixteenth the size of the U.S.'s, based on a population about a third the size—the U.S. is now competing internationally with a military power with a massive economy: China. China's GDP is about two-thirds that of the U.S.'s and is growing rapidly, based on a population four times that of the U.S. And China is very much pursuing a national industrial policy, including in areas that matter greatly to the U.S.—such as solar power, batteries, artificial intelligence, and electronics. The U.S. might want to consider a more muscular national policy to support U.S. companies in their competition against Chinese counterparts that have heavy backing from national policy. As we've said, while we favor market solutions wherever possible, some issues, including health care and climate change, will require changes in government policy that get some really tricky issues right.

State Governments

In many ways, state governments have even more freedom to experiment than the federal government does. Attempting something in, say, Rhode Island (population: 1.1 million) is rather different from rolling out a program nationally. Many states make bold moves, and some become national exemplars. For instance, after Hurricane Andrew devastated Florida in 1992, the state government worked with academics and insurers to create new insurance pools and strategies, to invest in new building codes and other resiliency measures, and to set up procedures so volunteers and NGOs could help in future emergencies. When four hurricanes hit Florida in 2004, the state was well-prepared—and other states took note.

While California has often positioned itself as the leader among states on environmental policies, any state could get out ahead of the federal government on carbon pricing, clean electricity standards, or a whole host of other issues. States could also band into regional alliances to increase their power—for instance, the current bipartisan U.S. Climate Alliance involves more than 60 percent of the U.S. economy and creates markets and scales ideas. And states have enormous procurement power they can direct toward any sort of Future Perfect goal.

Even overlooked public agencies, such as public utility commissions, can have a major impact. Texas' energy regulators let the state down in the deep freeze in 2021, but there's considerable upside, too, for regulators who build on the Laws of Zero to lower energy costs, to make the grids more reliable, and to reduce carbon emissions.

Local Governments

In addition to being able to take many of the actions states do, just on a smaller scale, local governments play an outsized role on public transportation, electricity, and zoning and building codes.

Already, many municipalities—including Milwaukee, Philadelphia, and St. Petersburg, Florida,—are switching to electric vehicles. Public buses lend themselves nicely to electrification because they tend not to travel very far, can have regular stops scheduled for recharging, and please constituents by not having any emissions.[220] Advances in electric buses are even making green transit more accessible for rural areas, where bus range, rough roads, and electrical infrastructure have historically been more of an issue.[221] Municipalities can also determine which electric utility serves the area and can make a utility's carbon profile a factor in the decision. And local zoning and building codes will play a big role in whether a locality is appropriately hardened for the increasing effects of climate change.

· · ·

We don't think President Reagan's famous line from his first inaugural address about how "government is the problem" is the end of the debate. Yes, we've all had our frustrations with government, and even those at its highest levels acknowledge it can do far better. But government has historically played a huge role in producing breakthroughs in science, medicine, business, and more. And government can do so again as we try to move to the Future Perfect. It must.

We prefer a different quote from President Reagan in that inaugural address: "[America is] too great a nation to limit ourselves to small dreams."

OVER TO YOU

Yes, we know books are supposed to have the prologue at the beginning. But we hope the past 225 or so pages are merely the start of a lot of work by all of us to invent the future, so we're putting our prologue here.

As you've seen, we have plenty of tools at our disposal—essentially an unlimited supply of computing power, communication, information, genomics, energy, water, and transportation to use as we think today about how to design 2050. And those abundant resources won't act in isolation. They'll work together, play off each other, compound each other. Genomics will drive incredible gains in health care—reinforced by all the AI, the imaging, the data storage, the brute computational force that will help sort through the unbelievable complexity of the human body. And the abundance of energy, clean water, and transportation will make living situations around the world become healthier, through abundant food, more heat, less pollution, better access to medical care, and much more. Other combinations of these vast resources will create opportunities for reimagining work, home life, and just about anything else we set our minds to tackling.

As exuberant friend wrote after reading an early version of this manuscript, "The future can be a fabric of continual innovation riffing off the platform-level improvements" allowed by the Laws of Zero.

We'll find more Laws of Zero as we head toward 2050. Nanotechnology holds great promise and could perhaps create breakthroughs in materials science that would allow for whole new classes of devices. And what if Sam Altman is right that AI creates a "Moore's law for everything"? He writes: "In the next five years, computer programs that can think will read legal documents and give medical advice. In the next decade, they will do assembly-line work and maybe even become companions. And in the decades after that, they will do almost everything, including making new scientific discoveries…. The price of many kinds of labor (which drives the costs of goods and services) will fall toward zero once sufficiently powerful AI 'joins the workforce…' [and] we can improve the standard of living for people more than we ever have before."[222]

Certainly, even with the Laws of Zero as we understand them now, we can lay out future histories for key areas that stretch well beyond the ones we probed in this short book—electricity, transportation, health care, climate, trust, and government services. The three of us have already begun work on education, which has proved confusing—online education, including so-called MOOCs (massive open online courses), hasn't panned out as many of us had hoped—but which absolutely must be re-envisioned and strengthened. Manufacturing, while a diffuse topic—lots of companies and people make lots of different things in lots of places—is another fertile area. Rethinking food is a must, and the Laws of Zero create all sorts of options just based on the possibilities of genetic improvements, plus the availability of infinite(ish) energy, water, and transportation. Cities can be rethought. Streets are really designed for cars at this point; let's redesign them for people.

Between now and the Future Perfect, a lot of people will get rich, and some nations will thrive. We're counting on it, because the lure of individual profit and national prosperity will drive the kinds of innovation we need. How much profit is available? Pick a number, any number, and it still won't be big enough. As costs plunge toward zero, all sorts of opportunities open up—try to imagine Amazon or Uber without the massive computing power and the ubiquitous communication available today, then multiply that power by a million and try to get your head around what someone will be able to do it by 2050. When economists and business types discuss an opportunity, they talk in terms of the total addressable market—how big an opportunity a product or company could conceivably address. Well, in this case, the total addressable market is… everything. The total addressable market is our future.

Even if you don't aspire to be the next Jeff Bezos or Jack Ma, we hope we've prepared you a bit for the future. It'll come at you fast and involve a lot of change, even if it's just in terms of where and how you live or what kind of car you buy next.

We also hope this book will help many of you with your kids—who are, after all, why we wrote this book. As we've talked with our kids about their potential careers, we've tried to point them at big problems that are, thus, big opportunities. While we know jobs will morph in coming years and decades, a problem like the electric grid or how to redesign cities or to move the needle on health care will still be with us. The three of us were fortunate enough to find our way into information technology and innovation almost from the outset of our careers and, through some twists and turns, have been involved in—and even helped drive—some fascinating work. We think any number of problems that can be tackled through the Laws of Zero and future histories can provide a focal point for the same sort of fruitful careers to our kids and yours.

At the least, we hope we've engaged you in thinking about what we see as the most profound problems—and opportunities—of our time. We think this book addresses the issues with our kids. Tim's son sees him understanding the existential threat of climate change. Paul's daughters know he gets that there's no Planet B. And Chunka's daughter is at least less inclined to wag her finger at him and say that, if he's really a futurist, then he'd better not screw up hers. We hope you and your kids find the same sort of common ground.

Science, through the Laws of Zero, has given us leverage on the universe. Let's use it wisely. Let's invent a great future together.

ACKNOWLEDGMENTS

This book began in the back of an Uber four years ago. Chunka and Paul were heading to the airport following a long day working with a group of business leaders on future strategies. The group had high ambitions based on many of the technology advances we've described in this book but were hobbled by a wide set of challenges and didn't see a way forward. Unlike those business leaders, however, Paul and Chunka weren't resigned to that vision of the future and wondered if there wasn't some way to provide one that was far more hopeful yet still plausible. Chunka had previously been noodling on the idea of a Future Perfect exercise, and Paul had begun using a Laws of Zero concept in some of his presentations. By the time they got to the airport, they agreed to merge their nascent ideas and attempt what you now hold in your hands.

But an awful lot of other things had to happen first, well beyond the voluminous research and workshopping of ideas that go into a book like this. In particular, the pace picked up when their old colleague Tim joined the project. Tim sharpened and broadened the thinking in a host of ways, in particular related to systems thinking, to AI, and to a number of the implications, including for the future histories of health care, trust, and government services.

The effort soon became a bit of a family affair, too. Beyond the encouragement (and forbearance) we've always received (and appreciated) from our spouses, our kids really leaned in to the effort. Tim's two sons, Paul's two daughters, and Chunka's son and daughter stretched our thinking in any number of ways, in particular related to the climate issues our generation is leaving them and related to social justice.

We thank them for their thoughts and encouragement, even when that meant a kick in the pants. Especially when that meant a kick in the pants. We realize there's no room for complacency if we're to get where we need to be by 2050. We love you guys.

The finished product really began to take shape once Booz Allen came on board, so we offer special thanks to Kristine Martin Anderson, who sponsored the project on behalf of the firm. Kristine, who leads the Civilian Services business at Booz Allen, thought the book resonated with the firm's values and history of innovating at scale and connected us with a vast array of experts at the firm. She also read the book numerous times herself—even setting aside time at the beach—and suggested any number of improvements.

Among those Kristine pulled into the fray, Dave Sulek provided steady guidance and numerous examples, especially on government services. Katie Hermosilla helped us sketch out the first draft of the chapter on the topic—she began a vignette set in 2050 with a made-up character named Connie Citizen, and we considered changing the name to Katie Citizen in her honor.

Rich Goffi provided crucial help on energy, electricity, and climate change—he sharpened our thinking on where the cost curves could go from here for solar, wind, and batteries and offered considerable nuance about the many implications of moving to carbon-free energy sources. Mike Miller, Joel Fetter, and Ben Getto added important thoughts on energy and electricity, as well, including on ARPA-E, which we think is such a good example of how government can drive needed innovation, in cooperation with the private sector.

Christina Marsh, Elise Roberts, and Jim Rojeski were part of the "book club" Kristine suggested to provide continual feedback to us as the project progressed (and, as it turned out, some much-appreciated encouragement from time to time)—Christina kept us honest in many ways, including on the challenges that driverless cars will face among her fellow Bostonians, and Jim was a sort of philosopher king, acquainting us with principles from an astonishingly broad amount of reading and thinking. The three were especially helpful on health care, as were Jocelyn Lewis and Kim Dalferes. Ravi Nagarajan, Jesse Goraya, Jeff Tunkel, and Steve Buchanan were core readers, too.

Kelly Rozumalski and some of her team made extensive comments that shaped the section on trust and privacy, and long conversations with Adam Weiner and Patrick Gorman also helped greatly. Frank DiGiammarino provided guidance on government services and on what government's role should be, and Stephen Labaton helped us shape the Intro and Laws of Zero section early on. Kevin Vigilante and Bill Phelps made valuable comments, too.

That brings us to Pam Rich and Guy Snodgrass. Pam coordinated many of the activities at Booz Allen, on behalf of Kristine, and somehow maintained her good humor even as many of us tensed up as deadlines came (and sometimes went). Guy, demonstrating his skills as a former Top Gun instructor and squadron commander, herded the proverbial cats as he helped generate feedback from Booz Allen's subject matter experts and, as a published author of two books of his own, proved to be an extremely careful and helpful reader of the manuscript. Thanks, as well, to Becky Rogerson for her usual organizational skills and attention to a million details.

We also want to thank a wider circle of mentors, colleagues, and friends who have shaped our general thinking and sharpened the ideas and details in this book. They didn't have time to spare, but they spared it anyway. They read the manuscript. They offered stories. They made this book better. So we'd like to heartily thank: Vince Barabba, Seth Bergstein, Kathy Blake, Dan Bricklin, Larry Cohen, Michael Golden, Paul Growald, Mira Irons, Chris Khoury, Karen Kmetik, Tom Kunetz, Andy Lippman, Jim Madara, Cheryl Martin, Toby Redshaw, Mark Richards, Karl Ronn, Ken Sharigian, Nancy Sulek, John Sviokla, Larry Weithers, and Steve Zwick.

Special thanks to Shannon Carroll and Mark Maltais. Shannon did an amazingly thorough copy-edit of the book, eliminating repetition and streamlining the logic, while always smoothing and polishing. Mark, the design genius we had the pleasure of working with in our days at Diamond, volunteered his time to walk us through numerous issues, and the book is the better for it.

Thanks, too, to Alan Barnett for indulging all our thoughts and changes on the cover and for doing such a lovely, careful job both on the cover and on the interior design and layout. Also to Brian Carroll and to Shannon Carroll again for giving the book such a hard proofreading scrub. The Carrolls have an allergic reaction to mistakes in grammar and just about anything else, and we're confident that those two bright 20-somethings found whatever were left in the manuscript. On the odd chance that one or two snuck through, blame us authors; we clearly changed something after their eyes made their final inspection.

Final thanks to two extraordinary people: Alan Kay and the late Mel Bergstein.

Alan won't surprise you, as his name is sprinkled liberally through the book. But we still want to thank him for having inspired us for so long and for always challenging us. We drew on another of Alan's famous lines, that the right context is worth 80 IQ points, when we named Diamond's thought-leadership magazine *Context* back in the mid-1990s, and, in many ways, that's been our guiding light for our careers: We've tried to find the right context for understanding and solving business issues, especially related to innovation. This book is really an exercise in trying to find the right context for planning for the future.

As for Mel: Beyond founding Diamond on the then-radical, now-obvious notion of digital strategy nearly 30 years ago, Mel was especially meaningful to Chunka and Paul, who had the privilege of knowing him both before and after Diamond and considered him a friend. When Mel was a mucketymuck at Andersen Consulting, now Accenture, and Chunka was a newbie hire, Mel decided Chunka's little AI project was cool and introduced it to Alan Kay, beginning the decades-long connection between them. When Paul covered technology at *The Wall Street Journal*, Mel was one of his favorite quotes and consistently provided keen insights—leading Paul to a very early piece on what became the massive IT outsourcing trend and even to a prediction of cloud computing ... in 1989. Mel would have been all over this book, and, even though cancer took him far too early, we tried to keep his memory as a little voice in the back of our minds as we wrote this, hearing him tell us to be broader, to be deeper, to be more inspiring, to use more examples, to cut the crap and get to the point—all with a big, warm hand clasping our shoulder as he made us feel much smarter than we are. We hope we did you proud, Mel. Mazel tov!

ENDNOTES

1   https://www.youtube.com/watch?v=XAfTXYa36f4

2   https://www.imore.com/history-ipad-2010

3   https://www.politico.com/agenda/story/2018/02/07/technology
    -interview-mit-david-autor-000629

4   https://www.nytimes.com/2015/03/29/magazine/the-radical
    -humaneness-of-norways-halden-prison.html

5   https://www.socialprogress.org/index/global/results

6   https://en.wikipedia.org/wiki/We_choose_to_go_to_the_Moon

7   "Resource Revolution: How to Capture the Biggest Business
    Opportunity in a Century," by Stefan Heck and Matt Rogers, with Paul
    Carroll; p. 7.

8   https://www.youtube.com/watch?v=0fKBhvDjuy0

9   https://www.forbes.com/sites/forbestechcouncil/2018/03/09/moores
    -law-is-dying-so-where-are-its-heirs/#325db9977a7b

10 https://www.forbes.com/sites/kenkam/2018/04/23/how-moores-law
    -now-favors-nvidia-over-intel/#1f63a8165e42

11 https://www.cnet.com/news/intel-3d-chip-stacking-could-get-you-to
    -buy-a-new-pc/

12 https://www.wired.com/2014/06/google-kubernetes/

13 https://www.weforum.org/agenda/2016/09/7-innovations-that-could
    -shape-the-future-of-computing

14 https://www.economist.com/leaders/2016/03/12/the-future-of-computing

15 https://www.theverge.com/2019/10/23/20928294/google-quantum
    -supremacy-sycamore-computer-qubit-milestone

16 Named after Bob Metcalfe, the principal inventor at Xerox PARC of
    Ethernet, an early and very important networking technology.

17 UCLA, Stanford Research Institute, University of Utah and UC-Santa Barbara

18 https://www.weforum.org/agenda/2016/12/by-2030-this-is-what -computers-will-do/

19 https://www.facebook.com/17043549797/posts/in-a-shocking -finding-scientists-discovered-a-herd-of-unicorns-living-in-a -remot/10159146577144798/

20 https://www.roadtovr.com/bell-says-latest-helicopter-was-designed-10 -times-faster-with-vr/amp/

21 https://interestingengineering.com/machine-learning-slashes-tech -design-process-by-a-whole-year

22 https://spacenews.com/spacex-submits-paperwork-for-30000-more -starlink-satellites/

23 https://www.zdnet.com/article/microsoft-spacex-and-t-mobiles -various-plans-to-bring-broadband-to-rural-america/

24 "The Victorian Internet: The Remarkable Story of the Telegraph and the Nineteenth Century's Online Pioneers," by Tom Standage

25 https://www.theguardian.com/society/2021/mar/11/bowel-cancer -screening-capsules-the-latest-in-at-home-care-trend

26 http://www.rmmagazine.com/2018/11/01/mini-meteorologists-how -satellite-technology-is-reducing-weather-risks/

27 https://www.technologyreview.com/s/613748/satellites-threaten -privacy/

28 https://www.independent.co.uk/news/world/americas/gold -mining-amazon-rainforest-south-america-mercury-jair-bolsonaro -raisg-a8677996.html

29 https://www.wired.com/story/we-need-data-rich-picture-climate -change/

30 https://www.nytimes.com/2020/12/12/opinion/sunday/biden-climate -change-al-gore.html

31 https://www.technologyreview.com/s/613748/satellites-threaten -privacy/

32 https://www.cnn.com/videos/world/2019/10/06/leaked-video-china -detainee-muslim-pkg-rivers-vpx.cnn

33 https://www.wired.com/story/mirrorworld-ar-next-big-tech-platform/

34 Mendel was no simple country friar. Mendel was immersed in the writings of his contemporary, Charles Darwin, and there's ample evidence that Mendel interpreted his data on nearly 30,000 plants with Darwin's theories on evolution and natural selection in mind. The German translation of Darwin's Origin of Species was published in

1860, in the middle of Mendel's research, and Mendel made numerous annotations in his copy of the book. Mendel's papers and letters also used Darwin's terminology to address evolutionary questions and concepts. https://www.nature.com/articles/s41437-019-0289-9.pdf

Some researchers believe that Mendel's embrace of science and his interest in studying evolution caused conflict with his church superiors. Mendel told his nephews that he had scientific papers he delayed publishing for fear of "clerical enemies" and that they should look for them upon his death. All of Mendel's papers, however, were burned by his abbey after his death.

35 Sanger and Gilbert shared the 1980 Nobel prize in chemistry. Sanger had already won a Nobel prize for his work in sequencing insulin; he is the only person who has won twice in chemistry.

36 https://www.nobelprize.org/uploads/2020/10/popular -chemistryprize2020.pdf

37 https://allianceforscience.cornell.edu/blog/2020/04/gene-editing-will -revolutionize-crop-breeding-in-africa-new-paper-predicts/

38 https://onezero.medium.com/the-7-craziest-ways-crispr-is-being-used -right-now-bcf3bd203f23

39 https://www.synthego.com/blog/crispr-cure-diseases

40 https://www.nytimes.com/2020/01/08/magazine/gene-drive -mosquitoes.html

41 https://www.wired.com/story/30-years-since-the-human-genome -project-began-whats-next/

42 https://www.scientificamerican.com/article/reflections-on-the-20th -anniversary-of-the-first-publication-of-the-human-genome/

43 Green, E.D., et. al., "Strategic vision for improving human health at the Forefront of Genomics," *Nature* 2020

44 Denny JC, Collins FS. Precision medicine in 2030-seven ways to transform health care. Cell. 2021 Mar 18;184(6):1415–1419. doi: 10.1016/j.cell.2021.01.015. PMID: 33740447.

45 https://www.freeingenergy.com/why-does-the-cost-of-renewable -energy-continue-to-get-cheaper-and-cheaper/

46 https://www.carbonbrief.org/solar-is-now-cheapest-electricity-in -history-confirms-iea

47 https://arstechnica.com/science/2019/04/with-tax-credit-idaho-power -secures-record-low-price-for-utility-scale-solar/

48 https://www.forbes.com/sites/jeffmcmahon/2019/07/01/new-solar -battery-price-crushes-fossil-fuels-buries-nuclear/

49   https://www.electricchoice.com/electricity-prices-by-state/

50   https://www.sciencemag.org/news/2018/06/skyscrapers-could-soon
      -generate-their-own-power-thanks-see-through-solar-cells

51   https://www.strategy-business.com/article/From-smokestacks-to-solar
      -panels-Asia-starts-embracing-renewables?gko=3f04e

52   https://spectrum.ieee.org/view-from-the-valley/energy/renewables/
      forget-cats-this-neural-network-spots-solar-panels?TrucksFoT

53   https://www.theguardian.com/environment/2021/mar/16/good-
      vibrations-bladeless-turbines-could-bring-wind-power-to-your-home

54   https://www.wired.com/story/ai-is-throwing-battery-development-into
      -overdrive/

55   https://medium.com/@nitinvaish/vehicle-electrification-energy
      -storage-indias-opportunity-66d30854c7ed?TrucksFoT

56   https://www.bloomberg.com/news/articles/2018-12-19/gates-bezos
      -among-billionaires-backing-alphabet-energy-spinoff

57   https://www.wired.com/story/the-batteries-of-the-future-are-weightless
      -and-invisible/

58   https://www.cbsnews.com/news/griddy-energy-texas-files
      -bankruptcy/#:~:text=The%20storm%20with%20record%2Dlow,for%20
      bankruptcy%20since%20the%20storm.

59   https://www.scientificamerican.com/article/the-other-reason-to-shift
      -away-from-coal-air-pollution-that-kills-thousands-every-year/

60   https://www.brookings.edu/opinions/the-real-costs-of-u-s-energy/

61   https://www.technologyreview.com/s/601242/qa-bill-gates/

62   https://www.greentechmedia.com/articles/read/alphabets-energy
      -moonshot-startups-makani-dandelion#gs.grmx1k

63   https://www.energy.gov/articles/doe-releases-new-study-highlighting
      -untapped-potential-geothermal-energy-united-states

64   https://qz.com/1402282/in-search-of-clean-energy-investments-in
      -nuclear-fusion-startups-are-heating-up/

65   https://www.cnbc.com/2021/02/12/commonwealth-fusion-backed-by
      -gates-bezos-for-unlimited-clean-energy.html

66   https://www.bloomberg.com/news/articles/2020-11-09/japan-eyes
      -replacing-oil-with-hydrogen-amid-carbon-neutral-push

67   https://www.technologyreview.com/2021/02/24/1017822/green
      -hydrogen-clean-energy/

68   https://www.bloomberg.com/news/articles/2021-02-08/climate-seen-as
      -next-race-for-global-supremacy-bofa-says?sref=Cg936Uu2

69   In its early days, DARPA was known as ARPA.

70   https://www.bloomberg.com/news/articles/2021-02-08/climate-seen-as
     -next-race-for-global-supremacy-bofa-says?sref=Cg936Uu2

71   https://www.wsj.com/articles/why-your-next-home-might-not-use-any
     -energy-at-all-11545454801

72   https://www.technologyreview.com/2020/09/01/1007762/
     air-conditioning-grid-blackouts-california-climate-change

73   https://www.popularmechanics.com/science/energy/a35092898/
     air-force-solar-power-beaming-spacecraft/

74   https://www.ozy.com/the-new-and-the-next/the-inventor-trying-to-
     suck-water-from-the-worlds-driest-air/86895/

75   https://www.xprize.org/articles/waxp-grand-prize-winner

76   https://venturebeat.com/2019/01/12/how-cody-friesen-extracts-water
     -from-air-and-kindles-hope-at-zero-mass-water/view-all/

77   https://www.globalwaterintel.com/global-water-intelligence
     -magazine/21/5/general/selling-water-at-150-m3-to-the-world-s
     -poorest-people-with-billionaire-backing

78   https://qz.com/africa/1272589/how-cape-town-delayed-its-water
     -disaster-at-least-until-2019/

79   https://earther.gizmodo.com/why-chennai-indias-sixth-biggest-city-has
     -run-out-of-1835736767

80   https://www.stuff.co.nz/world/middle-east/106941489/plan-to-tow
     -icebergs-from-antarctica-to-parched-dubai

81   https://www.wired.com/story/desalination-is-booming-as-cities-run
     -out-of-water

82   https://www.mercurynews.com/2018/01/29/california-water
     -desalination-projects-move-forward-with-new-state-funding

83   https://www.iflscience.com/health-and-medicine/watch-bill-gates
     -drink-water-5-minutes-after-it-was-sewage/

84   https://www.washingtonpost.com/graphics/2018/lifestyle/led
     -growing/?utm_term=.0f27c1510397

85   Kroger is already testing such an autonomous delivery service: https://
     arstechnica.com/cars/2018/12/kroger-owned-grocery-store-begins
     -fully-driverless-deliveries

86   https://www.nytimes.com/2012/01/08/arts/design/taking-parking-lots
     -seriously-as-public-spaces.html

87   https://www.alumniportal-deutschland.org/en/global-goals/sdg-06
     -water/water-drinking-water-freshwater-chile/

88   "Four billion people facing severe water scarcity," https://advances.
     sciencemag.org/content/2/2/e1500323

89 https://cen.acs.org/environment/water/stripping-air-moisture-quench -worlds/96/i41

90 http://www.ipsnews.net/2012/08/women-spend-40-billion-hours -collecting-water/

91 https://news.un.org/en/story/2010/03/333182-unsafe-water-kills-more -people-war-ban-says-world-day

92 https://www.wsj.com/articles/solar-power-booms-in-texas -11606579200?mod=e2tw

93 https://www.bbc.com/future/article/20161129-the-colossal-african -solar-farm-that-could-power-europe

94 https://spectrum.ieee.org/energy/the-smarter-grid/chinas-ambitious -plan-to-build-the-worlds-biggest-supergrid

95 https://www.bloomberg.com/news/articles/2020-09-16/are-batteries -the-trade-war-china-s-already-won

96 https://www.power-eng.com/2019/08/13/is-thorium-the-fuel-of-the -future-to-revitalize-nuclear/#gref

97 https://www.scientificamerican.com/article/putting-solar-panels-on -water-is-a-great-idea-mdash-but-will-it-float

98 https://www.bizjournals.com/austin/news/2019/12/10/ut-positions -itself-as-leader-in-clean-geothermal.html

99 https://www.irena.org/-/media/Files/IRENA/Agency/Publication/2018/ Apr/IRENA_Global_Energy_Transformation_2018_summary_EN.pdf

100 https://www.vox.com/2014/4/14/5604992/us-power-grid-vulnerability

101 https://www.ncsl.org/research/energy/modernizing-the-electric-grid -state-role-and-policy-options.aspx

102 https://www.youtube.com/watch?app=desktop&v=cdgQpa1pUUE

103 https://rudermanfoundation.org/wp-content/uploads/2017/08/Self -Driving-Cars-The-Impact-on-People-with-Disabilities_FINAL.pdf

104 http://www.leonardo3.net/en/exhibitions/1420-leonardos-cart.html

105 https://spectrum.ieee.org/cars-that-think/transportation/self-driving/ the-electronic-highway-of-1969

106 https://www.popsci.com/scitech/article/2004-06/darpa-grand -challenge-2004darpas-debacle-desert/

107 https://worldlandscapearchitect.com/toyota-woven-city-bjarke -ingels-group/

108 https://www.theatlantic.com/magazine/archive/2019/07/american -health-care-spending/590623/

109 https://www.strategy-business.com/article/Plumbing
-the-depths?gko=33e0b&utm_source=itw&utm_
medium=itw20200407&utm_campaign=resp

110 Approximations already exist, including at this site: https://en.wikipedia
.org/wiki/RealAge. They will improve and become widely available and
used.

111 https://jamanetwork.com/journals/jama/article-abstract/2752664

112 https://qz.com/1010259/the-100-billion-per-year-back-pain-industry
-is-mostly-a-hoax/

113 Such a glove is already being developed. https://www.gatesnotes.com/
About-Bill-Gates/My-visit-to-a-Harvard-robotics-lab

114 Already well underway. https://www.ozy.com/fast-forward/finding
-your-inner-doctor-the-rise-of-new-age-diy-tools

115 USGCRP, 2017: *Climate Science Special Report: Fourth National Climate
Assessment, Volume I* [Wuebbles, D.J., D.W. Fahey, K.A. Hibbard, D.J.
Dokken, B.C. Stewart, and T.K. Maycock (eds.)]. U.S. Global Change
Research Program, Washington, DC, USA, 470 pp, doi: 10.7930/
J0J964J6.

116 This is a categorization used by Bill Gates in his 2021 book,
"How to Avoid a Climate Disaster: The Solutions We Have and
the Breakthroughs We Need."

117 https://www.worldbank.org/en/country/mic/overview#1

118 https://en.wikipedia.org/wiki/Projections_of_population_growth#cite
_note-:484858585858583-10

119 https://www.bloomberg.com/news/articles/2021-03-02/bill-gates-led
-group-shows-u-s-grid-emissions-can-fall-45?sref=Cg936Uu2

120 http://energyfuse.org/americas-aging-vehicles-delay-rate-fleet
-turnover/

121 https://www.statista.com/statistics/185216/age-of-us-light-trucks/

122 https://www.nytimes.com/interactive/2021/03/10/climate/electric
-vehicle-fleet-turnover.html

123 https://www.wsj.com/articles/gm-sets-2035-target-to-phase-out-gas
-and-diesel-powered-vehicles-globally-11611850343?mod=article_
inline

124 https://www.nytimes.com/2021/03/02/business/volvo-electric-cars.html

125 https://www.nytimes.com/2021/02/17/business/ford-says-it-will-phase
-out-gasoline-powered-vehicles-in-europe.html

126 https://www.cnn.com/2020/10/03/cars/california-2035-zev-mandate/
index.html

127   https://www.cnbc.com/2020/11/18/the-uk-plans-to-ban-sales-of-diesel
      -and-petrol-cars-from-2030.html

128   https://www.forbes.com/sites/chunkamui/2016/02/08/the-virtuous
      -cycle-between-driverless-cars-electric-vehicles-and-car-sharing
      -services/?sh=30bb3e187143

129   https://www.wired.co.uk/article/the-strange-war-against-cow-farts

130   https://www.worldwildlife.org/stories/fight-climate-change-by
      -preventing-food-waste

131   https://www.greenbiz.com/article/5-feed-companies-could-relieve-
      cow-burp-methane-problem

132   https://energyefficiencyimpact.org

133   https://www.aceee.org/sites/default/files/publications/researchreports/
      u1907.pdf

134   https://www.resourcepanel.org/reports/resource-efficiency-and-
      climate-change

135   https://www.blackrock.com/corporate/investor-relations/blackrock
      -client-letter

136   https://www.blackrock.com/corporate/literature/whitepaper/
      bii-portfolio-perspectives-february-2021.pdf

137   https://www.ipcc.ch/sr15/chapter/spm/

138   https://carbonengineering.com/frequently-asked-questions/

139   https://www.gatesnotes.com/Energy/Introducing-the-Green-Premiums

140   www.1kosmos.com

141   https://www.nfpa.org/About-NFPA/NFPA-overview/History-of-NFPA

142   https://www.washingtonpost.com/graphics/2020/technology/
      trump-twitter-tweets-president/

143   https://www.theatlantic.com/magazine/archive/2021/04/the-interne
      t-doesnt-have-to-be-awful/618079

144   https://www.washingtonexaminer.com/news/trump-targeted-by
      -tehran-as-russians-and-iranians-meddle-in-2020-election-intel
      -officials-say

145   https://www.nytimes.com/2020/10/18/us/elections/voting-machines
      -paper-ballots.html

146   https://trustthevote.org/wp-content/uploads/2019/04/01Apr19_
      VotingSystemNewArch_v4Final1.pdf

147   https://www.pewtrusts.org/en/research-and-analysis/blogs/
      stateline/2021/02/17/despite-security-concerns-online-voting-advances

148   https://ericstates.org/

149 https://www.brennancenter.org/our-work/research-reports/automatic
     -voter-registration-summary

150 https://www.behavioraleconomics.com/resources/mini-encyclopedia
     -of-be/default-optionsetting/

151 https://www.brennancenter.org/our-work/research-reports/waiting-vote

152 https://www.washingtonpost.com/politics/2020/11/19/gops-post
     -election-tactics-are-causing-more-concern-about-suppressing-black
     -vote-even-after-it-happened/

153 https://www.pewtrusts.org/en/research-and-analysis/blogs/
     stateline/2018/02/01/how-voters-with-disabilities-are-blocked-from
     -the-ballot-box

154 https://www.ncsl.org/research/elections-and-campaigns/electronic
     -pollbooks.aspx

155 https://marker.medium.com/what-everyones-getting-wrong-about-the
     -toilet-paper-shortage-c812e1358fe0

156 https://en.wikipedia.org/wiki/2019_Midwestern_U.S._floods

157 https://en.wikipedia.org/wiki/2020_United_States_federal_
     government_data_breach

158 https://www.cisa.gov/sites/default/files/publications/Guide-Critical-
     Infrastructure-Security-Resilience-110819-508v2.pdf

159 https://www.ceres.org/sites/default/files/reports/2017-03/Ceres_
     RiskAwareElec_2014Update_111714_final.pdf

160 https://www.wired.com/2016/03/inside- cunning-unprecedented-hack
     -ukraines-power-grid

161 https://rmi.org/wp-content/uploads/2020/07/reimagining_grid_
     resilience.pdf

162 https://www.gridassurance.com/faq/

163 https://engineeringonline.ucr.edu/blog/the-future-of-smart-grid
     -technologies/

164 https://rmi.org/reimagining-grid-resilience-in-the-energy-transition/

165 https://www.waterworld.com/water-utility-management/article/
     14177750/accelerating-urban-water-resilience-through-innovation
     -and-technology

166 https://www.epa.gov/crwu

167 https://epa.maps.arcgis.com/apps/MapSeries/index.
     html?appid=03d35ca84b5944f8b3ab59bf3a981462

168 https://www.waterworld.com/water-utility-management/
     article/14177750/accelerating-urban-water-resilience-through
     -innovation-and-technology

169 https://medium.com/imagineh2o/announcing-imagine-h2os-2021
     -accelerator-cohort-the-latest-innovations-in-water-809fe1e15c74

170 https://medium.com/imagineh2o/the-future-of-water-how-innovations
     -will-advance-water-sustainability-and-resilience-worldwide-
     854ee2039e6f

171 https://www.timesofisrael.com/scientists-say-it-is-too-late-to-stop
     -climate-change/

172 https://leadthechange.bard.edu/blog/too-late-to-stop-global-warming
     -a-response-to-franzen

173 https://www.gatesnotes.com/Podcast/Is-it-too-late-to-stop-climate
     -change

174 https://www.theguardian.com/media/2017/feb/02/amusing-ourselves
     -to-death-neil-postman-trump-orwell-huxley

175 https://www.smithsonianmag.com/smart-news/how-aldous-huxley
     -118-today-predicted-the-present-far-more-accurately-than-george
     -orwell-7797626/

176 https://news.un.org/en/story/2020/01/1055681

177 https://www.un.org/development/desa/dspd/world-social
     -report/2020-2.html

178 https://www.oecd-ilibrary.org/social-issues-migration-health/trends-
     in-income-inequality-and-its-impact-on-economic-growth_
     5jxrjncwxv6j-en

179 https://openknowledge.worldbank.org/handle/10986/18825

180 http://blogs.lse.ac.uk/usappblog/2016/07/08/how-neighborhood-
     inequality-leads-to-higher-crime-rates/

181 https://www.inverse.com/article/38457-inequality-study-nature
     -revolution

182 https://www.theguardian.com/commentisfree/2019/jul/06/usa-womens
     -world-cup-netherlands-title-xi

183 https://www.sfweekly.com/culture/film-culture/looking-back-at
     -howard-jarvis-and-prop-13/

184 https://calmatters.org/politics/california-election-2020/2020/11/
     california-so-liberal-prop-13-tax-revolt-prop-15

185 https://www.allianzlife.com/about/newsroom/2019-press-releases/
     socially-responsible-investing-and-esg

186 https://www.cnbc.com/2021/03/04/sustainable-esg-investments-surged
     -in-asia-pacific-in-2020-msci.html

187 https://www.wsj.com/articles/tidal-wave-of-esg-funds-brings-profit-to
     -wall-street-11615887004

188   https://www.wsj.com/articles/green-finance-goes-mainstream-lining
      -up-trillions-behind-global-energy-transition-11621656039?mod=hp_
      lead_pos7

189   https://vulcanpost.com/741849/eat-just-making-alternative-meat
      -mainstream-singapore/

190   https://www.cnbc.com/2021/03/25/plant-based-food-company-eat-just
      -nabs-200-million-investment.html

191   https://www.bloomberg.com/graphics/2020-renewable-energy
      -supermajors/

192   https://www.internationalinsurance.org/sites/default/files/2020-11/
      Insurers%20Can%20Change%20the%20World%2011.2.2020.pdf

193   https://www.nytimes.com/2021/04/22/climate/climate-change
      -economy.html

194   Michael Hammer, "Reengineering Work: Don't Automate, Obliterate,"
      HBR, July–August 1990. https://hbr.org/1990/07/reengineering-work
      -dont-automate-obliterate

195   https://www.msci.com/documents/1296102/22910163/MSCI
      -Investment-Insights-2021-Report.pdf

196   https://www.forbes.com/sites/forbesbusinesscouncil/2021/03/25/
      family-offices-identifying-and-incorporating-sustainability-into-an
      -investment-strategy/?sh=4ded13f72c20

197   ibid

198   https://www.wsj.com/articles/venture-firms-bask-in-a-surge-of
      -blockbuster-profits-11619608939?page=1

199   https://hbr.org/2019/05/rd-spending-has-dramatically-surpassed
      -advertising-spending

200   The cost estimates were provided to us by Alan Kay.

201   https://18f.gsa.gov/2017/11/30/improving-government-outcomes
      -through-an-agile-contract-format/

202   https://www.transform.af.mil/Portals/18/documents/OSA/OTA_Brief
      .pdf?ver=2015-09-15-073050-867

203   https://grantsgovprod.wordpress.com/2016/07/19/what-is-a
      -cooperative-agreement/

204   https://arpa-e.energy.gov/sites/default/files/REPAIR%20
      Presentation%20-%20Contracting%20and%20Legal%20-%20Final%20
      v2.pdf

205   https://arpa-e.energy.gov/about/our-impact

206   https://jalopnik.com/a-whopping-80-billion-has-been-invested-so-far
      -in-the-1819504421

207   https://environment.princeton.edu/grandchallenges/research/energy

208   https://datasciencebowl.com/about/

209   https://www.wri.org/blog/2013/01/4-grand-challenges-energy-food
      -and-water

210   https://www.weforum.org/agenda/2016/01/what-are-the-10-biggest
      -global-challenges/

211   https://obamawhitehouse.archives.gov/administration/eop/ostp/
      grand-challenges

212   http://www.engineeringchallenges.org/8938.aspx

213   https://gcgh.grandchallenges.org/about

214   https://www.childfund.org/infographic/malaria/

215   https://arstechnica.com/science/2019/04/malaria-vaccine-rollout-is-a
      -gamble-an-imperfect-tool-used-imperfectly/

216   https://www.forbes.com/sites/chunkamui/2019/03/07/part-3-the-urgent
      -goal/

217   https://www.washingtonpost.com/graphics/2020/climate-solutions/
      empire-state-building-emissions/

218   https://energynews.us/2018/02/05/midwest/this-chicago-building
      -retrofit-program-saves-90-million-kwh-a-year/

219   https://www.osti.gov/opennet/manhattan-project-history/publications/
      DE99001330.pdf

220   https://www.natlawreview.com/article/consumers-focus-electric
      -vehicles-municipalities-look-to-electrify-their-bus-systems

221   https://greatlakesecho.org/2021/05/13/advancements-in-electric-buses
      -making-green-transit-more-accessible-for-rural-areas/

222   https://moores.samaltman.com/

INDEX

ABOUT THE AUTHORS

 **Chunka Mui** is a futurist and innovation adviser who helps organizations design and stress test strategies focused on making the world a much better place.

Chunka is the best-selling author of four other books on strategy and innovation, including (with Paul Carroll) *The New Killer Apps: How Large Companies Can Out-Innovate Start-Ups* and *Billion Dollar Lessons: What You Can Learn From the Most Inexcusable Business Failures of the Last 25 Years*. One reviewer wrote that *The New Killer Apps* "absolutely nails how to and how not to innovate." *Kirkus Review* named it a book of the month selection and awarded it a coveted Kirkus Star for Excellence. *Inc., The Globe and Mail* and other publications named *Billion Dollar Lessons* one of the best business books of the year. In 2005, *The Wall Street Journal* named Chunka's first book, *Unleashing the Killer App*, one of the five best books on business and the internet.

Chunka is also a longtime contributor to *Forbes*, where he has published more than 200 articles and garnered millions of views.

He was previously the Chief Innovation Officer and a Managing Partner at Diamond Management & Technology Consultants (now part of PwC), a publicly traded multinational firm that pioneered the idea of digital strategy more than 25 years ago. He created and led The Exchange, an innovation learning community for senior executives (now PwC Exchange). He co-founded and directed Vanguard, a global research and advisory service that helped senior executives explore the intersection of strategy and emerging technology (now TTI Vanguard). Chunka started his professional career at Andersen Consulting (now Accenture), where he was an early member of that firm's AI group and co-founded its Center for Strategic Technology Research (now Accenture Labs).

Chunka holds a B.S. in computer science and engineering from MIT.

 **Paul Carroll** has excelled at the highest levels of journalism for decades, while pushing the state of the art on business strategy and innovation.

For 17 years, he was a reporter and editor at the Wall Street Journal, where he wrote about information technology. The WSJ nominated him twice for the Pulitzer Prize, and he was a finalist once. He left to become a partner at Diamond Management & Technology Consultants, where he founded and edited a magazine that was a finalist for the National Magazine Award for General Excellence. For the past eight years, Paul has been the editor-in-chief at Insurance Thought Leadership, an affiliate of The Institutes that drives innovation in insurance.

He is the best-selling author of numerous other books, beginning with *Big Blues: The Unmaking of IBM*, published by Crown in 1993. In 2008, Paul and Chunka Mui published *Billion Dollar Lessons: What You Can Learn From the Most Inexcusable Business Failures of the Last 25 Years*, based on 20 researchers' two years of analysis of 2,500 corporate disasters. While Jim Collins looked at success stories and said, Here's how to be like those guys, *Billion Dollar Lessons* looked at failures and said, Here's how *not* to be like *those* guys. The *Wall Street Journal* review called the book "fascinating…, insightful and crisply written."

Paul was the writer on the National Broadband Plan, which the FCC submitted to Congress in 2010, and on a report that the Department of Energy produced later that year on a $36.5 billion innovation initiative funded by the Stimulus Act.

He and Chunka have founded a boutique consulting firm, the Future Histories Group, which stress tests corporate strategies. They have worked with senior management at numerous major organizations.

Paul graduated magna cum laude from Michigan State University's Honors College at age 19 and earned a master's degree in journalism from Northwestern University the following year.

 **Tim Andrews** is a renaissance person and problem solver and an expert in emerging technology and innovation.

A technology leader in Booz Allen Hamilton's Civilian Services business, Tim also has broad expertise beyond technology, including in strategy, cognitive psychology, health care, and life sciences. He has significant experience in large-scale system design and development and advances client missions through pragmatic use of leading-edge technology. He has been a prolific writer and public speaker throughout his career.

Tim has been an independent adviser and in leadership positions in firms ranging from startups to large corporations. Prior to Booz Allen, he helped create New York's innovative health information network as Chief Architect and worked with large corporations to develop and implement their technology strategies. In the late '90s, Tim was Chief Technology Officer for Viant, one of the first and most successful publicly traded internet consulting companies, where he led the innovation group and worked with clients to help them understand and capitalize on the internet. Tim was a partner at Diamond Management & Technology Consultants (now part of PwC), where he led the development of the digital strategy practice in the mid-'90s. Early in his career, in one of his most exciting experiences, he worked on the software for the original Macintosh computer and was a founder and Chief Technology Officer of one of the first unstructured database startups.

Tim holds an A.B in engineering from Dartmouth College and an MS in computer science and electrical engineering from Worcester Polytechnic Institute.

Made in the USA
Las Vegas, NV
09 September 2022

54905663R00163